CLIMATE@WORK

CLIMATE@WORK

EDITED BY
CARLA LIPSIG-MUMMÉ

FERNWOOD PUBLISHING • HALIFAX & WINNIPEG

For Jimmy Lipsig —
Trade unionist, socialist, civil rights activist
(1910–1976)

Editing: Marianne Ward
Cover design: John van der Woude
Printed and bound in Canada

Published in Canada by Fernwood Publishing
32 Oceanvista Lane, Black Point, Nova Scotia, B0J 1B0
and 748 Broadway Avenue, Winnipeg, Manitoba, R3G 0X3
www.fernwoodpublishing.ca

Fernwood Publishing Company Limited gratefully acknowledges the financial support
of the Government of Canada through the Canada Book Fund and the Canada Council
for the Arts, the Nova Scotia Department of Communities, Culture and Heritage,
the Manitoba Department of Culture, Heritage and Tourism under the
Manitoba Publishers Marketing Assistance Program and the Province of Manitoba,
through the Book Publishing Tax Credit, for our publishing program.

Library and Archives Canada Cataloguing in Publication

Climate@Work / edited by Carla Lipsig-Mummé.

(Labour in Canada ; 3)
Includes bibliographical references.
ISBN 978-1-55266-564-0 (pbk.)

1. Climatic changes--Economic aspects--Canada. 2. Climatic
changes--Government policy--Canada. 3. Work--Canada. 4. Labor--
Canada. 5. Employment (Economic theory). 6. Canada--Economic
conditions--21st century. I. Lipsig-Mummé, Carla, editor of
compilation II. Title: Climate at work. III. Series: Labour in
Canada (Halifax, N.S.) ; 3

QC903.2.C3C52 2013   363.738'740971   C2013-902466-2

CONTENTS

LABOUR IN CANADA SERIES

This volume is part of the Labour in Canada Series, which focuses on assessing how global and national political economic changes have affected Canada's labour movement and labour force as well as how working people have responded. The series offers a unique Canadian perspective to parallel international debates on work and labour in the United States, Great Britain and Western Europe.

Authors seek to understand the impact of governments and markets on working people. They examine the role of governments in shaping economic restructuring and the loss of unionized jobs, as well as how governments promote the growth of low-wage work. They also analyze the impacts of economic globalization on women, minorities and immigrants.

Contributors provide insight on how unions have responded to global labour market deregulation and globalization. They present accessible new research on how Canadian unions function in both the private and public sectors, how they organize and how their political strategies work. The books document recent success stories (and failures) of union renewal and explore the new opportunities emerging as the labour movement attempts to rebuild the economy on sound environmental principles.

Over the past thirty years, the union movement has increasingly been put on the defensive as its traditional tactics of economic and political engagement have failed to protect wages, maintain membership and advance progressive agendas. Yet there has been far too little discussion of how the terrain of Canadian politics has shifted and how this has, in turn, affected the Canadian labour movement. There has also been far too little acknowledgment of working people's attempts to develop new strategies to regain political and economic influence. This series aims to fill these major gaps in public debate.

The volumes are resources that can help unions successfully confront new dilemmas. They also serve to promote discussion and support labour education programs within unions and postsecondary education programs. It is our hope that the series informs debate on the policies and institutions that Canadians need to improve jobs, create better workplaces and build a more egalitarian society.

Series editors
John Peters and Reuben Roth

Labour in Canada series editorial committee:
Marjorie Griffin Cohen, Julie Guard,
Grace-Edward Galabuzi, Joel Harden, Wayne Lewchuk,
Stephanie Ross, Larry Savage, Mercedes Steedman and Erin Weir

INTRODUCTION

Carla Lipsig-Mummé

Globally, the world is browning, not greening. In 2010 greenhouse gas emissions rose 5.9 percent, the largest increase since measurement began. Global warming is likely to be the most important force transforming work and restructuring jobs in the first half of the twenty-first century. What is Canada doing to shape that transformation?

In 2008, a group of friends and colleagues with a long, shared history in the labour movement began talking about Canada's political refusal to take global warming seriously and what this meant for work, jobs, young workers and the next working class. And for the labour movement.

For the group, linked through labour research and activism in and for the unions, Canada's conservative silence represented a powerful threat. It also represented a source of embarrassment. In 2010, following a presentation I made with Donald Lafleur of the Canadian Union of Postal Workers about "climate change and the dilemma for labour" at an International Labour Organization (ILO) workshop on climate change and unions in Brussels, a speaker from Bangladesh came up to me. He said, "I have despised Canada for its stand on global warming. It's good to know that there are some people who are active in the right way in Canada." Ooof! A moment of truth about our changed place in the eyes of the world.

Throughout 2008, our group chewed over how to turn our conversations into useful contributions. Our focus became research: what do we really know about the impact and implications of climate change and policies to respond to climate change for jobs in Canada? Low carbon adaptation of work will necessarily change not only the labour process but the economies of regions and supply chains. What do we need to know?

We received research funding in 2008 from the Canadian Institutes of Health Research, the Social Science and Humanities Research Council of Canada and the Natural Science and Engineering Council to evaluate the state of knowledge about climate and work in Canada. Searching non-traditional research sources such as grey literature as well as the traditional peer-reviewed sources, we gathered more than 1,700 documents, which are now available to the public in an online bibliographic database. We found that while research on climate and work was certainly happening, its publication as reports or briefs often limited its dissemination. Very little research existed at all on the role of workers and their unions in responding to the impact of climate change and climate policy. In addition, Canada suffered from a fatal disconnect between research and public policy. The partial exceptions were Quebec and British Columbia. The Canadian situation was in contrast to the European Union, where research factors in to policy from the beginning.

By 2010 our research group had grown. Inevitably, our first research had thrown up new questions such as: What is being done to adapt the world of work to lower its greenhouse gas emissions? What role can labour play? In 2010, the Social Science and Humanities Research Council of Canada (SSHRC) funded Work in a Warming World (W3), a six-year project with thirty-three researchers, twenty-one community partners and ten universities in four countries. SSHRC is also funding a companion grant to make the research available to the non-academic public. Twenty-eight projects have been completed, a Climate, Youth and Work Institute is in place and regional forums have been held in New Brunswick, British Columbia and Ontario. The Work and Climate Change Report (WCR), a monthly bulletin of the most important research, legislation and policy worldwide on jobs, work and climate change, now has over one thousand readers.

The first section of *Climate@Work* is "Contexts," which explores three themes. First, the nature, sources and limits of available research. Elizabeth Perry discusses the surprising silence in English-language academic publishing on climate warming since 1995, finding that four-fifths of the research published is grey literature: reports and commissioned research, rather than publications in traditional, peer-reviewed journals. Why have the mainstream social sciences failed to invest in this important new field of research? What are the implications?

The second chapter is by Carla Lipsig-Mummé. It describes the international state of play for bringing the world of work into the struggle to green advanced economies, analyzing the EU, Australia, the US, profiling Canada's strategic paralysis. What makes a successful national strategy for emissions reduction? What is the range of roles that trade unions can and do play? In our decentralized collective bargaining system, neither the "social partnership" of the European Union nor the traditional labourism of Australia is available or necessarily desirable. Canadian labour needs a burst of strategic creativity, and this has yet to emerge.

The third chapter explores the role of international agreements in advancing or impeding integrated transition policy in Canada. Steve McBride and John Shields examine the trade challenges to Ontario's *Green Energy Act*, exploring both the obstacles that international agreements pose to building an integrated economic strategy around the transition to cleaner energy and the opportunities.

The second section of the book is "Sectors." Six chapters analyze the impact of both climate change and climate policy on employment in construction (John O'Grady), energy (Marjorie Griffin Cohen and John Calvert), tourism (Steve Tufts), postal and communications (Geoff Bickerton, Sarah Ryan, Meg Gingrich), transportation equipment (John Holmes with Austin Hracs) and forestry (John Holmes). The sectoral studies share a common set of questions: Has climate change affected the availability of jobs? What role does the government play in responding to climate change? What new green training and green re training is available for the sector? Who offers it? How widely is it taken up? Have domestic and international political economy played a role in the employment futures for this sector?

While the industries span the Canadian economy — public and private sector, services, manufacturing and resource-based — some surprising parallels and links emerge.

The sectoral studies highlight the need for robust government intervention in four ways. First is the need for regulatory policy to reduce firms' carbon footprint. Second is the need for serious government investment in training. Third is the need for integrated and inclusive government intervention to shore up struggling industries. Fourth is the hope that government leadership would take over from market-driven decision making.

Holmes and Hracs (transportation), Calvert and Cohen (energy) and Holmes (forestry) find similarities between the sectors in terms of their supply chains. Forestry, energy and transportation equipment are "hubs," linking with the other sectors and with each other. If there were a national policy of low-carbon transition, what role might these hubs play?

In the "hub" sectors as well as postal and communications, it looks like sectoral low-carbon transition will not change how the job is done, much. Cohen and Calvert, writing about the energy sector, do note that many green energy companies are non-union. Should the green energy sector remain largely unorganized, employment security and health and safety will be more difficult to protect. For tourism, Tufts found that high-road and low-road options for low-carbon transition were crystallizing among tourism sub-sectors in Canada, and the choice of which way to go had not yet been made. The prospects for the construction sector contrasts to the above. Representing 7 percent of the Canadian workforce and 35–40 percent of emissions (in life-cycle terms), continued growth in construction employment is assured, because of retrofitting. O'Grady observes that the industry has traditionally had an excellent record in adapting training to new circumstances; that the trades have been slow to pick up on green training; and that one consequence of this is that turf wars over long-established professional jurisdictions are breaking out.

1. CHANGING PATTERNS IN THE LITERATURE OF CLIMATE CHANGE AND CANADIAN WORK
The Research of Academics, Government and Social Actors

Elizabeth Perry

It comes as no surprise that there is an enormous, constantly expanding body of research on global warming and climate change. Isa Lang entitled her 2008 bibliographic essay about general climate change resources "Wrestling with an elephant" and characterized the literature as "daunting," "vast and overwhelming" (Lang 2008). Can the same be said of research about climate change and the world of work? This chapter examines the intersections between the vast climate change literature and the literature of the world of work, which is itself notoriously fragmented, including as it does the academic and practitioner output of economics, industrial relations, business, sociology and public policy. After a brief presentation of the literature search and its results, we discuss the contribution of the academic social sciences and the emerging importance of other sources of research and information, especially social actors and think tanks. Finally, we consider some implications of these new patterns of research and publication.

Writing in UNESCO's *World Social Science Report*, Roberta Balstad states that "there is a widely acknowledged need for social science contributions," yet "social science contributions to climate change have been less than many had expected. To date, climate change research remains a small specialty within the social sciences" (Balstad 2010: 210).

The results of our literature search confirm this: of all the documents, books and articles we discovered about climate change and the world of work, less than 20 percent were produced by the academic social science community.

Current discussion about social science research points to the growth of research organizations outside the traditional academic environment. Again, our results confirmed this trend, as we found many university organizations publishing without peer-review, producing what is generally known as "grey literature": documents produced by organizations whose primary purpose is not the publication of research.

BRIEF OVERVIEW OF THE LITERATURE SEARCH

Our literature search was done in support of a large research project coordinated by Professor Carla Lipsig-Mummé at York University in Toronto. The design of the search was dictated by the complex purpose of the research project, which was to discover and evaluate the state of knowledge concerning the interaction between climate change and Canadian work and employment. Key topics of interest were employment tenure and employment transitions, labour market restructuring, implications for skills and training and public policy and regulation.[1]

Our scope included important research relevant to these topics, produced in or about Canada, in either English or French, from January 1995 to December 2009. From the beginning, our interest went beyond the academic literature to include the research and publications of the social actors in this issue: government, business, labour and civil society. Different techniques and sources were required to find the publications of the social actors, which normally are published by the organizations themselves or in the popular or alternative press. The literature search was organized according to six economic sectors: energy, construction, forestry, postal services, tourism and transportation equipment. In addition, we captured any overviews on the issue of climate change impacts on multiple sectors or on jobs and work internationally. For each of these seven topics, the same search was replicated, consisting of three basic phases: 1) a search of academic literature; 2) a search of the websites of relevant stakeholders; and 3) an examination of the documents cited in phases 1 and 2, to ensure relevance and standards of quality and impartiality and to discover related documents using the bibliographies and footnotes in the documents from phases 1 and 2.

RESULTS OF THE LITERATURE SEARCH

Our literature search was conducted over four months in 2010, and though admittedly some minor publications might not have been recorded, we discovered and catalogued 1,414 documents relevant to the intersection of climate change and the world of work in our economic sectors in the years 1995–2009. The resulting bibliographic database allowed us to analyze the citations according to date, type of publishing body, format and economic sector. The analysis that follows focuses on the sources in English, including sources that were translated from the French. Details are provided in Tables 1.1, 1.2 and 1.3.

Of the entire database, academic documents accounted for only 18.5 percent of the documents found; 81.5 percent were "grey literature." Grey literature has been defined by the Grey Literature Network as "Information produced on all levels of government, academics, business and industry in electronic and print formats *not controlled by commercial publishing*, i.e., where publishing is not the primary activity of the producing body" (italics added).[2]

By far the most common publication format was the report: 715 documents, as compared to 227 journal articles and 81 books. Of the 796 reports and books, approximately 350 were published in Canada. We also identified 177 credible and authoritative websites.

Although our interest was in information about Canada, the global nature of the issue required an awareness of the international literature. Many social actors are working in collaborative arrangements and often in international collaborations. At the governmental level, high profile examples such as the Intergovernmental Panel on Climate Change, the United Nations Environment Programme (UNEP) and such sector specific agencies as the World Travel and Tourism Council, the Collaborative Partnership on Forests and the International Energy Agency reveal the importance of the international forum.

International collaborations among labour market actors — for example,

Table 1.1 Total Number of Documents by Economic Sector and Category

Industry Sector	Advocacy Groups	Government	Labour Market Actors	Popular Press	Research Organizations	Academic	Total
Context	25	62	46	4	22	28	187
Transportation Equipment	18	92	75	18	26	43	272
Construction	19	41	50	5	17	3	135
Energy	72	103	87	35	34	44	375
Forestry	9	76	30	3	14	39	171
Postal Services	4	15	51	8	1	7	86
Tourism	7	42	24	5	1	76	155
Ressources en français	1	30	65	0	6	0	102
Column Totals	154	461	428	78	121	233	1414**

1,414 is the total number of documents listed in the database as of September 2010. Some documents are listed in multiple sectors.

Table 1.2 Percentage of Grey Literature Documents and Academic Documents by Sector

Industry Sector	Grey Literature Documents Number (%)	Academic Documents Number (%)	Total Documents
Context	159 (85%)	28 (15%)	187
Auto	229 (84%)	43 (16%)	272
Construction	132 (97%)	3 (3%)	135
Energy	331 (88%)	44 (12%)	375
Forestry	132 (77%)	39 (23%)	171
Postal Services	79 (91%)	7 (9%)	86
Tourism	79 (50%)	76 (50%)	155
All sectors	1177 (83%)	237 (17%)	1414

Table 1.3 Publication by Year

	1995-1999	2000	2001	2002	2003	2004	2005	2006	2007	2008	2009	No date
Number of documents	81	32	32	41	49	55	76	108	145	247	321	Approx. 200

the International Electricity Partnership (of which the Canadian Electrical Association is a member), the European Trade Union Confederation, Universal Postal Union, Global Wind Energy Council and the World Business Council on Sustainable Development — also produced documents relevant to Canada. Similarly, international advocacy groups such as Greenpeace, Sierra Club and the Worldwatch Institute have Canadian offices or include Canada in their areas of interest.

THE IMPORTANCE OF THE WEB AND GREY LITERATURE

The crucial feature of grey literature — the fact that it is produced outside the mainstream of commercial publishing — renders it difficult to identify, locate, obtain and preserve. It is frequently published in web-only formats, which are often not archived and sometimes available only to a limited audience in sections of websites that enforce restricted access, part of what information specialists call the "deep web" or "invisible web."

Given the heavy concentration of grey literature in our database it is not surprising that there are so few documents available from the before the year 2000. However, the increase from 32 documents in the year 2000 to 280 documents in 2009 argues that there is also an expanding interest and awareness in the socio-economic issues relating to climate change. Based on our results, this interest is clearly coming from government agencies (461 documents), labour market actors (428 documents) and advocacy groups (154 documents).

Our literature search emphasized web searching for two reasons: firstly, one of the goals of the research project was to find publications that would be easily and publicly available; secondly, another goal was to learn what the social actors and labour market actors were researching, and these groups do not normally publish through the established commercial or academic channels. While one could argue that the search process itself has been responsible for the heavy concentration of grey literature, the results for the tourism sector show a 58 percent proportion of scholarly documents and serve as a reminder that the literature search included a complete review of academic indexes and catalogues in addition to the web search. The explanation for the heavy weighting of grey literature can be understood better by reviewing some of the current discussion about trends in social science research in general.

ARE SOCIAL SCIENTISTS IGNORING CLIMATE CHANGE?: THE EVIDENCE

The following themes in the current discussion about social science research can confirm and help to explain the results of our literature search:

1. A lack of interest in climate change in the traditional disciplines of management, economics, political science and sociology.
2. The development of new journals outside the traditional, core journals.
3. The growth of research centres outside the traditional academic environment: think tanks and collaborative bodies.

Our results are consistent with the observations made by Balstad and O'Brien in the UNESCO *World Social Science Report*: academic social science research about climate change is needed but not yet well developed (Balstad 2010; O'Brien 2010). More specifically, our results reflect the findings of Amanda Goodall in her analysis of the leading academic journals in the disciplines of business, management, economics, sociology and political science (Goodall 2008). Since these are the core disciplines of the field of employment relations, her work is highly relevant and her conclusions are of interest.

In researching her 2008 article, "Why have the leading journals in management (and other social sciences) failed to respond to climate change?," Goodall collected citation data from thirty leading English-language management journals, from 1970 to 2006. She found that only nine articles mentioned the terms "global warming" or "climate change" in the title, abstract or keywords. (This out of a total of 31,000 published articles.) When expanding her search to all management and business journals (not just the top thirty), she found forty-four articles. She replicated her search in the disciplines of economics, sociology and political science and found similar results (Table 1.4).

Table 1.4 Summary of Goodall's Results re: Climate Change Articles in Scholarly Social Sciences Journals

Academic discipline	Total number of articles published, 1970-2006	Number of articles mentioning global warming or climate change in title, abstract, or keyword
Business & Management	31,000	9
Economics	51,000	63
Sociology	25,000	40
Political Science	30,000	11

Source: Goodall 2008: 411

Replicating Goodall's paper for the literature of the world of work, we searched five core academic industrial relations journals for the term "climate change" from 1995 to 2011. The five core journals — *British Journal of Industrial Relations, Journal of Industrial Relations, Industrial Relations Journal, Industrial & Labor Relations Review* and *Industrial Relations/Relations industrielles* — yielded only one relevant article.[3] We expanded the search to encompass a broader selection of industrial relations journals, including formats such as peer-reviewed electronic journals, which yielded nine further articles (seven of which were published in the March 2011 issue of *Labour Studies Journal* in a special issue dedicated to the theme of "Labour and the Environment").[4]

If the literature search had been expanded even further to use broader terms such as "environment," it would have also uncovered pioneering work in Europe by Gregory, Hildebrandt, LeBlansch and Lorentzen in 1996: "Industrial Relations and the Environment — Some Theses" in the *European Review of Labour and Research* and in 1999, "Industrial Relations and the Protection of the Environment: Research Findings from a New Policy Field" in the *European Journal of Industrial Relations*. Such a broad search was not indicated in our original task but would form an interesting line of inquiry for future bibliographic work — work that would need to transcend the disciplinary and regional silos of publication.

SOCIAL SCIENCES AND CLIMATE CHANGE RESEARCH: POSSIBLE EXPLANATIONS

Goodall considers the possible reasons why the core academic business and management journals have not represented the climate change debate well — the relative newness of the issue, political bias, climate skepticism, career incentives in the discipline — but she ultimately hypothesizes that research on climate change has been "sidelined intellectually" and is being reported in fields (for example, environmental studies) that are considered peripheral to the central, traditional disciplines (Goodall 2008: 418).

Genevieve Patenaude uses Rogers's diffusion of innovation theory as her framework to explain the diffusion of the idea of climate change in the academic community of management studies (Patenaude 2011). Patenaude relies on Goodall's analysis and her own replication of it in the business and "prestige press" to conclude that "the communication channels favoured by the academic community to disseminate knowledge significantly contributed in hindering the diffusion of the climate change idea" (Patenaude 2011: 268). Her lengthy paper provides recommendations for how the academic community might break down their "silo-based" disciplines and departments within academia and increase engagement with other audiences.

DEVELOPMENT OF NEW JOURNALS

Goodall refers to new, peripheral fields, and these are spawning new professional associations and their own new journals. Although mainly a summary of bibliometrics about the scientific climate change literature, an analysis of research trends by Gert-Jan Geraeds points out that there has been remarkable growth in climate change studies in the social sciences, as reflected in the launch of several specialized journals. Geraeds points to the journals *Mitigation and Adaptation Strategies for Global Change, Climate and Development* and *Carbon and Climate Law Review* as examples (Geraeds 2009).[5] Other titles discovered in our search could be added to the list: *AMBIO, Climatic Change, Climate Policy, Climate Research, European Environment, Global Environmental Change*, as well as discipline specific journals such as *Energy and Environment, Energy Economist, Energy Policy, Greener Management Journal, Journal of Environmental Management, Journal of Sustainable Tourism* and *Renewable Energy*. In 2011 the prestigious Nature Publishing Group launched *Nature Climate Change*, in print and online, to link research in the physical and social sciences.

The growing number and quality of "open access" electronic journals offers a new publication model whereby academics can publish more quickly without forsaking some level of peer review, and the public can enjoy convenient and sometimes free access. As with all new endeavours, some titles disappear and others arise quickly: in 2011, work and climate change issues were being published in the *Journal of Environmental Economics, International Journal of Environment, Workplace and Employment* and *Global Labour Journal*.

NEW RESEARCH ORGANIZATIONS STRADDLE
ACADEMIA AND THE PROFESSIONAL WORLD

What are some of the new organizational models that might break down the "silos" Patenaude talks about? On the Canadian academic scene, the Social Sciences and Humanities Research Council of Canada has funded Research Chairs in aspects of climate change and society at at least three universities: University of Guelph, University of Victoria and University of Waterloo. These scholars are actively researching climate change issues within the traditional academic framework but also in some cases publishing outside the traditional peer-reviewed process. The Pacific Institute for Climate Studies at the University of Victoria, for example, brings together faculty and graduate students from University of Victoria, University of British Columbia, Simon Fraser University and the University of Northern British Columbia. It coordinates graduate student fellowship research, publishes in peer-reviewed journals and academic books and also has a mandate to ensure that research is meaningfully transferred to government, industry and the public. Accordingly, it publishes its own working paper series, briefing notes and a free online news scan service.

Environments is a refereed, interdisciplinary journal published by the Department of Geography and Environmental Studies at Wilfrid Laurier University, Waterloo, Ontario. The stated purpose of this journal is to promote scholarship and discussion in a multidisciplinary and civic way, providing ideas and information that people might use to think effectively about the future. This is also an open access journal (Department of Geography and Environmental Studies n.d.).

In the U.S., research organizations such as the Center on Wisconsin Strategy (COWS) at the University of Wisconsin, Madison; Center on Globalization, Governance & Competitiveness (CGGC) at Duke University in Durham, North Carolina; and the Political Economy Research Institute (PERI) at the University of Massachusetts, Amherst, have all produced publications relating to the economic impacts of climate change. And finally, a very pro-business example of a new academic-professional model is the Smith School of Enterprise and Environment at Oxford University in the United Kingdom. The school does not teach students but publishes working papers and reports. At its first world forum in 2008, the director stated, "the Smith School is a global hub to facilitate governments, the private sector and academia to meet the climate challenge" (Plume 2009).

And what exactly is a "think tank"? The Think Tanks and Civil Society Program at the University of Pennsylvania clearly links the academic world to this more accessible organization. In the program's very complete definition from the 2011 Global Go To Think Tanks Rankings, it states:

Think tanks or public policy research, analysis, and engagement institutions are organizations that generate policy-oriented research, analysis, and advice on domestic and international issues in an effort to enable policy-makers and the public to make informed decisions about public policy issues. Think tanks may be affiliated with political parties, governments, interest groups, or private corporations or constituted as independent non-governmental organizations (NGOs). These institutions often act as a bridge between the academic and policymaking communities, serving the public interest as an independent voice that translates applied and basic research into a language and form that is understandable, reliable, and accessible for policymakers and the public. (University of Pennsylvania Think Tanks and Civil Society Program 2011: 22; italics added)

The annual rankings produced by the program include a category for the top thirty think tanks in the world for environmental issues. Top ranking goes to the Pew Centre on Global Climate Change (now The Center for Climate and Energy Solutions [C2ES]). The only Canadian think tank among the top thirty is the International Institute for Sustainable Development (IISD), ranked twelfth. Although the IISD is a Canada-based non-profit, it has no direct academic links, and its main activity is its web-based reporting of UN and other multilateral agencies' international environmental and development activities (Geraeds 2009).[6]

QUESTIONS FOR THE FUTURE OF RESEARCH ON CLIMATE CHANGE AND WORK

The results of our literature search are consistent with other evaluative articles regarding the state of social science publishing about climate change to date. We identified a growing number of valuable, well-researched documents that exist outside the established, traditional channels of publication and, just as important, outside permanent libraries and repositories.

These documents are largely available on the web, although those published before 2005 are much less certain to be available. With web archiving inconsistent among publishing bodies, even among government departments and university research organizations, there is a pressing need to capture and preserve these documents before they disappear or move so that they are available for future researchers and for public discourse. Who can or will take on this challenge?

Approximately 81 percent of documents concerning Canadian workplaces and climate change were produced by governments, labour market actors (businesses and unions), advocacy groups and research centres from 1995 to 2009. We see that increasingly, research and its dissemination is not limited to academic venues and intra-academic discussions and that the government, unions and other social actors are bringing the results of their research out to the wider public. How is that changing the questions being asked and the ways in which the answers are used?

Notes

1   The documents discussed by this literature search are catalogued and described in the bibliographic database at the Work in a Warming World website, hosted by York University in Toronto, Canada. The online catalogue is publicly available and searchable at <workinawarmingworld.yorku.ca/bibliographic-database/>.

2.   Definition used by the Grey Literature Network Service, Amsterdam, and reproduced at their GreyNet website at <greynet.org/greynethome.html>.

3.   The search of the five core academic industrial relations journals yielded only one article: Preston, Alison. 2009. "Labour markets and wages in 2008." *Industrial Relations Journal* 51, 3: 313–30.

4.   The theme of *Labour Studies Journal* (March 2011) volume 36, 1, was "Labour and the Environment."

5.   Patenaude (2011: 263) provides detailed methodology of the sources searched. Of her use of the term "prestige press" she states: "I distinguish between prestige and tabloids as quality and popular sensationalist newspapers, respectively."

6.   The main focus of the Geraeds article, which appeared in a special issue on "Research into Environmental Challenges," is to summarize the bibliometric work by Gerald Stanhill, who found that the annual number of publications on climate change in the journal of the American Meteorological Society increased from 14 to 372 in the period between 1970 and 1995.

7.   The International Institute on Sustainable Development website is at iisd.org/default.aspx.

2. CLIMATE, WORK AND LABOUR
The International Context

Carla Lipsig-Mummé

We are far off course. (OECD 2012b: 1)

In the past five years, Canada has diverged increasingly from the rest of the developed world in terms of policy and action in the struggle to slow climate warming. On the international scene, Canada's Conservative government is a late-onset climate denier, withdrawing from Kyoto and dismissive of the science of climate warming. Nationally, the government has weakened environmental assessment and protection, downloaded responsibility for environmental protection to the uneven mercy of the provinces, removed charitable status from the more effective environmental groups and closed hundreds of climate science positions in the federal environment agencies. The federal-level industrial sector councils, which for decades have been the lead training organizations in occupational and industrial sectors in Canada, have been quietly dissolved, destroying their ability to play a lead role in any serious effort to deal with the economic effects of climate warming (NRTEE 2012; Buzzetti 2011a and 2011b).

A recent policy briefing about what Canadians can learn from U.K. climate change policy offers the following observations:

- "Canada has a comparatively weak level of commitment to international and national climate change action";
- "Canada's federal government is pursuing a sector-by-sector regulatory approach, with fragmented action between the federal government and the provinces";
- "Canada's emissions do not appear to be on a fundamental downward trajectory and with existing policies, Canada is unlikely to meet its 2020 Copenhagen Accord target" (Sustainable Prosperity 2012: 1–2).

In the face of the federal government's lack of a national climate strategy, provinces are moving to fill the void. But even if all fourteen provincial and federal emissions-reduction programs were combined and worked as projected, Canada would still, by 2020, be approximately 50 percent short of its target (NRTEE 2012). The Canadian government is, with the exception of the U.S., the developed world's lead climate skeptic, a spoiler in the international arena. The internal impact of the federal government's stance is still unfolding.

Responding to climate change[1] is a social issue. In the European Union and Australia, the impact of climate change on jobs and the impact of the policies to control climate change on jobs are central to the politics of emissions reduction and to the introduction of the Australian carbon tax. "If the questions of employment and human resources are not more closely integrated into climate policies, we may expect them to become a major barrier to the transformations demanded" (Dupressoir et al. 2007a: 3).

The United Nations Environment Programme (2008, 2011), the International Labour Organization (ILO 2011) and a prolific body of U.S. research focus on the opportunities that a transition to clean energy could unlock for massive job creation, if the political will were willing. But key groups in the American polity continue to ignore the findings of research, demonstrating both the disastrous divide between research and politics, and between the U.S. and the rest of the developed world.[2]

Except Canada. The effect of climate change on jobs greatly concerns Canadians, but doing something about climate's impact on work and employment has been obscured by the larger political campaign against the science of global warming. In the eyes of the present Canadian government, action to reduce GHGs at work will destroy jobs and the economy — and the economy comes before the environment. But the volatile, warming climate has already changed how we work, what we produce, where we are able to produce it and what new or adaptive skills we may need (Lipsig-Mummé 2008a). The climate effect is uneven, between provinces, industries, age groups and genders. It is shifting employment between regions and communities, dislocating people and industries and futures (Lemmen et al. 2008). New professions and occupations are springing up, established occupations are "green-branding" and the possibilities of new ways of working are crystallizing. These shifts are also challenging training and education, influencing the school-to-work trajectory and making broad environmental literacy a necessity for all ages in the workforce (Lipsig-Mummé 2008a).

Does a national policy to reduce greenhouse gases destroy jobs? Internationally, there is mounting evidence that *not* reducing GHGs will destroy jobs in the immediate and middle distance (Richardson, Kammen, Stern 2009; Thomson 2010). In Canada, as in every industrialized country, the world of work is one of the most significant producers of greenhouse gas emissions. Fields and mines, as well as offices, hospitals, factories, stores, universities, virtual offices and studios, all produce goods, services and ideas, and all produce greenhouse gases. New "green" job creation does not necessarily reduce the production of GHGs, but reducing the carbon footprint of the present suite of jobs and workplaces will reduce GHGs. Decarbonizing the work world changes work itself.

There are, however, two faces to the jobs/climate dilemma. First, there is the issue of the impact of climate warming on jobs. Some jobs will inevitably be churned from the most polluting industries and from single-industry communities such as agriculture and forestry where climate warming has destroyed or shifted the geographic location of work. However, European research indicates that with well-integrated government-led active labour market pathways, the dislocation of people and jobs remains within economic sectors and is projected to lead to a small increase in aggregate employment in the European Union by 2030 (Dupressoir et al. 2007b).

Second, there is the question of how work itself can adapt its practices in order to slow global warming and what impact the adaptation of work will have for employment, job creation, technology and new work practices, and for the reduction of emissions.

However, concerned as they may be by Canada's national political refusal to deal seriously with the threat of climate warming, very few of Canada's most important climate think tanks factor in the future of jobs or the potential contribution of greening work to the reduction of our carbon footprint.

Globally, the world is browning, rather than greening.

It is hard to avoid the fact that the struggle to slow climate warming is being lost: in 2010, greenhouse gas emissions rose 5.9 percent worldwide, the largest increase recorded in history (*New York Times* June 27, 2012). In the face of strategic failure of this magnitude, national governments in developed countries, of Left and Right persuasion, have turned to beefing up their own roles. "Bringing the state back in" has manifested itself in actions to regulate and tax carbon emissions nationally, incubate green R & D, encourage domestic manufacture of domestically-developed green tech, educate for environmental literacy and create and fund active labour market pathways for workers at all stages of their working lives. Germany, whose green transition is the most developed of the industrialized countries, has been able to decouple greenhouse gas emissions "absolutely" from economic growth (OECD 2012a).

In Canada, however, "The hard reality of developing an effective and acceptable national climate policy plan within a federation that shares responsibility for emissions management ... and needs to speak with one voice internationally, has been too tough [for Canada] to overcome" (NRTEE 2012: 20).

There are also neglected opportunities. Although climate science has recently become interested in the role of the economy and policy-makers in mitigating GHG production, and the need for strong interventionist governments to reduce GHGs is now widely accepted, work itself as a driver of emissions reduction is still neglected, and the potential contribution of every job and every work site to "green adapt" its practices in order to mitigate emissions, has been largely overlooked. The role of workers, their unions and their professional associations as agents of adaptation and mitigation in the work world is even more rarely considered.

This chapter reviews international research and policy on the climate/work interface in developed countries in the context of the rapid growth of climate warming. We focus particularly on three international debates that frame the limits and possibilities of bringing the work world in to the struggle against climate warming. The first debate asks: how has climate science's understanding of the role of economic activity and economic actors in slowing global warming evolved? The relation between mitigation and adaptation has of necessity changed. The second debate asks: what is the role of the state in the struggle to slow global warming? The combination of the global financial crisis and its aftershocks with the unexpected speed of climate warming has made strong state intervention increasingly acceptable to governments of the Right as well as of the Left, while placing new demands on national governments in regional, continental and global policy negotiations. In both national and international policy however, environment policy is too often employment-blind and vice versa (McBride 2010; Dupressoir et al. 2007b). The third debate concerns the future of jobs and the role of work in the transition to a lower-carbon economy. In conclusion, we consider Canada's policy approaches in the context of the international state of knowledge and action.

THREE DEBATES

Worldwide, the combination of unequal globalization and global warming is creating an uneven convergence of dangers. *Suffering the Science: Climate Change, People and Poverty* (Oxfam International 2009) predicted that hunger will become this century's most brutal legacy of climate change. A European Commission study predicted that as many as 20 percent of the world's population may become "environment migrants" (European Commission 2008). Among developed and prosperous countries, heat-related deaths are growing, seasons are disappearing, drought is destroying crops and agricultural futures, communities and livelihoods, and extreme weather events are wreaking havoc with growing seasons. "This summer is 'What Global Warming Looks Like,'" says Seth Borenstein of the Associated Press (Borenstein 2012). In *Man-Made World: Choosing between Progress and Planet*, Andrew Charlton observes that hunger and vulnerability define the life chances of the majority of the world's population, and poverty and the environment are "the twin imperatives of the twenty-first century" (Charlton 2011:7). He notes that the inability of rich countries to acknowledge the legitimacy of the survival needs of climate-threatened poor countries is central to the failure to develop a global strategy to slow climate warming.

THE FIRST DEBATE: CLIMATE SCIENCE AND ECONOMIC ACTIVITY

> It is crucial to reduce CO_2 emissions and thus mitigate climate change. (ILO 2011: 7)

> Neither adaptation nor mitigation alone can avoid all climate change impacts. (Intergovernmental Panel on Climate Change 2007a: 65)

The first debate develops within the international climate science community and concerns two relationships: first, the relationship between strategies to reduce greenhouse gas emissions and economic activity; second, the changing relationship between strategies of mitigation and adaptation. Serious science has established that human activity is responsible for climate warming. But the most influential climate syntheses continue to reflect the legacy of struggle over the role of human society in warming as they grapple with economic activity as both creator and reducer of greenhouse gas emissions (see, for example, Intergovernmental Panel on Climate Change 2007b).

What measures can be used to slow global warming, and how can economic activity play a role (Stern 2007; IPCC 2007)? For climate scientists, mitigation is "anthropogenic intervention to reduce the sources ... of greenhouse gases" (IPCC 2001 Annex B). Adaptation is "adjustment in natural or human systems in response to a new or changing environment ... which moderates harm or exploits beneficial opportunities" (ibid.). Until recently, both climate science and social science focused on mitigation as the main game — reducing the production of greenhouse gases. But in recent years there has been a complex and shifting relation between mitigation and adaptation. The climate scientist A. Lynch traces a longer picture.

> A primary finding [of the IPCC First Assessment Report, completed in 1990 and updated in 1992] was that mitigation and adaptation strategies should be considered as an integrated package and should complement each other to minimize net costs. But by the early 1990s, debate over climate change focused on the political positions for and against the reduction of green-house gas emissions and support of adaptation implied neglect of mitigation. (Lynch 2008: 1)

The turn against adaptation became extreme in the 1990s. Lynch quotes Al Gore's statement that "a focus on adaptation is a kind of laziness and an arrogant faith in our ability to react in time to save our skins" (ibid.: 4).

Since the beginning of this century, however, support for adaptation within the climate science community has re-emerged. Developing ways in which adaptation and mitigation can work together is now both a virtue and a necessity. It also opens the door to greater collaboration between social science and climate science. In its five-year synthesis of research in 2007, the IPCC observed that the potential for economic activity to make mitigation more effective was so considerable that it could "offset the projected growth of global emissions or reduce emissions below current levels" (IPCC 2007: 158). However, the economy's contribution would not be realized unless there was good policy in place.

In the past half-decade, the need to move beyond simplistic either/or strategic choices — either mitigation or adaptation — has become pressing (DesJarlais et al. 2004; DesJarlais and Blondlot 2010). This, for four reasons. First, climate warming is occurring more rapidly than expected and continues to worsen regardless of efforts to mitigate. Civil society and mid-level institutions, between the individual or household and the state, need to be involved. Between 1990 and 2008 global emissions grew by 40 percent (ILO 2011: 2). In 2010, CO_2 emissions grew more rapidly than in any other year in recorded history (*New York Times* June 27, 2012). Second, mitigation requires government intervention to effectively reduce emissions — self-regulation by private enterprise has proven inadequate both internationally and within developed and developing economies (ILO 2011: 1). To date, few governments among the industrialized nations outside of the E.U. have crafted and implemented effective national mitigation strategies.

Third, slowing greenhouse gas production calls for producing goods and services differently. "*Approximately 80 percent of all* CO_2 *emissions [in the European Union] occur in the production process and not from the direct energy consumption of households.* Lowering CO_2 emissions is likely to be associated with significant change for firms and workers, especially those concentrated in the high-carbon industries" (ILO 2011: 7–8; italics added).

"Producing differently" requires adaptation of part or all of the production process of goods, services and ideas. This includes inputs, work organization, technology, the physical environment in which work takes place, distribution and disposal. It also requires new or revised skills training, which will have an impact on education and training institutions.

Fourth, developed societies have tended to dismiss adaptation. It has traditionally been an international development strategy for building resilience in poor communities and economies grappling with a cluster of systemic vulnerabilities, of which climate exposure is one (UNEP 2007, 2008, 2009a,

2009b, 2011). To be of strategic use in developed economies at this point in time, adaptation needs to be adapted to prepare for the vulnerabilities of industrial and post-industrial societies.

Burton, a leading proponent of adaptation, emphasizes the links between development policy and adaptation. Observing in 2002 that "adaptation is much less developed than mitigation as a policy response," he suggests that it could be further developed in two ways: biological adaptation and adaptation for the poorest communities that focuses "on the social and economic determinants of vulnerability in a development context" (Burton et al. 2002: 145).

In its influential state of knowledge study on the impacts of climate change in Canada in 2008, Natural Resources Canada mentions the need for a larger role for adaptation in the spectrum of Canadian strategic responses to climate warming. "Although adaptation processes are not well understood, institutions and civil society will play a key role in mobilizing adaptive capacity" (Lemmen et al. 2008: 7). Giddens, however, goes further. "Adaptation is a misleading term. It implies reacting to climate change once it has occurred" (Giddens 2011: 163). He proposes to "refocus" adaptation for developed societies to map and respond to vulnerabilities before they crash — proactive or preemptive adaptation (ibid.: 162–5). Giddens singles out the organization of work as a site for proactive adaptation. Proactive adaptation in the work world calls for collective implementation.

As central as the world of work and its associations are to economic and social life (and therefore to the struggle to slow global warming), the International Labour Organization draws attention to the worldwide failure of environmental policy to consider work and workers as actors rather than acted upon.

In the climate debate, employment only features marginally and is regarded as merely a "co-benefit" of mitigation measures. This view overlooks the fact that the benefits for employment and development are vital for making many mitigation measures technically feasible, economically viable and socially acceptable (Belèn-Sanchez and Poschen 2009: 11).

The idea that new links between mitigation and adaptation may be developed in the world of work is promising. Yet, as a recent article by Fankhauser et al. notes, there is as yet very little research on climate's impact on the quality of jobs and on the organization of work itself (Fankhauser et al. 2008).

The need for jobs will neither disappear nor shrink. Tim Jackson's and Peter Victor's writing to the contrary notwithstanding, the need for paid employment is likely to grow, rather than shrink (Jackson 2009; Victor 2008). Paid employment and work itself are essential to maintaining life, identity and social inclusion. A focused strategy for adapting work in all its dimensions can mitigate the greenhouse gases produced by work. While Fankhauser et al. agree with the pioneering European Union study (Dupressoir et al. 2007a, 2007b) that reducing GHGs will lead to a modest increase in jobs in the short term, Fankhauser et al. adds that long term reduction of GHGs will transform "the way economic activities take place" (Fankhauser et al. 2008: 427). Surely this is a place where the world of work can contribute significantly to transitions to a greener world economy.

THE SECOND DEBATE: THE ROLE OF THE STATE

> To date, markets alone have been inadequate in addressing climate change. (ILO 2011: 1)

> A majority of people now want more active, creative and leading governments in the response to climate change. (Richardson, Kammen, Stern 2009: 7)

In the two decades since the Intergovernmental Panel on Climate Change (IPCC) issued its first report, the role of the state in slowing global warming has moved from the margins to the hot centre of climate policy. Since the global financial crisis (GFC) unfurled in 2008, it has become increasingly clear that national governments must play a deeper and broader role in catalyzing, coordinating and enforcing national environmental policies that reduce greenhouse gases. The global economic crisis and the global environmental crisis are inextricably linked. Globalization's trope notwithstanding, it is national governments that craft and activate climate strategy — or fail to do so (UNEP 2011; Giddens 2011). With the partial exception of the E.U., the focus now is on national government rather than subnational units; on economy-wide measures that operate on several levels of society; on government as regulator rather than facilitator; and on the urgency of acting before 2020 (OECD 2012b; UNEP 2011; ILO 2011; NRTEE 2012). In UNEP's 2011 report *Towards a Green Economy*, there are six enabling conditions for transition to a green economy. The state is the prime mover in all six. In the OECD's *Environmental Outlook to 2050*, national governments are called upon to "set more ... stringent mitigation targets," "put a price on carbon," "complement carbon pricing with well-designed regulations," and enforce the regulations (OECD 2012b).

In *Reality Check*, Canada's National Roundtable on the Environment and the Economy (NRTEE) highlights a policy gap for Canada that parallels the emissions gap. To achieve all the required least-cost emission reductions, Canada therefore requires either 1) an economy-wide national policy approach, or 2) coordination between different levels of government and among different policy mechanisms. Neither approach currently exists in Canada (NRTEE 2012: 109).

For the developed economies, this interventionist role for the state at the end of the first decade of the twenty-first century marks a double break: first, with the neoliberal posture of governments in the 1980s and 1990s that had hollowed out the welfare state and defined "the market" as equivalent to society as a whole. The second break was with the Stern Review, which, from its first publication in 2006, was a game-changer. It proposed, and legitimized, an economic turn for politics. After three decades of government abdication from regulating economy and society in developed countries, Stern had placed politics at the heart of the climate response, but a certain form of politics: national governments were to be pro-active agents for "climatizing" the market. "Policy must promote sound market signals, overcome market failures and have equity and risk mitigation at its core" (Stern 2007: i). Stern saw the economy as a key site for slowing global warming before it becomes catastrophic. But within the economy, Stern's view of the world of work is passive: acted upon rather than actor.

By 2009 it had become clear that the GFC was not a minor shock from which globalized capitalism would quickly recover. A new cluster of frailties now distracted attention from climate warming in developed societies. The continuing global financial crisis with its widening threat to the European Union's integration, coupled with U.S. economic decline, a growing economic gap between global North and global South and deepening inequality within the global North all turned attention away from global cooperation over climate strategies, allowed the reductiveness of "environment vs. economy" to resurface and signalled the renewed importance of regionalisms. The unexpectedly rapid pace of global warming combined with the approach of Kyoto's expiry in 2012 and the regionalization or abandonment of CO_2 reduction strategies made it more difficult to maintain a link between environment and economic policy and to retain hope for a new global climate pact. In this besieged climate, Giddens's recognition that "the state will be an all-important actor" (Giddens 2011: 5) and that it is national governments that control the implementation of international agreements, offers a return to the familiar terrain of politics at the level of the national state.

The return to the national state has been remarkable for the ideological range of those who espouse it. The inability of the world economy to emerge from the GFC has made for strange ideological bedfellows in the field of climate policy. In the U.K., Cameron's Conservative government pursues a multilevel program to reduce emissions and publicly finds common ground with Gillard's Labor government in Australia, whose carbon tax began on July 1, 2012 (Jotzo 2012; Patay and Sartor 2012). Both need effective strategies for transitioning employment from brown jobs to greener jobs. But Cameron's job cuts in the public sector and their flow-on effects are so enormous that the U.K. economy is slipping into recession, endangering the U.K.'s emissions strategy but mobilizing the broader labour movement. Australia and Canada are returning to resource-based economies of their colonial past after a century of building domestic manufacture. The economy of Australia has become so dependent on its brown resource industries and on China's consumption of these, that Australia's mining companies have gained the political clout to craft a broader agenda to reshape the Australian labour market around temporary (unorganized) workers from low-wage countries. Although mining employs a tiny fraction of the Australian labour force, the mining companies' opposition to a carbon tax contributed to the demise of Kevin Rudd as Labor prime minister in 2010 and may contribute to the election of the (conservative) Liberals in 2013. The Liberals' leadership group is climate-denying and opposed to the carbon tax.

The conservative turn in politics in the developed economies has not produced a uniform, conservative approach to environmental responsibility. On the one hand, the conservative governments of Germany and the U.K. pursue ambitious programs of decarbonization. Germany, the leader among developed countries in reducing greenhouse gas emissions, has managed to link an "ambitious environmental policy" (OECD 2012a: 1) with rapid economic recovery from the GFC. While there has been rapid growth in employment in the environmental goods and services sector, "taking account of the job losses in declining sectors, the net ... effects on employment are difficult to assess" (OECD 2012a: 3).

Environmentally speaking, an environmentally-committed, activist, Centre-Right government like Germany has much in common with environmentally-committed, activist, Centre-Left governments elsewhere in the European Union. Both Centre-Left and Centre-Right governments strive to make and enforce international climate agreements, set domestic carbon taxes and emissions trading schemes, incubate leading-edge green R & D, encourage domestic manufacture based on the R & D, aid the development of export markets, reward existing businesses for reducing their CO_2 production, provide active labour market transition for workers caught by the green transition and protect the highly skilled environmentally-trained workers upon whom so much depends.

What distinguishes environmentally progressive Left from Right governments where work is concerned? Their commitment, or lack of it, to creating the conditions for good employment transitions — or any transitions at all — for workers in brown sectors whose jobs are likely to disappear.

Conservatism in the U.S. and Canada, in contrast, is a more primitive affair. The U.S. and Canada are conservative political regimes that share, at differing levels of government, a visceral hostility to government itself. U.S. politics are starkly divided, and neither the U.S. nor Canada has a climate policy or strategy. President Obama favours a cap-and-trade scheme, which passed the House of Representatives in 2009 but failed to pass the Senate in 2010. U.S. federal political action to slow global warming is now pursued by the federal Environmental Protection Agency (EPA), whose mandate includes protecting public health. In the last five years, the EPA has often seemed the most courageous and creative body in U.S. environmental politics.[3]

In an article in *The Guardian*, Will Hutton refers to the U.S. "ideological imperative" to deny climate warming based in the fundamentalist antigovernment ideology of the Republican Party:

> Climate change sceptics, most vividly in the U.S. where it has become a basic credo of the modern Republican party, are sceptics because to accept the case [for global warming] is to accept the need to do something collectively and internationally that must involve government. But government is bad. It is inefficient, obstructs enterprise, inhibits freedom, regulates and taxes. Climate change activists want carbon taxes and to set targets for efficient resource use; they also want regulations to encourage environmentally friendly behaviour. This is the back door through which socialism will be reinvented — and scientists have been unwittingly captured by wild leftwing environmental ginger groups. (Hutton 2012)

Nevertheless, California and the New England states have managed to implement their own clean energy plans.

Canada's Conservative government under the leadership of Stephen Harper has no national plan for reducing GHGs and dismisses global warming as scaremongering. Like the U.S. Republicans (although without their "live free or die" extremism), Canadian Conservatives elide measures to reduce greenhouse gases with a threat to the economy and conflate climate policy with big government. Like Australia, the Canadian economy has again become dependent on the dirtiest of its national resources. In Canada, that is the tar sands. The federal government is also politically dependent on the tar sands corporations. In this toxic environment, Ontario, Quebec and British Columbia (like California and the New England states) are pursuing emissions reductions programs of their own, with some links to California (World Bank 2012: 80–90; NRTEE 2012: 42–61).

The question of jobs is nowhere on the Harper government's retrograde agenda, although Canadian provinces have green job creation within their climate plans.

Based on existing and proposed federal and P/T (provincial and territorial) policies, Canada is currently on track to achieve just under half of the emission reductions required to meet its 2020 target. A national emissions gap exists, and additional policies will be required to drive further emission reduction in order to achieve the 2020 target. Provincial policies account for most of these emission reductions — approximately 75 percent of forecasted reductions in 2020 (NRTEE 2012: 89).

THE THIRD DEBATE: WHAT ABOUT THE JOBS?

> If adaptation strategies for developed economies focus "proactively" on transforming economic activities and the organization of work, they have the potential to significantly mitigate the emission of greenhouse gases. (Lipsig-Mummé 2011: 20)[4]

> Robust action on climate change, made up of both mitigation and adaptation measures, should be based upon two crucial elements: the immediate setting in place of the political options which are most effective in delivering the double dividend of the fight against climate change and the creation of quality jobs, on the one hand; and on the other hand, the introduction of instruments to anticipate and provide socially responsible support for the economic and social changes demanded, and to make workers into the players in that change. (Dupressoir et al. 2007a: 4)

In their 2008 review article on climate and jobs, Pearce and Stillwell outline "three waves" in the development of thinking about climate change and the economy in the developed world: the 1960s, 1980s and 2000s (Pearce and Stillwell 2008). Writing of the third wave, they mark the Stern Review of 2006, Al Gore's campaign that same year and the Fourth IPCC Assessment in 2007 as turning points for political change on climate. Reviewing almost fifty years of engagement between climate and economy, they note, "What differentiates the latest of these waves [of climate focus on the economy] is the sustaining of momentum, culminating in the commitment to environmental economic policy change (ibid.: 121).

Pearce and Stilwell wrote as the global financial crisis was unfolding. Their measured optimism about the role that national governments needed to play in transitioning to a greener economy was set within a political economy framework. They noted that "labour redeployment" (job churning) had still not been included in the agenda of most government climate policies outside the European Union. And they drew attention to the important analyses that bring workers and jobs back in: the work of the Apollo Alliance in the U.S.[5] and the Canadian Labour Congress, which had created the idea of Just Transition. But they also noted that the research that did bring forward the questions of jobs and of workers was usually produced by progressive groups and scholars, often based in the labour movement.

JOBS AND CLIMATE CHANGE

The climate and jobs debate today is in reality two debates: the first concerns employment, the second concerns work. While research on the impact of climate change on employment in developed economies has grown in recent years, research on climate and work itself is still remarkably underdeveloped.[6]

For the past three decades, the focus of workers in developed economies has been on the quantity of jobs rather than the quality of work and industrial citizenship. This has undone the considerable gains made between the end of World War II and the 1970s for worker voice in the labour process, technological change, job security, decent wages and pensions, occupational health and safety and reducing demographic and systemic inequalities. The flow-on effects from collective bargaining to the wider workforce in this "golden era of the welfare state" were considerable. Since the mid 1980s, however, precarious employment has spread like an oil slick throughout North America, Australia and Europe as well as the countries of the former Soviet bloc, Latin America and Asia. Coupled with late twentieth-century globalization, governments of the Left and Right in Europe, North America, Australia and New Zealand stood back while precarious employment grew, unions weakened and manufacturing migrated either to the global South or to the poorer hinterlands of their own regions. As the struggle for the quantity of jobs eclipsed the struggle for the quality of work, the fragmented nature of employment and the vanishing link between identity, work and jobs have eroded not only working conditions and job security but the ability of unions in many developed countries to collectively bargain for workplace citizenship, occupational health and safety and environmental responsibility. In the present "climate era," the struggle for quantity of jobs vs. quality of work is translated into employment transition for workers in brown industry, and green adaptation of the labour process for all industries, sectors and occupations. At this point in the climate era, both are essential.

The erosion of union engagement with the quality of work is significant in the collective bargaining regimes of the U.S. and Canada, where the union movements' links to social democratic or mildly progressive parties are so ineffectual that the party in office is dependent upon union campaigning for election but itself cannot be counted on to factor the employment concerns of workers into trade, environment or labour market policy. In countries where labourism is a century or more old — U.K., Australia, New Zealand — the union-party relationship is now intermittently effective for unions when Labour is in office but cannot be counted on to make a place for unions and threatened workers when environmental policy is in debate.

In Europe's social partnership regimes, unions have pursued a coherent policy goal of double integration: integrating emissions-reduction policy with a policy of active labour redeployment and green skills training; and integrating both with a broadened social welfare policy that takes into consideration the employment and community upheavals caused by climate warming and by policies to slow climate warming. However, sectoral or national action plans for transitioning workers from jobs in the deep-brown industries and agriculture to greener jobs, remain underdeveloped (European Industrial Relations Observatory 2009).

Two large European studies of employment and climate, in which European unions played a key role, demonstrate the impact of the global financial crisis on union research and policy recommendations. They also demonstrate the confidence that European political leadership vests in trade union and para-union research and the ongoing influence of that research on policy.

Climate Change and Employment: Impact on Employment of Climate Change and CO_2 *Emission Reduction Measures in the E.U.-25 to 2030*[7] (Dupressoir et al. 2007b) is the path-breaking study that set out the parameters for workers' active role in greening the European economy. Carried out by a consortium of research think tanks and the European Trade Union Confederation (ETUC) and funded by the European Union and member governments, it studies the employment impact of climate warming and of policies of response to climate warming in E.U.-25.

The 2007 study has become an international model. It takes an industry and sector approach to projecting the future of employment in function of the impact of three GHG reduction targets for E.U.-25 over 20 years. The sectors studied are energy production, transport, steel and cement, construction/housing. The research maps predicted industry and sector job movement for each scenario onto three geographic regions: the Iberian Peninsula, Germany and Scandinavia; and the study discusses needs for active labour market transitions for workers in the sectors and regions. It concludes that if "business as usual" defines E.U. policy to 2030, job loss will be significant. But, it notes importantly, "the large-scale redistribution of jobs that will result from the implementation of climate policies will occur within rather than between sectors" (Dupressoir et al. 2007a: 8). Geographic dislocation, however, presents a threat that links environment, economic and social policy. Will new jobs be located in proximity to the jobs lost? How will single-industry communities fare as their industry or crop shrivels and crops or tree species move north (or south)? On the other hand, if emissions targets are pursued by actively integrating workers and unions into the low-carbon transition, there will be modest employment growth — with much job churning — by 2030. Above all, the study seeks to "make workers into the players in the [economic and social] change [demanded]" (Dupressoir et al. 2007a: 3).

The dislocations noted in the study — vocational, sectoral and geographic — took the study in five directions. First, climate change is a social issue (Dupressoir et al. 2007b: 5). Second, analysis of the impact of climate change on jobs is best approached on the sectoral level, because it is there that skills needs can be assessed and responded to. Third, "the E.U.'s drive to reduce greenhouse gas emissions cannot continue to be built primarily on industry and the energy production sector" (Dupressoir et al. 2007b: 8); E.U. climate action needs to extend to other economic sectors as well. Fourth, trade unions need to be actively involved in crafting transition policies and designing strategies for mitigating GHGs — to become "players," in other words. Fifth, there is need for double policy integration: first, integration between employment and environmental policy; then, between these policies and a suite of social safety policies.

Two years later, in the midst of the global financial crisis, the European Trade Union Confederation commissioned *Climate Disturbances, the New Industrial Policies and Ways Out of the Crisis* (Syndex et al. 2009). In this study, recommendations for policy shift to the state: expand the power of governments at national, subnational and regional levels. Governments are to develop industry strategies for low-carbon transitions in industries and regions and governments are to enable active labour market pathways for those churned out of jobs (Decaillon and Panneels 2010). The study calls for more government intervention, new regulatory measures and an end to "soft law." It links Europe's perceived weakening in the global climate arena to increased international competition, the threat of job loss, internal division and the possibility that climate change policy will be undermined. The commitment to greening more industries and more occupations is meant to continue.

American research, in the meantime, was focusing on modelling future job growth over ten, fifteen, twenty-five years on the basis of the hoped-for enactment of national, state or regional policies of transition to clean energy (Barrett et al. 2002; Global Insight 2008; Heintz et al. 2011; Kammen et al. 2006; Pew Center 2009; Roland-Holst 2008; United States Congressional Budget Office 2011; United States Department of Commerce, Economics and Statistics Administration 2010). Although the promise of masses of new job creation is a potent political lure in the tenacious U.S. recession, projections that tens or hundreds of thousands of amorphously-defined new green jobs would be created by major new investment in alternate energy have not been realized. With New England and California as exceptions, the U.S. political will has stymied the development of national climate — and jobs and climate — plans. Without these, how to discuss job churning: jobs lost and jobs gained, new training for the unemployed and young workers in the production of environmentally responsible goods and services, pathways between brown jobs and greener jobs for individuals and communities?

FROM GREEN JOBS TO GREENING THE ECONOMY

Although defining green jobs became a veritable growth industry in the last decade, no common definition has emerged.[8] The early, widely adopted definition of green jobs, derived from the United Nations Environment Programme, was "work in agriculture, industry, services and administration that contributes to preserving or restoring the quality of the environment (UNEP 2008: 5). UNEP cautioned that a green job might become more or less green over time as technology changed. But three fundamental conceptual problems ultimately limited the socio-political value of labelling (Lipsig-Mummé 2008b; Demerse 2011). First, to label a job green is static — a snapshot that describes the job or the economy at a point in time. Second, some "green jobs" as defined above may well produce more emissions than many jobs not labelled green. Third, the UNEP definition was vulnerable to political capture. In Canada as well as the U.S. it is politically tempting for governments and employers who have done little to reduce greenhouse gas emissions to expand the jobs that can be called "green," inflating the number of new "green jobs" and demonstrating the "greenness" of the national, provincial or state economy (ECO Canada 2012).

In the light of the proliferation of definitions, there has been a shift away from counting green jobs toward "greening work" and "greening the economy." "Greening" is the transition of economic activity toward more environmentally responsible practices. It describes a process of change — becoming greener.

The semantic and strategic struggle over what constitutes a green job is still most heated in countries without a serious national climate policy, like the U.S. and Canada. In contrast, in the E.U., the concept of "green" is both a description and a process; "green" includes "greening." "Greening" includes both creating new jobs that contribute to decarbonization and the greening of existing work and workplaces to lower carbon inputs and outputs.

GREENING WORK: THE ROLE OF WORKERS

The second component in the debate about the role of the work world in reducing emissions is work itself and the workplace. "Work" is the process of producing or creating a product or service or idea. Reducing emissions requires restructuring work itself. Restructuring how work is organized and carried out entails green-adapting the long chain of production.

There are six points in the chain of production where greening, or adaptation of work, can occur (Lipsig-Mummé 2012). These are: the inputs into the labour process; the organization of work; technology used; the physical environment in which work takes place; distribution; and disposal of both the results of production, and what is left of the inputs and technology. Green-adapting the long chain of production may also require new or revised skills training, which will touch education and training institutions (Lipsig-Mummé and Mummé 2009).

The reality for Canada and any other developed economy is that to green-adapt existing work will reduce more emissions than will the "green" jobs newly created. Why? First, jobs in the environmental goods and services sector are not necessarily green in their production processes. Second, there are vastly more existing jobs in the service-based economies of the developed countries than there are in the newly-defined environmental services. Third, greening work can reduce the carbon footprint of any and every workplace, in established and emerging sectors and professions. Fourth, green-adaptation of existing jobs has flow-on effects throughout their supply chains and in creating efficiencies of water use and waste disposal as well as energy efficiency. "All work can be green" (Decaillon and Panneels 2010: 28).

Greening the long chain of production and concentrating on greening the present jobs we have will entail sharpening the responsibility of workers at each stage. "The question is, whether a demand for green jobs leads to 'shallow reforms' or whether it transcends the present forms of production" (Räthzel and Uzzell 2013).

The world of work, then, can provide a practical locus to link adaptation to mitigation of GHGs in industrial societies. *Towards a Greener Economy: The Social Dimensions* draws attention to the fact that four-fifths of Europe's GHGs are created by production rather than household energy consumption (ILO 2011: 7–8).

Adaptation in work can be seen as a dynamic process in which changing how work is carried out changes the expectations of workers, the technology they use, the physical environment in which they work, their productivity and their responsibility for outcomes, at the same time as it mitigates the production of greenhouse gases.

The scope of concrete projects by European trade unions to adapt work in order to reduce emissions is analyzed in *Social Partner Initiatives in Europe on Climate Change and Employment Study* (Syndex 2011) and summarized in *Collective Bargaining and the Green Economy: A European Trade Union Perspective* (De Wel et al. 2011). The authors, trade unionists, have direct knowledge of the projects. They bring together examples from six European countries as well as pan-European activities. Four areas of worker action are covered: greening the workplace, green collective bargaining, national dialogue on the green economy and national dialogue on green training. In the social partnership environment of the E.U., which was frayed but not torn by the GFC, four major forms of European trade union intervention stand out. First, "tripartite consultation is well developed" (ibid.: 14). Second, unilateral trade union initiatives in green education and training are widely but unevenly developed. Third, bipartite, tripartite, and "tripartite-plus initiatives" (which include NGOs and researchers) work through policy proposals on energy efficiency, industrial relations and working conditions, in response to climate warming. Here again, there is uneven development: "Germany and Belgium [are] positively teeming, compared to the vast majority of the cases studied" (ibid.: 15). Fourth, the unions have initiated workplace-based green initiatives. These, particularly in the U.K., contribute to engaging members in the struggle to reduce emissions and educate them — its own form of empowerment. It is to be noted that the authors attribute to union-led activities "importance in contributing to … the dialogue between the social partners" (ibid.).

This is a far cry from the static and narrow vision of adaptation as a reactive strategy of adjustment to whatever the environment throws up. It links research to policy on the one hand and on the other, to worker action. The adaptation-to-mitigation-to adaptation relationship in the workplace — any workplace — can become a virtuous spiral for slowing global warming.

INTERNATIONAL CONCLUSIONS AND CANADA

An assessment of the international debates about responding to climate warming in developed economies over the past two decades offers some conclusions.

First, despite efforts over the past two decades, the planet is warming more quickly than predicted — the world is browning, not greening. Successful transitioning to a lower carbon society is measured by reduction of GHG emissions.

Second, in the developed countries, successful GHG reduction plans are led by national governments.

Third, the most successful national GHG reduction programs are multilevel and characterized by national government leadership with the involvement of subnational government units and the participation of private enterprise and the labour movement. This collaboration is legislated, developed through taxes and markets and also works through regional green development programs and bipartite, sectoral management-union programs. More rarely, GHG reduction is achieved through collective bargaining and union-led green technology redesign.

Fourth, national governments achieve GHG reduction most effectively when they combine regulation, taxation, incubation of green R & D and domestic green manufacturing, support robust exports, active labour market skills training and retraining and support unions and employers as they green-adapt their technology and labour process.

Fifth, in every developed country, the work world remains an underdeveloped site for reducing GHGs. The ILO's recent finding that four-fifths of Europe's emissions are produced by the production of goods and services challenges the current convenient wisdom about the importance of house-hold energy consumption (ILO 2011: 7–8). Even in the most sophisticated emissions reductions programs, such as Germany's, mitigation has been the preferred instrument. But mitigation alone has not achieved enough, fast enough. Rather, it is now recognized that strategies of work and workplace adaptation are also needed. But adaptation, still only vaguely understood at governmental and metapolicy levels, is nevertheless treated as a yet-to-be-developed panacea.

Adaptation in the world of work requires green-adapting all the stages of the labour process, from inputs through disposal, including technology and the physical environment in which work takes place. Adaptation, in other words, originates at the "mid level" of society and calls upon labour-market actors to craft a "green shift." The green shift may enjoy govern-ment support or funding as it does in some E.U. countries and Australia, or it may be a product of collective bargaining in North America's more conflict-oriented and patchwork industrial relations regimes, in which unions rely more heavily on the engagement of their membership. But adaptation of work in developed economies always includes the active engagement of workers and their unions, assessment of vulnerability, articulation and use of workers' knowledge and redesign: greening the long chain of production.

Sixth, even in the most successful of GHG-reducing countries, develop-ing, funding and making accessible the extensive skills retraining/training that is required are topics discussed enthusiastically in the political arena, but in reality are treated as add-ons and inadequately developed and funded.

HOW DOES CANADA STACK UP?

First, Canada has no national plan for reducing GHGs. As the National Round Table on the Environment and the Economy summarizes in *Reality Check*:

> Canada signed the Kyoto Protocol and is now withdrawing from it. Canada announced a national plan and new targets and then sought to align with developments in the United States, leading to a different plan and different targets. Provinces and territories acted both independently and banded together to reduce carbon emissions through a range of innovative, diverse, and traditional measures. Canada now has 14 climate policy plans on the books, one for the federal government and each province and territory. How is this to be reconciled? (NRTEE 2012: 20)

As the E.U. has shown, countries need *national* emissions reductions programs. Plans limited to one or a cluster of subnational jurisdictions, like the Western Initiative, can contribute to GHG reduction, but cannot be effective enough.

At present, Canadian provinces provide 75 percent of the country's reduction in emissions, and if we continue on the path we are on today, nationally we will be almost 50 percent short of our Kyoto target in 2020 (NRTEE 2012).

Finally, the Canadian government has no commitment to preparing the work world to produce less GHGs. Quite the opposite. The government's support for and enthusiasm about the spectacularly polluting oil sands industry is a harbinger of rising emissions. The termination of Canada's federal industrial sector councils in early 2013 is shutting down the most important institutions that prepare Canada's workers for the skills and technologies needed to work greener. That training will now shift to the provinces in a messy mosaic or to for-profit private trainers. In the construction industry, the union-led training institutions will survive. But ceding training for other industries to the for-profit sector or to provinces with an unequal commitment to greening work weakens an important component of adaptive capacity and takes Canada further from the goal of GHG reduction.

Notes

1. Climate change is defined as recent changes in climate attributable to human activity.
2. U.S. President Obama favours a cap-and-trade scheme, which passed the House of Representatives in 2009 and failed to pass the Senate in 2010.
3. In June 2012 a federal appeals court in Washington, D.C., ruled that the EPA had the right to regulate heat-trapping devices (vehicles, industry) because they are a danger to public health. Fourteen states had sued to stop the EPA and may appeal the ruling (*New York Times* June 27, 2012).
4. In chapter 7 of the 2011 edition of *The Politics of Climate Change*, Giddens sets out a series of concepts for refining "adaptation." He distinguishes between "proactive or pre-emptive adaptation" and "reactive adaptation." Reactive adaptation takes place after the event has taken place. Proactive or pre-emptive adaptation is more complex, because it entails analyzing future vulnerabilities, their interaction with each other and with policies of response.
5. In 2011 the Apollo Alliance merged with Blue-Green Alliance.
6. There is a natural intersection between research on adapting work to respond to climate warming and the substantial applied literatures from occupational health and safety, life-cycle assessments of technology and buildings and sustainable engineering. That intersection has yet to be fully developed.
7. E.U.-25 refers to the twenty-five countries that were members of the European Union at the time of publication.
8. A partial list of current attempts to define green work and green jobs: Campaign against Climate Change 2010; D. Parsons & Associates 2009; ECO Canada 2010; GHK 2009; Global Climate Network 2010; GLOBE Foundation of Canada 2010; Renner 2008; UNEP 2008; United States Bureau of Labor Statistics 2010; United States Department of Commerce, Economics and Statistics Administration 2010; Workforce Information Council 2009.

3. INTERNATIONAL TRADE AGREEMENTS AND THE ONTARIO GREEN ENERGY ACT
Opportunities and Obstacles

Stephen McBride and John Shields

A mantra of how to adapt to globalization is "Think Global, Act Local." At first glance the Ontario *Green Energy Act* provides a perfect illustration. Concerned by global warming and the role of greenhouse gas emissions in triggering it, determined to close down Ontario's coal electricity generating plants and stimulate the production of clean energy, cognizant of the need to keep consumers and citizens onside with such initiatives that would have the unfortunate effect of substituting expensive for cheaper energy, the Ontario government introduced an intricate array of incentives and regulations designed to achieve these ends. Doing something about the environmental crisis without harming the economy and jobs has been a dilemma for governments for many years. All too often such environmental measures as have been taken ignore the employment implications of the measures they contain, and employment policy is often equally blind to the environmental effects. Public opinion tends to vacillate, ranking environmental protection high in times of economic prosperity and being willing to sacrifice the environment in times of economic difficulty (Bowen and Stern 2010). Industrial strategies that stimulate employment in sectors that help build a green economy are thus especially attractive since they hold the promise of escape from the environment versus jobs dilemma. Our work explores the potential and opportunities conferred by this type of economic strategy and, using the example of Ontario's green energy policy, also illustrates the obstacles to achieving that positive sum result posed by international economic agreements, the economic and financial crisis and fluctuating political will. Thus thinking globally and acting locally is more complicated than it seems. The "global" includes an international trade and investment architecture that inhibits the maximization of local benefit as states or, in this case, subnational jurisdictions move to devise energy strategies that can contribute to mitigating the effects of climate change.

THE POSITIVE-SUM POSSIBILITIES OF INDUSTRIAL STRATEGIES FOR GREEN JOBS

Conventional wisdom from mainstream political and economic circles has long posited the position that growth and environmentally-friendly public policies were ultimately irreconcilable. In short, that a zero-sum relationship exists between economic and job growth and environmentally sustainable policies (Whaples 2009: 337–8). This kind of thinking has been exemplified in *The Economist* magazine in article titles such as the 2009 example, "Saving the planet and creating jobs may be incompatible." Supporters of neoliberal models of growth have long downplayed the issue of environmental threat altogether, largely denying the near scientific consensus regarding global warming. They suggest that the intrinsic dynamic of unfettered global capitalism through technological innovation can address any serious environmental problems that arise (Heynen et al. 2007). The fact is that environmental degradation is too often seen, along with growing levels of inequality and exclusion, as the unavoidable but necessary collateral damage of neoliberal growth strategies (Bauman 2011).

By the end of the twentieth century a strong environmental movement had developed, gaining political currency. Concern for the environment has been expressed in two broad developments, one an "ecology" movement, which is associated with deeper more radical change, and those that identify themselves with "environmentalism," which is reformist in character (Giddens 1994: 203) and has had a strong applied policy orientation. This latter position adopts the approach that capitalism can be regulated and market mechanisms adapted to work in favour of environmentally-friendly goals in conjunction with economic growth. Third Way political developments have, in particular, advanced the policy position that a middle way is available within a reformed market framework where new and emerging risks like those associated with the environment can be successfully managed (Giddens 2011; Wills and Wilsdon 2003; Jacobs 2001).[1]

Such positive-sum approaches to the economy and environment are also associated with sustainable development. This involves the adoption of alternative clean energy sources, new directions in industrial production and enhancement of the service economy, which together minimize harm to the environment while promoting measured growth. Obstacles to the movement toward positive-sum sustainability approaches include the costs involved in conversion away from "dirty employment," overcoming powerful entrenched economic interests, resistance to unfettered profit making in favour of environmentally-regulated enterprise and managed development, among others.

Reports from prominent international bodies have presented some perspectives regarding the role of public policy in promoting environmentally-sustainable growth. The United Nations Environment Programme Green Economy Initiative offers some guideposts to aid governments in greening their economies "by reshaping and refocusing policies, investments and spending towards a range of sectors, such as clean technologies, renewable energies, water services, green transportation, waste management, green buildings and sustainable agriculture and forests" (UNEP n.d.).

Moreover, UNEP conceptualizes the greening process in the following way:

> Greening the economy refers to the process of reconfiguring businesses and infrastructure to deliver better returns on natural, human and economic capital investments, while at the same time reducing greenhouse gas emissions, extracting and using less natural resources, creating less waste and reducing social disparities. (UNEP n.d.)

The Organization of Economic Cooperation and Development (OECD) has acknowledged that the greening of the economy will result in substantive job losses in carbon-intensive economic sectors. But the OECD also has now come to the position that these job losses will be more than compensated for by the creation in other sectors of "green jobs" (OECD 2010: 40). In fact, UNEP sees by the year 2030 some ten times the number of jobs in the clean energy field compared to 2010 (*The Economist* April 2, 2009).

THE GENESIS OF ONTARIO'S GREEN ENERGY STRATEGY

In Canada as of 2005, the environmental industry was composed of some 7,500 companies employing greater than 160,000 people, and the supply of environmental goods and services was valued at about $14.4 billion in 2000 (OECD 2008: 26). However, the country is also on a per capita basis the third largest emitter of CO_2 and is generally acknowledged as a laggard in terms of climate change public policy (UNEP 2008:132, 11). For example, by 2008 Canadian greenhouse gas (GHG) emissions rested at 24 percent over its 1990 levels even though there was a commitment to reduce GHG emissions by 6 percent over this time period. The current federal Conservative government has steadfastly refused to unilaterally move the environmental policy agenda forward, instead delaying to pursue a harmonized cap-and-trade approach with a hesitant United States, a country now facing prolonged economic stagnation and political deadlock (OECD 2010: 14, note 2; White 2010: 23–24). The Conservatives have steadfastly sought to harmonize their environmental and energy policies with the United States, in effect surrendering their sovereignty on the issue and ensuring that Canadian climate change targets are set in Washington (Macdonald 2011).

The election of a majority Conservative national government in 2011 has extended the government's assault on environmental policies. This includes changes to environmental assessment processes to speed up decisions on measures like oil and gas pipeline rights-of-way through environmentally sensitive lands (Sandborn 2012). The federal government has also deeply cut jobs within environmental portfolios in the public service as part of its public sector austerity measures. This has seriously threatened the state's capacity for environmental monitoring and evidence-based decision making (*Montreal Gazette* May 28, 2012: Editorial). Additionally, civil society environmental organizations have been subject to state defunding, subject to verbal attacks as public enemies and threatened with the loss of charitable status because of their public opposition to Conservative policy (Ball 2012; McQuaig 2012). Together these developments constitute an intensification of the federal Conservative government's war on green policy and its defence of oil and gas and other carbon-based corporate interests in Canada.

Lack of progress on the environment front at the national level in Canada has, however, opened up space at the provincial level for environmental policy action and leadership. Many provinces have adopted substantive environmental reforms and strategies, with Ontario under the McGuinty Liberal government generally conceded to have led the way.

The Ontario Liberal government of Premier Dalton McGuinty (2003–2013), in contrast to the former Conservative administrations in Ontario, pursued an economic policy path that included prominent green directions. McGuinty, as a result of a Liberal leadership renewal, was replaced by Kathleen Wynne on February 11, 2013, and she has committed her Liberal government to continue and improve upon the environmental and energy policies of the McGuinty era (MacDermott 2013). Symbolically she reappointed to her cabinet Liberal environment minister Jim Bradley. Importantly, the McGuinty Liberal green policy was said to be "a centrepiece of [the government's] economic plan" (Radwanski 2011). The 2007 Climate Change Action Plan, which was centred on green job creation, building livable and sustainable communities and long-term GHG reductions, was the forerunner of the most prominent piece of environmental legislation, the 2009 *Green Energy and Economy Act* (generally referred to as the *Green Energy Act*). It is seen as a cornerstone in its commitment to make Ontario North America's leading green energy economy (Marshall 2011c). This Act was further designed to strategically position Ontario to fully participate in an emerging carbon trading market (Centre for Civic Governance 2011: 7). According to Tim Weis, Director of the Pembina Institute's renewable energy program, "Ontario's *Green Energy Act* is modelled off the most successful renewable energy policies in Europe — policies that create the long-term market stability necessary to attract continued investment and create jobs" (Burda 2011a: 6).[2]

Central to the *Green Energy Act* is its Feed-in Tariff (FIT) mechanism. The FIT is based on German legislation, which has helped to make that country a leader in wind and solar energy technology and which is credited with creating in excess of 300,000 jobs there (Marshall 2011c). The Ontario FIT enables:

> individuals, companies, municipalities and cooperatives to sell electricity from wind, solar, hydro, biomass, biogas and landfill gas projects back to the provincial energy grid at guaranteed rates for the next 20 years. The prices vary by technology, ranging from 10.3 cents per kilowatt-hour for landfill gas projects to 80.2 cents per kilowatt-hour for small residential solar rooftop projects. Incentives were also provided for Aboriginal and community-based projects. (Marshall 2011c)

Significantly, green generated jobs are designed to be created not just in energy production but also in the province's manufacturing, construction and installation sectors. The *Green Energy Act* requires that a minimum percentage of goods and services be sourced in Ontario in order to qualify for FIT contracts (ibid.). This "domestic content" requirement introduces a job multiplier effect. As of 2011 the government claimed that the *Green Energy Act* was responsible for the creation of some 20,000 jobs and was on track to generate a promised 50,000 jobs by 2012 (Province of Ontario 2011). The Pembina Institute calculated that green energy creates between three to ten times the number of jobs per hour of energy generation compared to fossil fuels and nuclear power (Burda 2011b).

The U.S. Bureau of Labor Statistics refers to this method of green job creation as being part of an "output approach" as opposed to a "process approach." In essence "the output approach ... identifies establishments that produce green goods and services and counts the associated jobs" while "the process approach ... identifies establishments that use environmentally friendly production processes and practices and counts the associated jobs" (United States Bureau of Labor Statistics 2010).[3] While not all of the jobs generated by the FIT component of the *Green Energy Act* may be truly green themselves, most of them are good jobs in the sense that they pay above twenty dollars an hour (Pollin and Garrett-Peltier 2009).[4]

An interesting feature of the *Green Energy Act* is that it is targeted at both large and small producers — corporate entities, as well as communities and individuals. This lends a populist flavour to the program that is an important component in its attempts to win over popular support. This populist appeal is also brought to the fore through the strong connection drawn by the government between green energy and job creation.

The Liberals' environmental strategy has encountered some challenges along the way. Their pledge to eliminate the heavily polluting coal power electricity plants had to be pushed back from 2007 to 2010 and now to 2014 due to cost factors (Talaga 2010). The expansion of nuclear power has also run into cost and construction problems. All of this in the context of a declining manufacturing base in the province hit hard by the 2008 recession, which has depressed provincial revenues and created new political pressures (Lorinc 2011).

Moreover, the siting regulation for wind farms has created considerable controversy in rural areas. The Ontario content regulations associated with the *Green Energy Act* have caused trade issues in the case of the $7 billion agreement with the Korean company Samsung, which is setting up operations in the province (Marshall 2011c). The content regulations of the Act are also blamed for greatly increasing the costs of green energy production in Ontario and for creating "supply chain problems" that have delayed production (Lorinc 2011).

THE GREEN ENERGY STRATEGY OUTLINED

The McGuinty Liberals distinguished themselves from hardline neoliberals by embracing a "Third Way" policy direction. The *Green Energy Act*, along with their strategic investments in education and anti-poverty strategy, was central to establishing their "progressive" credentials. As opposed to neoliberal free market approaches, they embraced "progressive competitiveness" involving policies that combine an active state centred around promoting higher-end employment through business incentives (Evans and Shields 2011: 140), while supporting broad social policies to address the risks produced by global capitalism, including environmental risks (Jacobs 2001: 325).[5]

The *Green Energy Act* has secured some prominent endorsements, which have enhanced its political and social credibility. For example, former U.S. Vice President Al Gore has called the Act "the single best green energy program on the North American continent" (Yuen 2009). Also, the prominent Canadian environmentalist David Suzuki heavily criticized Ontario Progressive Conservative leader Tim Hudak for his election campaign commitment to cancel the *Green Energy Act* and offered his endorsement of the Liberal program (Mcavoy 2011).

The 2011 Ontario election posed a significant test for the McGuinty government. Not only was it seeking a third term, but its green energy policies were at the heart of much of the campaign and they generated strong opposition with elements of the electorate. Both the Progressive Conservative and NDP opposition had targeted the Liberals' environmental policies, with the Right focusing in on tax cuts (Marshall 2011d), and the Left proposing a variety of initiatives aimed at other, family-friendly measures (including mass transit) to address environmental concerns (Marshall 2011b). The greatest threat came from the Conservatives who promised to scrap the Liberal

Green Energy Act and associated environmental proposals altogether (Marshall 2011a). The election outcome proved to be a victory of sorts for the Liberals, who won an unexpected third term. Their minority government was shy only one seat from a majority.

A post-election assessment suggested that "The green-energy file will now be at the heart of Mr. McGuinty's biggest challenge: shepherding his vision for transforming Ontario into a clean energy powerhouse with a minority government for the next four years" (Howlett and Ladurantaye 2011). Part of the challenge is that the world and Ontario economies remain fragile. The financial and political resources needed for green energy transformation in such an unstable environment will face stiff competition from demands related to more traditional economic and social concerns.

Another element of the challenge is that the Liberal government lost many of its rural seats in the 2011 election. These defeats cost them their majority and their environment minister John Wilkinson. A primary issue for rural voters was opposition to green energy initiatives and in particular to wind turbines (Butler 2011; Howlett and Ladurantaye 2011; Radwanski 2011). The Liberals had greater success among urban voters, especially in contrast to the Conservatives, in their appeals for an active pro-environmental policy agenda. In fact, a focus on green energy "offers the government some potentially significant electoral advantages, particularly among younger voters" (Winfield 2011). In the future, however, the environmental policy divide between rural and urban Ontario is one that will need to be carefully managed, especially in the context of minority government.

Since the election, the Ontario government has received mixed assessments on the green energy file. The Ontario Environment Commissioner Gord Miller criticized the government for lack of forward progress on energy conservation measures (Spears 2012). Yet Ontario was named the greenest province in a recently announced independent report card on the environment. It was noted further that "the single largest greenhouse gas reduction initiative in Canada" is Ontario's phase out "of coal-fired electricity generation" (Province of Ontario 2012). Ontario's green energy strategy remains central to the government's policy agenda.

OBSTACLES: TRADE AGREEMENTS

There are various obstacles to the development of green economic strategies, including austerity triggered by the economic and financial crisis, and fickle political support. Here, though, we focus on the provisions of international trade and investment treaties that may foreclose or render difficult certain policy options. Arguably, the agreements are intended to tie the hands of governments in areas such as intervention in the operation of markets and to make such neoliberal changes permanent. It is in this sense that Stephen Gill used the term "new constitutionalism" to refer to a system of "disciplinary neoliberalism" (Gill 1995). Such agreements reach into areas of investment, services and intellectual property rights. In so doing, they "condition" a large part of what was previously considered to be "domestic" policy (Grinspun and Kreklewich 1994). For these reasons, Third Way initiatives like those just described are vulnerable under the international trade regime.

Here we pay particular attention to the impact that such agreements, specifically the North American Free Trade Agreement (NAFTA) and the World Trade Organization (WTO), may have on state capacity to enact and implement industrial policies, since green economic strategies can be seen as a particular variant of an industrial strategy.

For example, NAFTA imposes a variety of obligations including the application of national treatment to trade in goods (chapter 3 of the Agreement), government procurement (chapter 10), investment (chapter 11), cross-border trade in services (chapter 12), financial services (chapter 14), intellectual property rights (chapter 17) and most-favoured-nation status for investment (chapter 11). Reservations to the various obligations are contained in annexes. The degree of obligation varies by topic, but to a greater or lesser extent all of the provisions operate to reduce a nation's discretion to discriminate in favour of domestic industries.

Article 105 commits the signatories to "ensure that all necessary measures are taken in order to give effect to the provisions of this agreement ... including their observance ... by state and provincial governments" whose actions, by this means, are covered by the agreements even if it is the federal government that must take responsibility under international trade law. Under NAFTA (article 10), some but far from all government procurement is covered and subject to national treatment provisions.

Nor may a government discriminate against a local supplier on the basis of foreign affiliation or ownership or on the basis that its goods or services are imported from another NAFTA signatory (Article 1003). The agreement's chapter 11 covers, subject to certain reservations, all forms of investment interests. With respect to provinces and states, the principle of "best in Province" treatment is to be applied (Article 1102.3). A noteworthy aspect of this article is its prohibition of a wide range of performance requirements and the creation of investor rights in dispute resolution. The lengthy list of prohibited performance requirement measures include requirements to export a certain proportion of goods or services produced, or achieve any specified level or balance of foreign exchange earnings, or target specific export markets. Particularly germane to the case of Ontario, the agreement bars domestic content or purchasing requirements, as well as provisions that insist on transfers of technology.

The WTO comprises a group of agreements, including the General

Agreement on Tariffs and Trade (GATT), which contain the essential principles of the liberalized trading system. According to the WTO itself the first principle is that the trading system should operate without discrimination. This means no discrimination in a country between its own and foreign products, services or nationals, all of whom are given "national treatment." Any benefit given to one is extended to all. Other principles include achievement of freer trade through lowering trade barriers, guaranteeing predictability through "binding" states' commitments on issues like tariffs and promoting fair competition through working toward elimination of subsidies and dumping (selling overseas below cost in order to gain market share).

The impact of GATT trade rules becomes far-reaching when extended under the WTO from trade in goods to trade in services and to investment. The agreement on Trade Related Investment Measures (TRIMs) (Das 1998: chapter 16) identifies a number of measures that are inconsistent with GATT. These include so-called domestic content provisions, such that an enterprise must use or buy a particular quantity or proportion of domestically-sourced products in its operations. This removes one of several "performance requirements" (e.g., domestic content) that countries often used before authorizing foreign investments. The domestic content provisions in Ontario's *Green Energy Act* (GEA) have already triggered trade complaints (see below).

There are, of course, other interpretations that suggest continued capacity for state intervention and activism. Linda Weiss argues that

> Rich nations as a group have carved out a multilateral order which best suits their current development trajectory — one that diminishes space for promoting industries critical to their climb up the development ladder, while increasing scope for sponsoring the technology-intensive sectors now critical to securing national prosperity. (Weiss 2005: 723)

In this view

> the measures prohibited under the WTO are those of diminishing importance to a relatively advanced level of development, which depends increasingly on knowledge-intensive technologies. Second, the measures permitted — or at least not explicitly prohibited — are advanced-country friendly: they enable the industrialized state to align its national growth goals with significant support for industry, technology and exports ... [T]he tighter rules of the WTO era, rather than constraining or limiting the scope for state activism, have made it more technologically focussed, hence unintentionally stimulating a more strategic or proactive approach to industrial governance, even in contexts not noted for industrial strategy. In

this respect, the new multilateralism appears to have served more generally as an upgrading device for the development economies. (Weiss 2005: 724–5)

Weiss looks at the impact of TRIMs and the WTO agreement on Subsidies and Countervailing Measures (SCM) on states' "room to manoeuvre": "No matter where a country stands on the development ladder, it can no longer apply with impunity the regulatory framework that virtually all industrial-izing countries have used to nurture fledgling industries" (Chang 2002, as cited in Weiss 2005: 726).

This is because key measures contravene GATT rules under TRIMs. These are: local content and trade balancing requirements, foreign exchange balancing requirements, foreign restrictions and domestic sales limitations (Weiss 2005: 726). However, Weiss suggests that against the limitations of the GATT and TRIMs, "we must weigh those requirements or 'bargains' that governments may negotiate, more or less formally, with foreign investment companies as a condition of access to generous state-provided benefits, in order to support domestic industry development" (ibid.).

This kind of strategic activism is active policy and is not necessarily reactive to or confrontational with trade agreements. Weiss identifies four key areas for governments to renew or increase participation: "governance of science and technology, venture capital promotion, *government procurement* and the enlargement of export capacity" (Weiss 2005: 732; italics added). Government procurement is significant; because

> it can be used both as a tool for creating national champions and supporting domestic producers and as a lever to entice foreign sup-pliers to comply with national development projects, government procurement has gained renewed importance as an instrument for accomplishing national development objectives. (Weiss 2005: 736)

As we shall see below, local content provisions and alleged subsidization lie at the centre of international trade challenges to Ontario's *Green Energy Act*. Government procurement is a central plank in its defence,[6] though one that in future is threatened by possibly enhanced procurement openness that Canada is negotiating, with provinces at the table, in new economic agreements such as the Canada-European Comprehensive Economic and Trade Agreement (CETA).

In December 2012, the WTO ruled that Ontario's *Green Energy Act*, more specifically the local content requirement attached to the feed-in tariff pro-visions, was contrary to WTO provisions. Canada subsequently announced that it would appeal the ruling. However, reviewing the general arguments and background information may be useful in understanding the inhibiting impact of trade and investment treaties more generally. On September 13, 2010, Japan filed an official dispute with the WTO against Ontario's *Green Energy Act* feed-in tariff (GEA FIT) program, citing GATT 1994 and the Trade Related Investment Measures (TRIMs). The E.U. launched a similar WTO complaint. The dispute is not with the *Green Energy Act* per se, but rather the requirements necessary to access feed-in tariff (FIT) payments. To qualify for FIT payments from the Government of Ontario, wind projects must have a minimum of 50 percent domestic content, and solar energy producers must use 60 percent local content (Brigham 2009). As highlighted by the Green Energy Act Alliance, "if a contract facility does not meet the Minimum Required Domestic Content Level, the Supplier will be in default under the FIT Contract" (ibid.).

In filing its request for WTO consultations in September 2010, Japan outlined its case against Ontario's FIT program (WTO 2010):

- It is inconsistent with Article III: 4 of GATT 1994 and is in opposition to the Most Favoured Nation (MFN) principle: "treatment [of imported products] is no less favourable than that accorded to like products of national origin in respect to laws, regulations and requirements affecting their internal sale, offering for sale, purchase, transportation, distribution or use";
- It violates GATT III: 4 not to "establish or maintain any internal quantitative regulation relating to the mixture, processing, or use of products in specified amounts or proportions which requires, directly or indirectly, that any specified amount or proportion of any product which is the subject of the regulation must be supplied from domestic sources" and not to "otherwise apply internal quantitative regulations in a manner contrary to the principles set forth in paragraph 1";
- It violates article 2.1 of TRIMs not to "apply any TRIM that is inconsistent with the provisions of Article III or Article XI of GATT 1994."

Moreover, Japan argues that under articles 3.1(b) and 3.2 of the Subsidies and Countervailing Measures (SCM) Agreement, FIT payments are contingent on the use of domestic products over imports (Todgham-Cherniak 2010). Japan officially filed a Request for Consultations with the WTO dispute settlement body (DSB) on September 13, 2010, and a number of other countries including the United States and the European Union (E.U.) requested third party status under WTO rules. Subsequently the E.U. launched its own case. Since the grounds of its complaint were virtually identical to that of Japan, this was probably to ensure the E.U.'s capacity to present more detailed argumentation than would be possible as a third party and also to obtain right of appeal should the decision be adverse.

The whole issue of subsidization or other supports for green energy initiatives is increasingly the subject of international trade adjudication. In an analogous, but far from identical case, U.S. complaints prompted China to end a system of subsidies for wind-generated electricity. The United States filed a complaint with the WTO on October 15, 2010, after receiving a complaint from the United Steelworkers (USW). The USW referred to section 301 of the *Trade Act of 1974* when calling for the U.S. federal government to challenge Chinese subsidies for wind power equipment that made U.S. producers less competitive in the Chinese market. The Act in question is "U.S. legislation (i.e., Sections 301–310 of the *Trade Act of 1974*) authorizing certain actions by the Office of the United States Trade Representative, including the suspension or withdrawal of concessions or the imposition of duties or other import restrictions, in response to trade barriers imposed by other countries" (WTO n.d.a).

The U.S. challenged China's Special Fund for Wind Power Equipment ("Special Fund") subsidies under Article 3 of the WTO Subsidies and Countervailing Measures (SCM) Agreement, which prohibits local content subsidies that give preference to a state's manufacturers over another state, therefore interfering with trade (WTO n.d.b). According to the website of the United States Office of the Trade Representative (USTR),

> the subsidies took the form of grants to Chinese wind turbine manufacturers that agreed to use key parts and components made in China rather than purchasing imports. The United States estimated that the grants provided to Chinese companies since 2008 could have totalled several hundred million dollars. The size of the individual grants ranged between $6.7 million and $22.5 million. (USTR 2011)

China revoked its wind power equipment subsidies on June 7, 2011. The U.S. has successfully challenged Chinese subsidies three times at the WTO (ibid.). Commenting on the decision, U.S. trade representative Ron Kirk said:

> The United States is pleased that China has shut down this subsidy program. Subsidies requiring the use of local content are particularly harmful and are expressly prohibited under WTO rules. This outcome helps ensure fairness for American clean technology innovators and workers. We challenged these subsidies so that American manufacturers can produce wind turbine components here in the United States and sell them in China. That supports well-paying jobs here at home. (USTR 2011)

Lawrence Herman of Cassels Brock Lawyers in Toronto had this to say on the possible relevance of China's cancellation of wind energy equipment subsidies to Japan's challenge of the *Green Energy Act*:

As an interesting development in a related case, China and the U.S. have just settled a U.S. WTO complaint over China's wind power subsidy program. The Americans complained that grants to Chinese wind turbine manufacturers, on condition that they use locally-produced inputs rather than foreign imports, were prohibited under the SCM Agreement. To settle the dispute, China voluntarily agreed to end the program. It is not clear the impact this will have, if any, on the Japanese case against Ontario when the matter comes before the WTO panel. (Herman 2011)

However, the dispute between the U.S. and China continued. In May 2012, the U.S. Commerce Department announced that it would be imposing duties to counter alleged dumping of Chinese-made solar panels (*Bridges Weekly* May 23, 2012). Shortly afterwards, China requested consultations at the WTO alleging that the U.S. countervailing duties were contrary to the WTO agreement (*Bridges Weekly* May 30, 2012).

Returning to the challenges to Ontario's FIT and local content provisions, several watchers of global trade policy argued that Japan had a winnable case. *Global Trade Alert*, which claims to provide "information in real time on state measures taken during the current global economic downturn that are likely to discriminate against foreign commerce," has marked the local content requirement of the *GEA* as a non-tariff barrier (NTB) to trade and therefore an "actionable subsidy" (Centre for Economic Policy Research n.d.). In 2010, Ontario's Energy Minister Brad Duguid, however, was quoted as maintaining that the *Green Energy Act* is "consistent with Canada's international trade obligations under the WTO" (Blackwell 2010).

Initial commentary suggested that there were three key arguments that could potentially secure a victory for Ontario. First, FIT payments are not government subsidies (Brigham 2009: 8). Second, FIT payments do not discriminate on national grounds. Finally, this type of government/public procurement is exempt from GATT/WTO local content disputes (Laing 2006). The WTO panel concluded that local content provisions were contrary to its rules but did not rule in favour of Japan's subsidies argument.

What are the implications of the WTO decision, assuming that Canada's appeal is unsuccessful?[7] It is a key political problem for Ontario that, without the creation of Ontario jobs (an estimated 50,000 by 2012), the high costs of the FIT payments are not worth the government's expense (Blackwell 2010). If Ontario eliminates the local content requirement, companies could import their equipment from abroad and still profit from high renewable energy rates, and green jobs will be removed from sustainable economy dialogue. Therefore, the WTO's ruling in Japan's favour could 1) put an end to high FIT payments provided by Ontario taxpayers, 2) end the GEA's local content requirement, but continue FIT payments to all investors, and/or 3) end consumer demand for renewable energy sources, due to higher costs and lower benefits (in terms of local content generated job creation). Even if Canada had prevailed in the case with Japan, on the grounds of government procurement, it may be weakening its capacity to win future cases by concessions on the procurement issue in the Canada-European Comprehensive Economic and Trade Agreement (CETA) negotiations.

Ontario's green energy strategy has also been the subject of a complaint under NAFTA Chapter 11. MesaPower Group, a U.S.-based renewable energy multinational, alleged favouritism (discrimination) in the award of contracts when it failed to win anticipated contracts under the feed-in tariff (FIT) provisions of the Ontario *Green Energy Act*. The company also mentioned local content provisions and alleged preferential treatment to other foreign investors like Samsung. Mesa claimed damages of $775 million.[8]

CONCLUSIONS

Ontario's green energy strategy is an interesting initiative designed to replace carbon intensive energy production with clean and renewable energy and, at the same time, ensure that a proportion of the jobs created by the strategy are homegrown. Sustaining the strategy in difficult economic times with uncertain political support will be a difficult task. The provisions of the trade agreements to which Canada is a signatory may make that task even more difficult. The WTO ruling in Japan's favour could further erode public support for the plan if it has the effect of reducing the benefits (in terms of local content generated job creation). Even if Canada prevailed in the case with Japan on the grounds of government procurement, it may be weakening its capacity to win future cases by concessions on the procurement issue in the CETA negotiations. An unfavourable result in the NAFTA Chapter 11 case could create "regulatory chill" by imposing damages on governments.

The consequences of the cases launched so far are uncertain, but the trade and investment agreements certainly pose a challenge to green industrial policies, especially if government procurement protections are sacrificed or substantially weakened in subsequent trade agreements. Aaron Cosbey has argued that the WTO dispute settlement process is the wrong place to forge international consensus on renewable energy support measures. He argues that the dispute will be corrosive and will seemingly pit trade against the environment (Cosbey 2011). Instead of focusing on the legal rights and wrongs, the dispute process should focus on what the law should say, including assessing the appropriateness of WTO rules given the growing focus on the need for green economies.

The stakes are high because the existing trade cases pose the question of whether trade law can or should trump legitimate environmental concerns, themselves often incorporated in international agreements.

These are the first international trade disputes that engender the potential for conflict between a nation's commitments under the World Trade Organization and its obligations under the Framework Convention on Climate Change and the Kyoto Protocol. It raises fundamental questions about whether the goals of trade liberalization can be reconciled with ecological imperatives to reduce greenhouse gas emissions, and if not, which are to prevail. (Blue Green Canada 2012: 1)

Notes

1. Of course the "third way" approach, which attempts to bind together progressive and neoliberal policy orientations, also reflects the inherent tensions within these divergent set of ideas (Jordan 2010: 63–83). These contradictory tendencies come to the fore during economic crises like that of 2008, which point to the limitations of middle way market-based solutions to deep problems of global scale. Meaningful policy solutions to climate change call for deep structural changes within capitalism itself (Held, Hervey and Theros 2011: 1–2).

2. The Pembina Institute is a national non-partisan think tank focused on sustainable energy with long-term goals for behavioural change to achieve environmental goals.

3. "In the output approach, BLS is concerned with jobs related to producing a specific set of goods and services, and is not concerned with the environmental impact of the production process. The output approach alone, however, would not cover some activities and associated jobs that favorably impact the environment although the product or service produced is itself not green. The process approach is intended to address this aspect of green jobs. In the process approach, BLS is concerned with whether the business uses practices or technologies that have a favorable impact on the environment, regardless of the good or service produced. The process approach is relevant to any industry. Each approach requires different measurement strategies and will tend to count different jobs, with some overlap in industries that produce green goods and services" (United States Bureau of Labor Statistics 2010).

4. There is still an open question about what constitutes a green job. The U.S. Bureau of Labor Statistics offers the following two definitions: "A) Jobs in businesses that produce goods or provide services that benefit the environment or conserve natural resources; OR B) Jobs in which workers' duties involve making their establishment's production processes more environmentally friendly or use fewer natural resources" (United States Bureau of Labor Statistics 2010).

5. The Liberal's Third Way strategy embodies contradictory tendencies. Alongside their green energy program, the provincial government supported the bailout of the auto industry in 2008–09; gave some $1 billion in support of the financially struggling forest industry between 2005 and 2010; and has made mineral development in the so-called Ring of Fire the centrepiece of a Northern Ontario development project (Winfield 2012: 180–1).

6.   An alternative line of defence, under Article XX of the GATT, has not been used
     by Canada. In an amicus curiae brief (May 10, 2012), the International Institute
     for Sustainable Development, Canadian Environmental Law Association and
     Ecojustice Canada requested the panel to consider the argument that the case
     fitted two exceptions permitted under Article XX, namely that WTO members
     might adopt policy measures otherwise inconsistent with WTO provisions in
     pursuit either of the protection of human, animal or plant life or health or
     the conservation of exhaustible natural resources. Panels may accept or reject
     amicus curiae briefs at their discretion.

7.   Excellent surveys of the complex legal arguments can be found in Wilke (2011),
     Ritson-Bennett (2011), Blue Green Canada (2012) and in the U.S. *Third Party
     Written Submission in the case of Canada: Certain Measures Affecting the Renewable Energy
     Generation Sector* (WT/DS412) January 9, 2012. The latter contains an effective
     interpretive critique of the Canadian case.

8.   Sosnow (2011) provides more details: (1) Mesa Power argues that Canada al-
     legedly failed to provide it a minimum standard of treatment as required under
     Article 1105. Originally under the FIT Program, wind power projects were
     evaluated in a way that produced a priority ranking that was to be used to award
     Power Purchase Agreements (PPAs) to applicants within a specified geographic
     region. Only a specified number of PPAs could be awarded for each geographical
     area, as each geographic region had a capacity cap. This has changed under
     the FIT Program. Now, projects can interconnect and build transmission lines
     in neighbouring regions. Mesa Power alleges that because of changes to the
     geographic area rules, it has lost two of its wind projects in the Bruce Region.
     Mesa Power argues that the Ontario Power Authority's (OPA's) change in rules
     was capricious, discriminatory and unfair and thus a violation of the require-
     ment to accord NAFTA investors and their investments a minimum standard of
     treatment; (2) Mesa Power argues that the various buy-local requirements under
     the FIT Program violate the prohibitions against performance requirements
     contained in Article 1106; (3) Mesa Power argues that Canada failed to provide
     it with either National or Most Favoured Nation Treatment under Articles 1102
     and 1103, respectively, since a Canadian and a non-NAFTA country competitor
     allegedly were treated more favourably under the FIT Program. Specifically,
     Mesa Power argues that Boulevard Associates Canada, a Canadian competi-
     tor in the West London Region, was able to bring four of its projects over to
     the Bruce Region after the change in rules. Mesa Power argues that Canada is
     in violation of Article 1503(2), which requires a NAFTA party to ensure that its
     state enterprises do not act in a manner that is inconsistent with its Chapter 11
     obligations.

4. THE IMPACT OF CLIMATE CHANGE ON EMPLOYMENT AND SKILLS REQUIREMENTS IN THE CONSTRUCTION INDUSTRY

John O'Grady

This chapter reviews published sources on the construction industry and climate change from two perspectives. The first is the impact on employment trends in the construction industry of investments that may be required to upgrade or replace infrastructure that will be stressed or made obsolete by climate change. The second is the effect on skill requirements of "green construction" principles, i.e., construction methods and design principles that increase the resource efficiency of the built environment and, in particular, reduce the built environment's "carbon footprint." The chapter focuses on four occupational groups that are central to the construction industry: engineers, architects, technicians and technologists and skilled trades.

While there is an extensive and growing literature on the implications of climate change for the design and engineering of the built environment, there has been relatively little research on the implications of green construction for skill requirements. There is a greater body of research that endeavours to estimate the employment implications of alternative energy and retrofitting investments that would mitigate the emission of greenhouse gases (GHG). As will be discussed, however, these employment effect models are of limited value to the governments, employer organizations, unions, training and educational institutions and professional associations that make human resources planning decisions.

Section 1 provides a brief description of the key institutional features of the construction industry and a review of the data and literature dealing with the contribution of both the built environment and the construction industry to GHG emissions. This section also examines the literature on the impact of climate change on infrastructure, i.e., roads, bridges, harbours, water distribution systems, etc. The focus of this review is on what can be derived from the literature about the employment effects of the major infrastructure investments that adaptation to climate change may require and whether the Canadian construction industry has the planning capacity to respond to these demands.

Section 2 reviews the literature on the employment impacts of green construction, principally on retrofitting the existing building stock to meet higher energy efficiency standards. This section also discusses how the literature interprets the impact of green construction on the skill requirements of both the design professions and the construction trades. Section 3 offers concluding observations on the gaps in our understanding of the impact of climate change on human resources in the construction industry.

SECTION 1: THE CONSTRUCTION INDUSTRY AND GHG EMISSIONS

Overview of Human Resources in the Construction Industry

In 2009, Canada's construction industry employed approximately 1.2 million persons or just fewer than 7 percent of the labour force. Around 73 percent of persons working in the construction industry are employed in trades occupations, while the remainder work in managerial, professional or administrative roles. This does not include the majority of architects, engineers and technicians and technologists whose work is wholly or substantially tied to construction. In 2006, the architectural and engineering services industry employed approximately 209,400 persons. Half or more of these individuals were likely linked to the construction industry. Others who might be included, but whose numbers cannot be accurately estimated, are persons employed by governments to administer the application of building codes and official development plans and persons who do "in-house" construction work, as is common in many resource industries and in some segments of the electricity industry.

The construction industry comprises several distinct subsectors. These include: residential construction (which is further divided between low-rise and high-rise construction), non-residential building construction (also known as industrial-commercial-and-institutional construction or ICI construction), civil or engineering construction (i.e., infrastructure and power generation and distribution), pipeline construction, residential renovation and repair and ICI repair work. Figure 4.1 shows the approximate share of these subsectors, based on the estimated value of construction output for 2008. These shares vary significantly across regions and also over the business cycle.

The contractors and workers who undertake construction have only limited influence on design decisions and the specification of materials. In the main these decisions are made by owner-developers on the basis of advice from architectural and engineering professionals. In turn, this professional advice is strongly shaped by the regulatory environment. Over the past ten

Figure 4.1 Approximate Shares of Construction Output, 2008

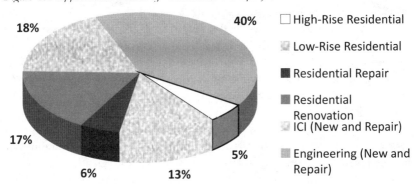

Source: Author's estimates based on Construction Sector Council's estimates <www.constructionforecasts.ca>

years, rating systems, such as LEED, have come to play an important role in design decisions. The influence of these rating systems is a function of both regulatory requirements and market demand. On the other hand, liability also plays an important role. Architects, engineers and contractors are financially liable for the performance of the structures they design and build. This liability can extend over many years. Liability instills a high degree of conservatism in the construction industry. Consequently, the industry is slow to abandon engineering and architectural solutions, building materials and construction methods that have worked in the past.

Unionization varies by province, by sector and by trade. Quebec has a distinct labour relations model, which results in an overall unionization rate of approximately 40 percent in the construction industry. In the rest of Canada, unionization in the construction industry is approximately 29 percent on a labour force basis. The engineering construction and ICI construction (especially the industrial segment of ICI) have higher rates of unionization. On the other hand, low-rise residential construction is predominantly non-union in most parts of Canada, with the exception of the Greater Toronto Area. Repair and renovation work is overwhelmingly non-union especially in the residential sector. In the construction industry, unions are generally, though not always, organized on a craft basis. Outside of Quebec, unions affiliated to the American Federation of Labor and Congress of Industrial Organizations (AFL-CIO) Building Trades Department predominate. In British Columbia and Alberta, "merit shop" contractors operate on a non-union basis but often provide benefits and skills training on a multiemployer basis. In these provinces, the Christian Labour Alliance (CLAC) also has a significant membership in the construction industry. Most construction bargaining is conducted under right-to-strike conditions. However, in some jurisdictions, some trades have opted for voluntary arbitration. CLAC generally pursues a non-strike policy. In the Greater Toronto Area, low-rise residential construction is subject to compulsory arbitration.

In the construction industry, the majority of employers are small and medium-sized enterprises. In 2009, approximately 51 percent of construction workers were employed in establishments with fewer than twenty employees. Self-employment is also a significant factor in the construction industry. In 2009, almost 15 percent of workers in the construction industry were self-employed.

Sector-based, or multiemployer, human resources planning is strongly rooted in the construction industry. The distinctive affinity for multiemployer human resources planning arises from the need to ensure an adequate supply of skilled labour in an industry that is dominated by small employers and specialized skills that must be acquired over time. At the national level, the Construction Sector Council provides detailed estimates of future trade requirements. In Ontario, the Ontario Construction Secretariat, as established by statute, supports the unionized ICI. The most highly developed sectoral management of construction human resources is found in Quebec where the Commission de la Construction du Québec (CCQ) is mandated by statute to oversee labour relations, training and human resources planning.

In the unionized sector, construction work is generally organized along trade lines with tasks parcelled out according to jurisdictions established by regulation, agreement or tradition. Construction crews comprise journeypersons, apprentices and, in some cases, helpers or labourers. In the unionized sector, forepersons are members of the bargaining unit. In the nonunion sector, employers use a greater proportion of semiskilled workers (Bourdon and Levitt 1980). The majority of craft unions operate dispatch services (historically known as "hiring halls") whereby the unions supply skilled workers to employers who, in turn, are required by collective agreements to hire only workers dispatched by the union. Dispatch priority is based on length of unemployment and the requisite skills. In contrast with other sectors, seniority rules play little or no role in the construction industry.

Most craft unions operate training programs for their members. Many of these programs are delivered through well-equipped training centres that are owned by unions or by trusteed funds. Training is typically financed by negotiated contributions to training trust funds, which may be operated by the union or jointly with employers (Prism Economics and Analysis 2005).

In all provinces, most or all construction trades are regulated occupations. A trade qualification (TQ) is issued by the provincial government or a provincial training authority following completion of trade examinations. Most, but not all, TQ-holders complete an apprenticeship before taking these examinations. Apprenticeships consist of a period of on-the-job learning and classroom-based learning ("trades school"). Both the duration of apprenticeship training and the amount of trades school training vary by trade. For trades such as electrician and plumber, apprenticeships are typically 7,200 to 9,000 hours with three periods of trades school, each of eight weeks duration. In Canada, occupational regulation is in provincial jurisdiction. Most construction trades, however, are "Red Seal" trades, meaning that the provincial standards adhere to a common national standard established by the Canadian Council of Directors of Apprenticeship. For Red Seal trades, occupational standards are based on a National Occupational Analysis (NOA), which is undertaken by the federal government in cooperation with industry and the Canadian Council of Directors of Apprenticeship.

Construction trades may be compulsory or voluntary. In compulsory trades, work that is encompassed by a trade regulation can only be performed by a TQ-holder or a registered apprentice. In Quebec, most trades are compulsory. In the rest of Canada, only a minority of construction trades require a worker to hold a TQ or to be registered as an apprentice in that trade. British Columbia has adopted a strategy of making specific skill sets compulsory, rather than trades per se. The functions of some trades may also be regulated by technical standards authorities, some of which are stand-alone bodies, while others are divisions within provincial ministries.

Both engineers and architects are licensed professions in Canada. Admission to both the engineering and architecture professions requires a professional degree from an accredited university program, the completion of additional courses and examinations specified by the professional associations and a significant period of practical experience under the supervision of a licensed professional. In both professions, university programs must be accredited by the profession to be recognized for licensure. This gives the professions significant leverage over the content and quality of professional education. Most professional associations in engineering and all associations in architecture require their members to undertake continuing professional development to maintain their licensure status.

For technicians and technologist occupations, the usual qualification is a community college certification. However, many technicians and technologists also hold university qualifications. Professional associations also accredit college technology programs. Technicians and technologists need not be licensed, but may obtain a voluntary certification from a professional association. Most low-rise, residential construction does not require a licensed architect to "stamp" drawings. Consequently, much of the design work in this segment of the industry — which accounts for 20–30 percent of total construction activity — is undertaken by architectural technicians and technologists.

The Built Environment as a Source of Greenhouse Gas Emissions

Partington and Bramely estimated that, in 2006, the ongoing operation of residential and commercial buildings accounted for 5.5 percent and 4.6 percent of CO_2 emissions respectively (Partington and Bramley 2010). The preponderance of these emissions pertained to heating and cooling needs. These estimates, it should be stressed, apply only to the *operation* of buildings; they do not reflect emissions caused by the manufacture of construction materials or by the construction process. When these factors are included, a significantly different view emerges. Cement, for example, is one of the most GHG-intensive construction materials, as well as one of the most widely used. Kruse estimates that cement production accounts for 5 percent or more of GHG emissions internationally (Kruse 2004). To determine the total impact of the built environment on emissions, many studies use a life-cycle model, which takes into account the emissions involved in the manufacture of construction materials, the construction process itself, the operation of buildings and the ultimate demolition and removal of buildings. These broader accounting frameworks put the contribution of buildings and the construction industry at around 30–40 percent of total GHG emissions (CEC 2008: 22; UNEP 2006).[1] Given these estimates, it is not surprising that the Intergovernmental Panel on Climate Change identified changes in the design and operation of buildings as providing the greatest opportunity for reducing GHG emissions.

Twenty-one countries, including most OECD jurisdictions, have established at least one green rating system for new construction (UNEP 2006: 137–8). Building rating systems are central to efforts to mitigate the impact of the built environment on the natural environment. The Canadian Urban Institute summarizes five of the most widely used systems of rating buildings that currently operate in Canada.

Leadership in Energy and Environmental Design (LEED) is the best known of the rating systems. A recent study of the cast-in-place concrete industry reported comments from the design sector that, in the near future, it would be impossible to obtain approval for a major commercial development that was not LEED certified. The study also reported that most of the leading engineering and architectural consultancies either had LEED accredited professionals in their senior ranks or were in the process of securing accreditation (Prism Economics and Analysis 2007b). Since 2001, the Canada Green Building Council has accredited more than 10,000 professionals (Canada Green Building Council n.d.). Indicative of the impact of LEED, Public Works Canada now requires new federal buildings to be constructed to the LEED Gold standard or higher.

The impact of building rating systems has been modest but may be approaching a tipping point. In 2009, the Canada Green Building Council certified only 587 projects, of which two-thirds were in the public sector.

Figure 4.2 Building Rating Systems

System	Description	Rating Levels
Leadership in Energy and Environmental Design (LEED)	Canada Green Building Council Evaluates new buildings and major renovations on the basis of five performance categories: site sustainability, water use efficiency, energy and atmosphere, materials and resources and indoor environment. Points are awarded under each category.	LEED Platinum: 52–70 points LEED Gold: 39–51 points LEED Silver: 33–38 points LEED Certified: 26–32 points
Green Globes	Existing Buildings: Building Owners Management Association New Buildings: ECD Jones Lang LaSalle Green Globes evaluates building environmental performance in seven categories: project management, site, energy, water, resources, emissions and effluents and indoor environment. The Green Globes system is derived from standards originally developed by the Canadian Standards Association.	Properties receiving a rating above 35% receive certification of one to four "green globes."
BOMA Go Green	Building Owners Management Association Building performance is evaluated in ten categories: energy use, water use, construction waste, recycling, hazardous waste, material selection, ozone depletion, indoor air quality, HVAC maintenance and tenant awareness.	Properties that meet all requirements receive Go Green certification.
Built Green	Built Green Society of Canada Evaluates sustainability based on: energy efficiency, indoor air quality, resource use (including waste management) and overall environmental impact. Relies on EnerGuide criteria for houses.	Platinum: 120 points Gold: 77 points Silver: 74 points Bronze 72 points
Energy Star	Natural Resources Canada (NRCan) Energy Star is an international energy efficiency standard that is administered in Canada by NRCan. In construction, the objective is to improve energy efficiency in heating and cooling systems, ducts, windows, walls, ceilings and ventilation.	Energy Star homes exceed building code requirements for energy efficiency by approximately 30%.

The 2008 report of the Commission for Environmental Cooperation (CEC) reported estimates that, in the United States, green building represented about 2 percent of new non-residential building. The commission did not expect this share to exceed even 10 percent by 2010. In the residential sector, the commission estimated that green buildings accounted for less than 1 percent of the new construction market. Notwithstanding the current low levels of green construction, there are reasons to believe that the trend could change significantly in the near future.

A study for the Pacific Institute for Climate Solutions estimated that applying green standards to new building construction and renovating existing buildings to green standards at the rate of only 2.5 percent per year would raise three-quarters of the total building stock to green standards within twenty years (Woodbury et al. 2008). The Canadian Urban Institute confirms this conclusion. In a 2008 study, the institute portrays the movement to green construction in Canada as approaching an acceleration point. "The potential impact of green construction on GHG emissions, therefore, is significant as would be the implications of green construction skill requirements in the construction industry" (Canadian Urban Institute 2008).

Construction Activity as a Source of Greenhouse Gas Emissions

Environment Canada has published estimates of GHG emissions by sector. For the construction industry, these estimates consider only the impact of construction activity. That is to say, the estimates do not attribute to the construction industry the GHG emissions arising from either the manufacture of building materials or the operation of buildings. Figure 4.3 summarizes this data.

Figure 4.3 Greenhouse Gas Emissions by Source, Canada 1990 and 2006

	GHG Emissions Megatonnes of CO_2 Equivalence		GHG Emission Intensity Kilograms of GHG/$ GDP	
	1990	2006	1990	2006
Total	592	728	0.84	0.66
All Industries	123	113	0.68	0.44
Construction Industry	3.78	3.11	0.08	0.05
Construction Share:				
Of Industry	3.1%	2.8%		
Of Total	0.6%	0.4%		

Source: Environment Canada 2008: Tables 1 and 3

As can be seen, in 2006, the construction industry accounted for approximately 2.8 percent of industrial emissions of GHGs and 0.4 percent of emissions from all sources (i.e., including non-industrial). The construction industry's emission intensity was substantially lower than the average for industry as a whole. Moreover, intensity declined by 41 percent between 1990 and 2006. Estimates for the United States attributed a somewhat higher share of GHG emissions to the construction industry (EPA 2009: 3).[2]

To reduce GHG emissions caused by the construction process, the U.S. Environmental Protection Agency (EPA) places the greatest emphasis on more efficient use of energy in operating construction machinery. The principal steps recommended are: reduced idling of equipment, improved maintenance and driver/operator training, switching to biodiesel fuels and improving energy conservation. The EPA also urges greater recycling of building materials. While these measures have some implications for training of onsite construction workers, in the main, EPA's recommendations are focused on construction contractors and their front-line management.

Climate Change, Infrastructure and Human Resources Planning in the Construction Industry

Among the more potentially profound impacts of climate are its possible effects on sea levels, the stability of the permafrost, the frequency of severe weather conditions, the water table and natural drainage systems. There is a substantial Canadian and international literature on the potential impact of these consequences of climate change for both buildings and infrastructure. Much of this literature has been collected by the Public Infrastructure Engineering Vulnerability Committee, which is jointly funded by Natural Resources Canada and Engineers Canada.

Climate science is an imprecise science. There is, therefore, no certainty about the scale, severity or timing of environmental developments. Consequently, there can be no certainty about the impact of climate change on roads, bridges, harbours, water distribution systems and other infrastructure. On the basis of some scenarios, the requirements to upgrade and replace infrastructure would put considerable strain on the economy and would increase significantly the size of the construction industry and its labour force. Other scenarios imply more manageable pressures, similar to those that arise whenever there is a large block of construction work undertaken in a short period of time. Moreover, the effect of climate change on infrastructure is not easily separated from the broader need to upgrade and expand Canada's dated infrastructure. In the 1980s and 1990s, Canadian governments at all levels deferred infrastructure investments as they struggled to restore fiscal balance to the public sector. This underinvestment led to what many observers have termed an "infrastructure deficit." Over the past ten years, most governments have significantly increased infrastructure investment. As a result, the share of engineering construction in total construction has grown from under 30 percent twenty years ago to approximately 40 percent today. It is notable that the construction industry adjusted to this significant increase in infrastructure spending without apparent difficulty. This should be taken as evidence of the industry's capacity to adapt to changed demand conditions as long as those changed conditions can be forecast.

From a human resources planning perspective, the key question is whether the labour market demands arising from increased infrastructure investment can be anticipated in time for planning measures to prevent serious bottlenecks in the supply of skilled labour. There are reasons to answer this affirmatively. As a result of work undertaken by the Construction Sector Council, Canada is now the recognized international leader in monitoring and forecasting labour requirements in the construction industry.[3] As well, two decades of investments in training centres have significantly increased the capacity of the construction industry to respond to changing demand conditions. In light of this planning capacity, it is unlikely that even a large increase in infrastructure investment would shock the labour market and put the supply of skilled construction labour under unsustainable pressure. The same is likely to be the case with the engineering profession. Current enrolment trends in engineering, together with immigration of internationally trained professionals, means that the current supply of engineers is likely greater than the current needs of the Canadian economy.

From the perspective of human resources planning, the principal challenge will not be to meet labour supply requirements per se. Rather, the challenge will be to meet the specific skill needs that arise from adopting green construction principles. It is to this topic that we now turn.

SECTION 2: THE POTENTIAL IMPACT
OF "GREEN CONSTRUCTION" ON EMPLOYMENT AND SKILLS

Employment Implications of Green Construction

For any given level of construction investment, the determinants of employment in the construction industry are: (1) the selection of building materials, (2) the degree to which pre-fabricated components are used and (3) the degree to which onsite tasks are mechanized. Green construction methods principles affect employment through these factors or not at all. While it would be useful to the industry to better understand how green construction principles might affect both the overall demand for construction labour and the demand for specific construction trades, this remains *terra incognita*.

Much more attention has been directed to the employment effects of retrofitting the existing building stock to meet higher energy efficiency standards. It should not be assumed, however, that significant amounts of retrofitting are currently being undertaken. With reference to the U.S., Rogers comments that the amount of retrofitting is negligible (Rogers 2007). He cites nine barriers that must be addressed before a significant increase in retrofit investments can be anticipated. These include: lack of access to capital; the muted incentives inherent in commercial tenancies, which typically pass operating costs through to tenants; and alternative uses for capital (including public capital). Several studies estimate the employment impact of proposed incentive programs. Among the more widely cited U.S. studies is one by Pollin et al. for the Center for American Progress. The study concluded that $100 billion invested in a range of green initiatives, including building retrofitting, would create only approximately 2.0 million jobs (Pollin et al. 2008). Roughly 50 percent of these jobs would be directly created, while the remainder would be indirect jobs (i.e., jobs in supplying industries) or induced jobs (unrelated jobs created by multiplier effects).

A study prepared by IHS Global Insight for the United States Conference of Mayors projected that green jobs would increase over the next thirty years at a rate of just slightly less than 6 percent per year (Global Insight 2008). The study concluded that green jobs will account for 10 percent of new job growth over the next thirty years (ibid.). Roughly 30 percent of this job growth will arise from the expected construction of renewable power generating capacity (Dupressoir et al. 2007b). Retrofitting accounts for only 2 percent of the job creation in the IHS Global Insight study (Global Insight 2008).

The European Trade Union Confederation (ETUC) modelled the employment effects of a range of policies to reduce GHG emissions. Construction was among the sectors studied. Unlike the previous studies, the ETUC examined only direct employment effects. The policies modelled include simple compliance with current policy directives to the adoption of an aggressive plan to reduce 75 percent of GHG emissions in the residential sector. ETUC concludes that the direct employment effects on the construction industry are under 1 percent of additional cost for the current policy option, but over 10 percent for the aggressive retrofitting option (Dupressoir et al. 2007b: 146–59).

In Canada, the Federation of Canadian Municipalities (FCM) cites an unspecified federal government report that investing in municipal building retrofits will generate full-time equivalent jobs at the rate of one job per $50,000 expended (FCM 2003). The nature of the retrofit renovations is not described. Given that nonlabour inputs account for around 50 percent of repair costs, this estimate could be high.

The trades that are generally seen as benefiting disproportionately from retrofit investments are carpenters, electricians, plumbers and pipefitters, sheet metal workers, general labourers, insulators and refrigeration and air conditioning mechanics. It should not be assumed, however, that green jobs will be good jobs. Mattera stresses the need for green investment to be linked to employment standards (Mattera 2009). A similar point is made in the UNEP study, *Green Jobs: Towards Decent Work in a Sustainable, Low-Carbon World*. In contrast with these studies, Tuerck et al. offer a sharply critical assessment of the methodologies and conclusions in a number of employment impact studies (Tuerck et al. 2009).

The employment effects of investments in retrofitting depend on three factors. The first of these are macroeconomic variables, most importantly the discount rate that is used to translate future cost savings into present values and the expected future cost of energy. Retrofit investments are only undertaken when the projected "present value" of future savings exceeds the cost of the investment. A second class of variables comprises assumptions about the breadth and intensity of retrofitting. The breadth of retrofitting is the amount of building space that is subject to retrofitting. The intensity of retrofitting refers to the types of renovations that are undertaken. Retrofitting may be limited to simply caulking and sealing air leaks. More intensive retrofitting entails upgrading or replacing insulation. More costly still is replacing or upgrading fenestration systems. And lastly, electrical and mechanical systems may be upgraded or replaced. The employment implications depend on what types of renovations are undertaken and the scale of those renovations across the existing stock of buildings. And finally, a third class of variables includes assumptions about wage rates, labour productivity, the take-up rate on government incentives and who does the retrofitting (i.e., the construction industry, in-house maintenance staff or homeowners on a do-it-yourself basis). Some employment impact models estimate multiplier effects (jobs that are indirectly created) by spending on retrofitting. In many cases, however, these multiplier estimates do not allow for the likelihood that spending on retrofitting is, to some degree, diverted from spending on other purposes. Hence, the multiplier effects are often larger than more cautious approaches would allow.

A study by Pollin and Garrett-Peltier, commissioned by the Green Energy Act Alliance, Blue Green Canada and the World Wildlife Fund–Canada, illustrates the complexities of forecasting employment impacts. The purpose of the study is to estimate the job creation effect of Ontario's *Green Energy Act*. The study projects that the legislation will create 90,442 jobs (Pollin and Garrett-Peltier 2009). However, almost 60 percent of these jobs are the result of multiplier effects. The directly created construction jobs are assumed to earn wages that range from $17.84 per hour for construction labourers to $24.56 for electricians. (The union rates for these occupations were more than double these amounts.) The report also assumes civil engineers can be hired for $31.37 per hour, which is significantly below the prevailing billing rates. Less aggressive multiplier assumptions and more realistic wage assumptions would necessarily reduce the projected employment effects, perhaps significantly. Employment forecasts of the type reflected in Pollin and Garrett-Peltier may play an important role in policy debates. However, they are of little value to those engaged in serious human resources planning.

Skill Implications of Green Construction: Design Professions

In a 2002 article in *Canadian Architect*, Peter Busby comments that "8,000 architects and 20,000 engineers control most of these processes [i.e., construction processes]. We can have an impact!" (Busby 2002: 18). Busby's comments raise two questions. First, are design professionals taking up the additional professional training that is required to apply green building rating systems? And second, are the curricula of college and university programs for design professionals responding to the need for greater understanding of green design principles?

For design professionals, one of the key implications of green construction is the need for competence in the application of building rating systems. Since these rating systems are evolving rapidly, there is also an implicit need for continuing professional development to maintain competence. The need for competence in green rating systems is over and above the need for design processionals to be fully knowledgeable of mandatory standards, such as building codes and environmental regulations. As noted earlier, there are already more than 10,000 Canadian professionals who are LEED Accredited Professionals (AP). This suggests a high degree of accessibility to accreditation. LEED AP status also requires enrolment in a credential maintenance program involving fifteen to thirty hours of continuing training every two years.

The professional associations that regulate licensure for architectural design all require continuing professional development (CPD) as a condition for remaining licensed. In Ontario, the professional association has designated "sustainable design / green architecture" as a core topic area. Most provincial associations in the engineering profession have CPD requirements. The Engineering Institute of Canada promotes CPD and designates quality providers. Additional research on engineering and policy issues is undertaken by the Canadian Academy of Engineering and more recently by the Ontario Centre for Engineering and Public Policy (OCEPP), which was established by Professional Engineers Ontario. Several recent editions of OCEPP's flagship publication address environmental issues. Further, the Public Infrastructure Vulnerability Committee has examined the implications of climate change for engineering curricula.

Within colleges and universities there has been a broad move to incorporate curricula that will equip graduates with a working knowledge of green design principles. In 2008, the Canadian Urban Institute commented that

> having found willing partners within industry and the design community to devise and implement whole building rating systems, the public sector is now beginning to focus on creating capacity within the education system — both postsecondary and continuous professional learning — to ensure that there is proper follow through over

the long term as well as an ability to translate theory into practice. (Canadian Urban Institute 2008: 4)

Skill Implications of Green Construction: Construction Trades

For workers in the trades, the skill implications of green construction primarily stem from engineering and architectural decisions on how buildings are to be constructed. Principally this affects the selection of building materials, the specification of electrical and mechanical systems and the design of roofing systems and building envelopes. Energy conservation also has implications for the efficient sealing of the building envelope. The elimination of landfill waste has been a regulation-driven priority for the construction industry for some time, under the reduce-reuse-recycle principles that underpin environmental regulations. There is awareness in the construction industry of the growing importance of environmental issues and environmental regulations. A survey reported by the *Daily Commercial News*, a Canadian construction industry publication, found that climate change was among the leading concerns of the plumbing industry (Williams 2008).[4] A survey of residential heating and ventilation contractors in Canada found that 69 percent of employers were having difficulty recruiting workers who were familiar with environmental requirements (Prism Economics and Analysis 2007a: Figure 25).

Some discussions of the skill implications of green construction take no account of the important role of the trades. For example, a study by Holmen Enterprises for the Canadian Urban Institute is silent on the issue of trade skills, although it comments on the need for green design skills (Holmen Enterprises Inc. 2006). Similarly, in a special issue on sustainable building and construction in UNEP's *Industry and Environment*, Wells makes only passing references to trade skill requirements (Wells 2003). Other studies, however, comment on the possibility that skills shortages in the construction trades may be a future constraint on green construction. For example, the Commission for Environmental Cooperation notes that

> one impediment cited repeatedly by many during the Secretariat's green building consultations, but not explored well in the literature and research, is rapid industry expansion threatening to compound the problem of the lack of experienced workers and thus increasing the risk of inexperienced or untrained service providers entering the green building market in search of a premium on their services. (CEC 2008: 56)

The view that the trade skill implications of green construction are poorly understood is also voiced by the European Trade Union Confederation (ETUC). ETUC comments that "the questions of human resources, underestimated by the majority of professionals concerned, are a significant hindrance to the transformation of the residential sector into distinctly less of a CO_2-emitting sector" (Dupressoir et al. 2007b: 159).

The manner in which skills are certified — whether trade skills or professional skills — is an important issue for public policy. Kleiner has identified occupational certification as one of the more important trends in the contemporary labour market (Kleiner 2006). An important issue, especially for trade unions, is whether green construction skills will be integrated into current trade standards or be the basis for new "niche occupations" outside the mainstream system of apprenticeship training. A study for the U.S.-based Apollo Alliance comments that "retrofitting American cites ... requires not 'green construction workers,' but rather workers with traditional construction skills who also have up-to-date training on energy-efficient construction" (White and Walsh 2008: 16). The study argues against creating what it terms "boutique" programs divorced from broader workforce development efforts (ibid.: 47). A similar view is advocated in a study by the GHK consultancy for the European Employment Observatory. The authors comment that green jobs in the construction trades entail "the same generic skills of those already in the building sector ... but jobs will require an 'add-on' in terms of e.g., renewable energy knowledge, installation [and] diagnostic techniques" (GHK Consulting Inc. 2009: 33). This is consistent with the view expressed by UNEP that "many existing jobs (especially such as plumbers, electricians, metal workers and construction workers) will simply be redefined as day-to-day skill sets, work methods and profiles are greened." The report continues: "it goes without saying that this last aspect is by far the hardest to document and analyze and the hardest for which to foresee the full implications" (UNEP 2008: 43). This approach is endorsed by B.C.'s Residential Construction Industry Training Organization, which operates under a mandate from the province's Industry Training Authority.

Training in green construction requires incorporating green construction principles into the training standards for apprentices and also designing and delivering upgrade training to persons who already have their trade qualification. Training for apprentices is governed by training standards that are based on a National Occupational Analysis (NOA). NOAs are undertaken by industry with federal government support. The focus of an NOA is on the job tasks and skills that are broadly needed by members of the trade. An important consequence of the NOA system is that the standards can be slow to accommodate emerging skill requirements, since these often lack the critical mass to warrant a change in the NOA. This conservatism has led some green industries to pursue training and certification strategies outside the framework of the established system of apprenticeship and trade regulation. In Canada, an important example of this phenomenon is the solar photovoltaic industry, where the industry has developed training and an industry-based certification outside the established trades system. Training is delivered through private trainers and community colleges.

A Toronto study by Penney et al., which was sponsored by the Clean Air Partnership Fund, the Canadian Urban Institute and the Toronto Training Board, reflects the tension between incorporating green construction skills into existing trades versus establishing "niche trades" parallel to, or outside, the established trade system. The study was based on a canvass of construction industry members. It noted that "anecdotal reports suggest that some energy efficient building designs fail to perform as predicted and that some of the shortfall may be due to inadequate knowledge and skills among the trades who execute the designs or operate the systems that have been installed" (Penney et al. 2007: 7). In the main, the Penney study concluded that the most appropriate training strategy was one that built on existing trade skills rather than one that endeavoured to displace the construction trades with new "green trades." However, the study acknowledged that new trades are emerging that are related to green construction strategies. These include: external insulation finishing systems mechanics, solar installers, geothermal installers and green roof specialists. To some degree, the emergence of these "niche trades" reflects a failure of the established trades to adequately address the new skills required by green technologies. The study commented that "rather than struggle to get the training system to integrate these skills, associations such as the Canadian Solar Industries Association and the Canadian GeoExchange Coalition have begun their own training and certification programs" (ibid.: 19). For the established construction trades, the Penney study identified two types of skill requirements. The first is a general understanding of energy efficient and sustainable construction.

The Penney study found that energy efficiency training was delivered through a number of channels, including colleges, union training centres, private trainers and technology suppliers. The study noted the lack of recognized standards and certifications. At the same time, Penney also commented that "the major barrier to expanded energy efficiency training for the trades is that the demand for energy efficient buildings is not yet sufficient to trigger the requisite changes in the training systems" (ibid.: 5). Penney raises important questions about the role of policy in driving the adoption of energy efficient technologies in buildings and the equally important role of policy in establishing appropriate competency standards and certifications for tradespersons and contractors. In a similar vein, a U.S. study undertaken by Mattera for the Sierra Club and a consortium of union advocates found that access to government monies for retrofitting should be linked to support for labour standards, training and apprenticeships, thereby linking green construction spending to broader trade union goals (Mattera 2009).

A number of construction unions are currently developing upgrade training to provide addition green construction skills to their members. The International Brotherhood of Electrical Workers (IBEW), for example, has introduced a 75-lesson course on green building fundamentals. Among the topics addressed in the course are: energy efficiency principles, photovoltaics, wind systems, programmable logic controllers, fuel cells, power quality and building automation. The union has established a dedicated website to address issues arising from "working green" (International Brotherhood of Electrical Workers n.d.). The IBEW in Canada has also developed training in the installation of solar photovoltaics. In the piping trades, the International Association of Plumbing and Mechanical Officials (IAPMO), the United Association of Journeymen and Apprentices of the Plumbing and Pipe Fitting Industry of the United States and Canada (UA) and Green Plumbers are collaborating on the development of training programs and accreditation. The UA also maintains a dedicated website to address green construction issues. In addition to training delivered through union training centres, colleges are also developing and delivering a range of courses on green construction methods. A 1997 study shows that the colleges have been responsive to the need for green construction skills for a considerable period of time (Prism Economics and Analysis 1997).[5]

SECTION 3: GAPS IN OUR UNDERSTANDING OF THE IMPACT OF CLIMATE CHANGE ON EMPLOYMENT AND SKILLS REQUIREMENT IN CONSTRUCTION

The preponderance of the literature on climate change deals with its potential consequences for arable land use, the sustainability of resource-based industries, the vulnerability of the built environment to increased occurrences of extreme weather conditions and the risks to coastal settlements of rising sea levels. The potential implications for the labour market of measures to adapt to climate change or mitigate its effects have only recently drawn the attention of researchers. The potential labour market effects of climate change depend to a large degree on policy decisions, especially those labour market effects that arise from efforts to mitigate climate change. Labour market effects fall broadly into two categories: changes in the pattern and trajectory of employment across and within industries and changes in skill requirements. Human resources planning involves anticipating both types of change and responding with appropriate adjustment programs to ease the transfer of labour across industries and human capital investments to re-skill labour.

The first key finding of this review is that relatively little research has been undertaken on the magnitude of public and private investments that may be required to update or replace infrastructure that could be stressed or made redundant by climate change. Consequently, relatively little is known about the potential consequences of such investments for long-run employment trends in the construction industry. That being said, it must be noted that the Canadian construction industry is an international leader in managing technical systems that support informed human resources planning. The industry also has a highly developed capacity to design and deliver training. Similarly, both the postsecondary system and professional associations in architecture, engineering and technology have responded to changing professional competency needs in these fields.

The second key finding is that currently available estimates of the employment impacts of green policies, including retrofitting, fall significantly short of the rigorous validation that is required to support properly informed human resources planning decisions.

The third finding is that building rating systems will play an increasingly important role in shaping how green construction principles are applied to new construction projects and, to a lesser degree, to retrofitting. The link between these building rating systems and their implications for construction methods and the resulting skill requirements has been insufficiently investigated. It may also be important to study the institutional characteristics of building rating systems and the degree to which appropriate accountability and validation standards are maintained.

The fourth finding is that while some construction trades have taken steps to incorporate the skill implications of green construction into trade standards and trade skills, this trend is limited. More work along these lines appears to have been done in the U.S., though the Canadian affiliates of international construction trades unions are able to draw on this work. Part of the reason for the lag in introducing green construction skills into mainstream trade standards is that the current demand for such skills is still a niche market. Credible insights into how the demand for such skills is likely to unfold would be helpful. The college system has been an early introducer of programs to meet emerging needs for green construction skills.

The fifth finding, one that is potentially important for some construction trades, is that the lag in incorporating green construction skills into trade standards is prompting some green industries to establish training and certification outside the mainstream trade system. From a policy and research perspective, the issue is when changes in skill requirements should be accommodated within existing occupations and certifications and when they should lead to the creation of new occupations and new certifications.

A sixth finding is that green certifications, such as LEED, are playing an increasingly important role in professional qualifications in the design professions and in the direction of design work. Green certifications, however, are entirely private certification systems. The entities that own and copyright these certifications are accountable to no one. This raises important public interest questions. It would also be useful to have an international context in which to review Canadian trends.

Understanding climate change and the steps that will be needed to mitigate it or adapt to its effects are among the leading policy and research challenges of our day. The labour market — in particular, the construction labour market — is an important area that has largely been outside the scope of most research. There is a pressing need to develop a research agenda.

Notes

1. The Commission for Environmental Cooperation's 2008 report, *Green Buildings in North America*, puts the contribution of the built environment to GHG emissions at 35 percent. The United Nations Environment Programme's 2006 study, *Buildings and Climate Change: Status, Challenges and Opportunities*, estimates that the built environment accounts for 40 percent of GHG emissions. However, it should be noted that this higher estimate is sensitive to building materials used. In much of the world, concrete is the dominant construction material. While concrete is used extensively in Canada, it is still less predominant than in many other parts of the world.

2. The U.S. Environmental Protection Agency's 2009 report, *Potential for reducing greenhouse gas emissions in the construction sector*, comments that "In 2002, the construction industry produced approximately 1.7 percent of total U.S. greenhouse gas emissions. Equivalent to 6 percent of total U.S. industrial-related greenhouse gas emissions, this quantity places construction as one of the top emitting sectors."

3. The Construction Sector Council's labour requirements tracking system is described in Watt (2005).

4. Ten percent of survey respondents were Canadian contractors (Williams 2008).

5. The study identified 392 courses in emerging or technology-related areas pertinent to the carpentry trade. Of these, 85 were described as green construction courses.

5. CLIMATE CHANGE AND LABOUR IN THE ENERGY SECTOR

Marjorie Griffin Cohen and John Calvert

Global warming (or climate change) will be Canada's most important environmental, economic and public policy challenge in the coming years. A growing body of research is interested in the various ways that dealing with climate change will affect Canadians, and the possible impact on labour is gaining attention in anticipation of a shift from a carbon-intensive to a different kind of economy (University of British Columbia 2009). These changes potentially could have both contractive and expansive effects. The contractive effects relate to the ways that actions taken to reduce carbon use could result in lower economic activity and, therefore, higher unemployment. The expansive effects relate to new industries and jobs that may arise as a result of abatement or mitigation policies. Of particular interest is how new forms of work could lessen the negative impacts on an economy if there is a switch to greater use of renewable resources in the energy sector (Marshall 2002).

The purpose of our study is to examine the impact of climate change on labour in one sector of the Canadian economy: energy production. This sector is significant for two main reasons: the production of energy is a major source of greenhouse gas emissions in Canada, and public policy in various jurisdictions is beginning to focus on the ways that some energy production, mainly electricity, could become more reliant on renewable resources (or green energy).

To explore this issue, we first examine some of the basic characteristics of the energy sector itself, including the major production trends in its various components — oil, gas, electricity and coal production — to understand output levels projected for the near future. Second, we analyze the policy context in which Canada's energy future is being determined and the role governments play and could play in determining that future. Most significant for green employment in the industry is the extent to which the future will be shaped by market-based decisions or by proactive government decisions that may move Canada in different directions.

Third, we examine what has been happening to the energy sector workforce to understand where people are currently employed and how this employment has changed over time. Included in this will be an examination of the characteristics of the workforce in terms of gender, age and other demographic characteristics and the extent that the labour force is represented by trade unions. Our fourth objective is to understand how climate change initiatives are likely to change the nature of work in the industry and the characteristics of the workforce.

CANADA'S ENERGY PRODUCTION SECTOR

Canada's energy production sector includes a broad range of different energy sources, technologies, facilities and employment patterns.[1] The principal sources of energy are: oil, natural gas, coal, nuclear power, large hydro and various renewable sources such as wind, run-of-river hydro, solar, biomass and geothermal. Despite the considerable attention governments have given to expanding low GHG sources of energy, in reality fossil fuels such as oil, natural gas and coal continue to dominate energy production. Also, new investments are occurring in the further exploitation of fossil fuels, particularly the expansion of the oil sands,[2] unconventional gas and offshore oil and natural gas.

Energy production is a major source of GHG emissions in Canada, accounting for 274.5 megatons of GHG emissions in 2008, an increase of slightly over 40 percent from the 196.7 megatons generated in 1990. In 2008, the energy production sector contributed 37.4 percent to Canada's total GHG emissions, an increase from 35.6 percent in 1990. Currently the oil and gas sector contributes over 21 percent of all GHG emissions and the electricity sector over 16 percent.[3]

While conventional oil output declined in recent years from its peak in 1973, output from the oil sands has been expanding rapidly. It now constitutes more than half of Canada's oil production. The oil sands' share of total oil production is projected to increase much more in the coming years due to major new investments planned by industry to exploit an estimated 173 billion barrels of bitumen. One recent study estimates that during the period from 2009 to 2025, total investment in the oil sands alone will amount to $373 billion (CERI 2009). The National Energy Board (NEB) expects the oil sands to constitute three quarters of the supply by 2020. Both shale and tight gas are similarly expected to increase significantly and account for two thirds of all gas production by 2020, compared with one third presently (National Energy Board 2009).

The large-scale investments in oil and gas create relatively few jobs compared to other sectors of the economy. Employment impacts tend to be concentrated in the planning, exploration, development and construction of energy projects and related infrastructure, as well as in the transportation requirements associated with building and servicing these projects. These jobs are mostly short-term in nature (CEP 2009; Newcomb 2004). Long-term employment in energy construction is contingent on continuing expansion of energy projects (Gardner Pinfold Consulting Economists Limited 2009). Manufacturing linkages for materials and equipment, as well as related administrative and technical services, do provide some additional employment, particularly in Ontario and Quebec (CAPP 2009). But imports also meet a significant share of the demand for manufactured goods needed in the energy sector.

Like production of oil and gas, electricity production shows no signs of abatement and has increased significantly since 1993, with minor downturns primarily reflecting fluctuations in economic activity.[1] The major structural changes in this sector relate to the shift away from coal for electrical generation, which has affected employment related to coal production, and the general change in the electricity market itself, as it moves away from a predominantly government-owned utilities model, where increased production and distribution is planned to meet growing needs, toward a more market-oriented model of production. Two factors have contributed to the changes in the industry: one was a response to pressures to adopt the U.S. move toward a more market-oriented approach, and the other was pressure from private power producers to have the ability to compete in the market (Electricity Sector Council 2007b: 25; CEA 2004: 12).

Also like oil and gas, Canada's electricity production is capital intensive, creating relatively few permanent jobs compared with other sectors of the Canadian economy. Total employment was 104,000 workers (Statistics Canada 2007: Table 7.1). Canada's utilities (excluding industrial self-generation output) produced 575 terawatt hours (TWh) of energy in 2009 (Statistics Canada 2009b). Electricity production is dominated by large hydro (58 percent), with coal (17 percent), nuclear (15 percent) and natural gas (6 percent) playing lesser but still significant roles in some provinces. Despite the increasing focus on new sources of "green" energy, large hydro remains the predominant source of renewable electricity and renewable energy in Canada. Some consider nuclear energy to be green energy and this may well play an increasing role in Canada in the future.[5] Nuclear generation accounts for 14.6 percent of Canada's electricity generation, with the greatest concentration in Ontario, where it provides 51 percent of the province's power needs. In addition to Ontario, nuclear power is also produced in Quebec and New Brunswick. According to Industry Canada, the nuclear generation industry employs about 21,000 people directly and 10,000 indirectly. The multiplier effect from direct and indirect work in the nuclear industry is about 40,000 jobs (Industry Canada n.d.b).

Figure 5.1 Total Electricity Production in Canada by Fuel Type

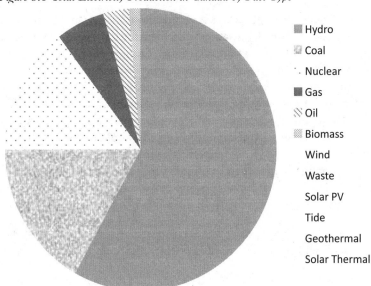

Legend:
- Hydro
- Coal
- Nuclear
- Gas
- Oil
- Biomass
- Wind
- Waste
- Solar PV
- Tide
- Geothermal
- Solar Thermal

Source: Electricity Sector Council 2008 (Note: Figure includes both utility and nonutility generation)

Proposals for expanding the share of renewable energy sources in Canada's energy production mix tend to focus primarily on further greening the electricity sector through the construction of new hydro, wind, solar, tidal, biomass and geothermal generating projects. So far, new renewable electricity (as opposed to existing large hydro) is still a relatively small contributor to overall energy supplies. Wind energy, the fastest growing and largest part of the renewable sector, still accounts for less than 1 percent of electricity output. Despite the attention given to the need to expand the role of new renewables in Canada's energy mix, they are unlikely to make a major impact in replacing fossil fuels or nuclear generation in the near future, however desirable this objective may be in reducing GHG emissions.

At present, renewable energy projects tend to be relatively more expensive per unit of energy produced compared with coal, oil and natural gas. Part of the reason is that they are also more labour intensive both to construct and, in some cases such as biofuels, to maintain and operate (Kammen et al. 2006). They are normally much smaller in size, reducing opportunities to benefit from economies of scale. While from an employment perspective this is beneficial, from the perspective of cost, it constitutes a major barrier to their expansion (Calvert 2007: 91–93). Consequently, governments wishing to expand green energy production have had to provide substantial subsidies, either by paying high prices for new renewable energy or providing tax breaks and other financial incentives to energy investors.

THE POLICY CONTEXT

Canada's ability to meet the challenges arising from climate change and consequently, the nature of the labour force demands and characteristics in the energy sector, will depend in part on the kinds of policies that federal and provincial governments follow in the coming years. The current federal government, along with most provinces, has adopted the view that the role of government is essentially one of supporting market-based, private sector solutions both to energy development and to Canada's response to climate change. The federal government has been explicit about its commitment to the energy sector's "market orientation," which it believes will provide the most efficient guide to meeting Canada's future energy needs. An example of the federal government's policy approach is explained on the Natural Resources Canada website.

> Canada's energy policy is guided by a series of principles, agreements and accords. The main principles of our energy policy are:
>
> • A market orientation: Markets are the most efficient means of determining supply, demand, prices and trade while ensuring an efficient, competitive and innovative energy system that is responsive to Canada's energy needs.
> • Respect for jurisdictional authority and the role of the provinces. Provincial governments are the direct managers of most of Canada's resources and have responsibilities for resource management within their borders.[6] (Natural Resources Canada n.d.c)

In relying on market forces and existing institutional and treaty arrangements, the federal government seems to assume that it does not need to carry out long-range planning or adopt an activist policy agenda that would take Canada in a direction different from that which market forces would otherwise dictate. The federal government seems prepared to intervene in some cases, but primarily through the support of market-based policy, while minimizing direct regulation of the energy market. The apparent approach is that national leadership will not be required to plan and shape how Canada will green its energy sector. The constitutional role of provinces/territories as resource owners reinforces the belief that national public planning should be limited to supporting private initiatives. This has led to a patchwork quilt of uncoordinated policies and a continuing reliance on the exploitation and export of fossil fuel (Doern and Gattinger 2003).

This market-oriented method also means a continuation of the very substantial fossil fuel subsidies currently in place.[7] The tax and royalty regimes of both levels of government have been shaped by the goal of expediting the exploitation of Canada's fossil fuel resources and, in recent years, a commitment to continued private ownership of the resource.[8] Industry payments to governments are low by international standards, while environmental regulations are widely criticized as being far too industry-friendly.[9] While the long-term costs of viewing the environment largely as an externality are not easy to calculate, in provinces such as Alberta they are likely to be very significant (Clarke 2008).

Reliance on market forces has also meant eschewing the development of an explicit industrial strategy that would move the energy sector toward more labour intensive green jobs. In a number of European countries such as Denmark and Germany — and to a lesser degree in parts of the U.S. — national and state/provincial governments have consciously attempted to link their efforts to build a green energy sector with the development of new manufacturing and related energy service industries. They believe that employment and skills development in these sectors can make a contribution equal to, or in some cases greater than, the creation of jobs in the construction and installation of energy generation facilities. These governments view subsidization of green energy initiatives as a springboard to the development of a world-class renewable manufacturing sector.

International experience indicates that most manufacturing in the renewable energy sector occurs in countries where there is considerable government support (Germany, U.S. [led by states], Spain, India and China) and where this support is part of a larger industrial strategy. Unfortunately, growing reliance on private sector development in Canada for green energy in all renewable energy projects reduces government leverage to encourage the domestic production of inputs.

To the extent that public pressure has encouraged governments to pursue green energy in Canada, provincial governments have generally taken the lead, although the federal government has provided some limited subsidies and tax breaks to stimulate private investment in this sector.[10] Where provinces, such as British Columbia, have encouraged expansion of private green energy projects, they have normally chosen not to impose local or national industrial offset requirements as a condition of public support.[11] Rather, using the excuse of commitments to various trade agreements (e.g., the Agreement on Internal Trade; Trade, Investment and Labour Mobility Agreement [TILMA]; and other provincial trade agreements), they have sought to eliminate this type of public policy tool, leaving corporations free to source components and services in national and international markets.[12]

CURRENT EMPLOYMENT IN THE ENERGY SECTOR

While the energy production sector has a major impact on Canada's economy, direct employment in the sector provides only a small share of the nation's jobs. Total direct employment is slightly under 300,000 workers, or roughly 1.8 percent of Canada's 17 million employed workforce in 2009.

Employment in the energy sector in Canada has increased steadily in the twenty-first century, and all projections by the government and the industries indicate that it will continue to increase into the future. However, there are fluctuations in the long-term upward trend. For example, during the 1990s employment in the largest sectors — electricity, oil and gas and services — dropped dramatically. The electricity sector went from employing 112,600 workers in 1993 to 85,900 in 2000 (Electricity Sector Council 2008). Oil and gas extraction employed about 32,200 workers in 1991, but dropped about 10,000 workers by 1996 (Statistics Canada n.d.b). However, employment in the electricity and oil and gas industries, which account for over half of all energy sector jobs, has almost completely recovered from the economic downturns of the 1990s. The oil and gas sectors are now growing more rapidly than the electricity sector, which still has employment levels slightly below what it experienced in the early 1990s. Support services have expanded dramatically and this area is now the second largest source of employment in the energy sector, after electricity.

As can be seen in Figure 5.2, of the entire energy sector only employment in coal mining has declined steadily since 1991; by 2008 it employed about half of what it did in 1991.[13] This specifically relates to shifts from coal-fired electricity production to cleaner forms of energy, much of which has been driven by public policy such the Ontario government's decision to phase out its coal-fired power stations (Province of Ontario 2009).

Canada's employment growth in the oil and gas sector, for the most part, reflects an increase in nonconventional types of fossil fuel production. These methods tend to be environmentally even more problematic than conventional oil and gas production due, in part, to the significant volumes of natural gas required to create steam for bitumen extraction or the need to clear large areas for surface mining and tailings ponds.

Because of the increased production of nonconventional fossil fuels, employment trends in Canada are diverging from those in the U.S. and Europe. Unlike those jurisdictions, Canada is not experiencing overall reductions in employment in the fossil fuel (or dirty) energy sectors. In Europe and the U.S., job losses in fossil fuel industries reflect a decline in resource availability, rather than environmental regulations or conservation (Kammen et al. 2006). Like the E.U. and the U.S., Canada is experiencing a decline in conventional oil, and conventional gas production remains flat (PHRCC 2010). The major difference in Canada is that it has large deposits of unconventional forms of fossil fuels, such as shale and tight gas, that are beginning to be developed.

Canada is also planning to increase extraction of oil from the oil sands,

Figure 5.2 Employment in the Canadian Energy Sector

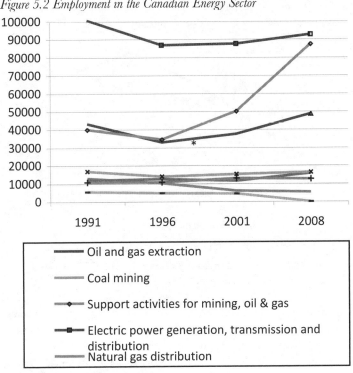

Source: Calculated from Statistics Canada, Table 281-00244 Employment (SEPH). (Note: Pipeline data is not available past 2001 to meet the confidentiality requirements of the Statistics Act.)

including proposals for major new pipelines to export this oil. In 2009, synthetic and bitumen production (77,266 thousand cubic metres) overtook conventional oil production (70,615 thousand cubic metres) for the first time in Canada's history.[14] These new oil sources indicate that fossil fuel resource availability will continue to generate expanded labour demands in these areas.

The major drivers for employment in the electricity sector in the future will be in new infrastructure to meet growing demand (both for domestic use and exports) and replacement needs (Electricity Sector Council 2007b; CEA 2004). Given the age of much of Canada's electricity infrastructure, considerable investment will be required to replace existing transmission lines, turbine generators and aging power plants. Although Canada is a major consumer of electricity and uses more on a per person basis (at 17,307 KWh) than does the U.S. (at 13,640 KWh), according to the Electricity Sector Council, per capita electricity consumption is not expected to decrease in the future.[15] As can be seen from Figure 5.3, electricity consumption is rising faster than population growth in Canada.

According to a 2006 Natural Resources Canada (NRCan) forecast,

Figure 5.3 Changes in Canadian Population and Electricity Demand

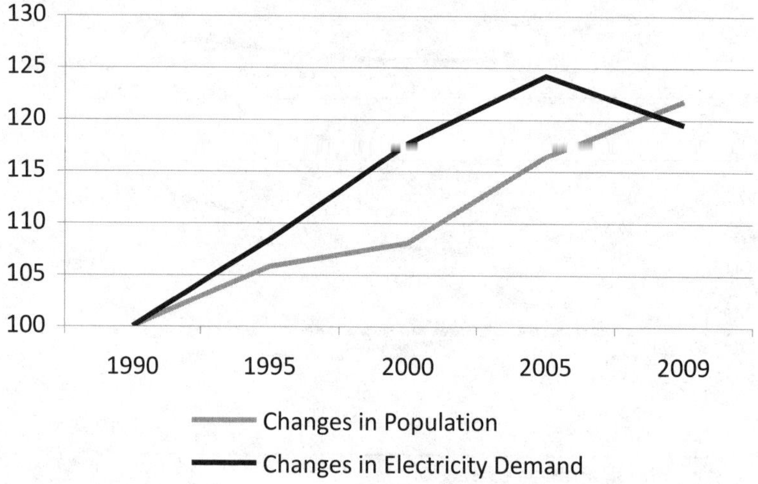

Source: Statistics Canada. *Energy Statistics Handbook, January to March 2007 as cited by Electricity Sector Council (2008: 42) (Index: 1993 = 100)*

electricity consumption is projected to increase by 1.3 percent annually until 2020 with most growth occurring in the commercial market (Natural Resources Canada 2006). Increases in exports are likely to occur as well, since provinces like Quebec, B.C. and Manitoba rely heavily on electricity exports for provincial income and have initiated clean energy plans with substantial export components.

EMPLOYMENT TRENDS IN OIL AND GAS PRODUCTION

The oil and gas sector constitutes four major types of activities and thirty-seven core occupations. The four main types of activities are exploration and production (E & P), the oil sands, services and pipelines. E&P includes exploration and production activities associated with both conventional oil and gas reserves and unconventional reserves, such as coal bed methane, tight gas and shale gas and oil. Forty percent of the oil and gas sector workforce is employed in E & P. The oil sands include producer-operated extraction and the upgrading of bitumen and employs about 7 percent of the oil and gas sector's workforce.

Services include contracted exploration, extraction and production services to the conventional E&P and oil sands sectors. More specifically, these services include well services, oilfield construction, production services, maintenance and turnaround, transportation services, drilling and geophysical services. Workers in services account for about 50 percent of the oil and gas labour force. Pipelines refer to mainline transmission, and employment in pipeline work accounts for about 3 percent of the industry's labour force.

Figure 5.4 Petroleum Industry Employment

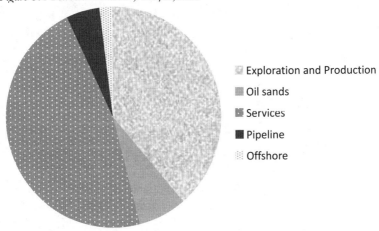

- Exploration and Production
- Oil sands
- Services
- Pipeline
- Offshore

Source: PHRCC 2010

The historical hiring practices in the oil and gas sector resulted in a largely white, male labour force, with an under-representation of immigrants and women. The increased demand for labour associated with expanded production in the future, coupled with an aging workforce and natural mortality rates (replacement demand) is forcing the industry to consider workers that previously had low participation rates in this industry (PHRCC 2010; Alberta Employment and Immigration 2007). According to 2006 census figures, women account for about 28 percent of those working in engineering, trades and technology in the Canadian labour force, but they accounted for only about 8 percent of these positions in the petroleum industry. Immigrants fare slightly better, accounting for 20 percent of the comparable labour force, and 9 percent of the workers in the petroleum industry. New entrants to the labour force and aboriginal workers represent a slightly larger share of the petroleum industry's labour force than they represent in the comparable total labour force.

Altogether women account for 28 percent of the employees in the oil and gas sector, an increase from 25 percent in 1997. Generally the labour force is characterized as being younger than the rest of the labour force, with a greater percentage of workers under thirty-five than in other sectors of the economy.

As can be seen from Table 5.1, union coverage in the sector is low and declining. Where 32 percent of the workers in Canada were unionized in 2006, only 12.3 percent of those in the oil and gas sector were in trade unions. Most of these unionized workers are in manufacturing and gas distribution. In the manufacturing sector about 32 percent of the labour force is unionized, a figure that is relatively unchanged since 1997. In gas

Figure 5.5 Petroleum Industry — Share of Labour Supply (Census 2006)

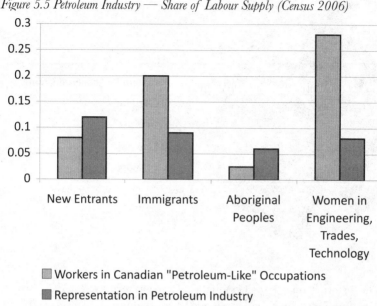

☐ Workers in Canadian "Petroleum-Like" Occupations

■ Representation in Petroleum Industry

Source: PHRCC 2010: 34

distribution about 45 percent is unionized, down from 50 percent in 1997. The level of unionization is very low in extraction (9.2 percent) and support industries (10.2 percent), but both have experienced about a 2 percent growth in unionization over ten years.

There is almost no unionization of gas station workers (4.8 percent) even though this sector of the industry is a major employer. Of the 74,000 gas station workers, 35 percent had part-time jobs in 2006. Almost 60 percent were under the age of thirty-five and average hourly wage rates were only $8.61. A much higher proportion (42 percent) were women as well. Employment in this sector has declined slightly in recent years as a result of rationalization of the number of service stations and a shift to greater customer self-service (Williams 2007).

FUTURE EMPLOYMENT GROWTH IN OIL AND GAS

The Petroleum Human Resources Council of Canada (PHRCC) estimates that by 2011, 100 percent of the Canadian labour supply growth will come from immigration, and, given the fierce competition that is likely to arise from a tight labour market in the future, the industry will need to diversify its workforce. Considerable pressure will come from employee losses due to retirement and natural deaths over the next ten years, with the greatest pressure from this in the pipeline sector.

Oil sands production and related services are the primary sources of

Table 5.1 Characteristics of Oil and Gas Labour Force

	All Industries		Oil and Gas Related	
	1997	2006	1997	2006
Employed	13,706.00	16,484.30	244.7	297.6
Self-Employed	2,349.40	2,498.00	28.6	34.9
Sex				
Men	54.5	52.9	74.6	71.8
Women	45.5	47.1	25.4	28.2
Age				
15 to 34	40.1	36.8	48.8	44.8
35 to 54	50.1	49.1	45.4	46
55 +	9.7	14.1	5.8	9.3
Union Coverage (excludes self-employed)	33.7	31.7	13.8	12.3
Work Schedule				
Full-time	80.9	82	85.5	88.3
Part-time	19.1	18	14.4	11.7
Avg. $/hr	12.92	16.73	14.8	20.64

Source: Williams 2007: Table 2

projected expansion in new demand for workers, as new operations and production come on stream. The main driver in services is the support that is required by in-situ oil sands extraction. The industry estimates that the following occupations will need the largest number of additional workers by 2020 (PHRCC 2010: 9):

- oil and gas drilling, servicing and related labourers
- oil and gas well drillers, servicers, testers and related workers
- operators (steam and non-steam)
- heavy equipment operators, supervisors, oil and gas drilling and service
- oil and gas well drilling workers and service operators
- drilling coordinators/production managers
- truck drivers, millwright and machinists
- petroleum engineers
- geologists and geophysicists

The employment growth in some occupations will be very large, with the demand for mining engineers up 66 percent over the 2008 workforce. The demand for almost all core occupations is expected to rise between 30 and 50 percent over the same period. Altogether the petroleum industry

Figure 5.6 Petroleum Industry Employment Growth Scenario 2006–2020

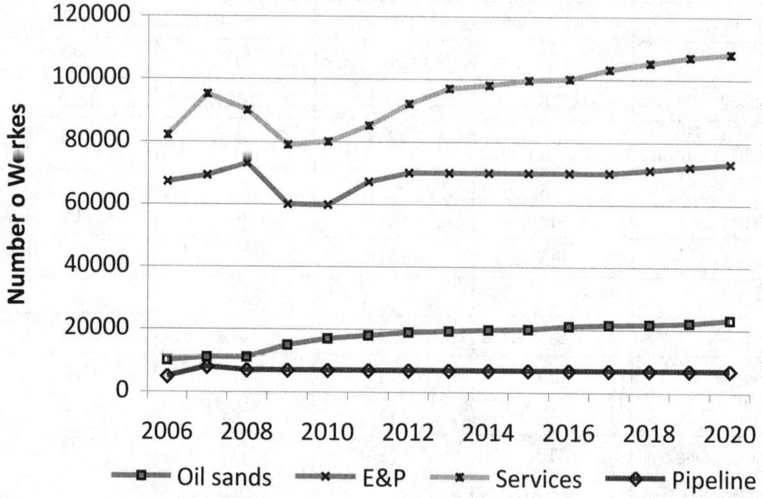

Source: PHRCC 2010: 8

will need to hire about 105,000 workers between 2010 and 2020 to meet replacement demand and to support new industry activity. In the short term, that is, by 2011 or 2012, labour shortages are expected in five groups of the industry's core occupations: engineers, geologists and geophysicists, trades, operators (steam and nonsteam) and services (drilling and geophysical workers, operators and labourers). Most of the labour market growth will occur in provinces that focus on oil and gas production: British Columbia, Alberta, Saskatchewan, Newfoundland and Labrador and Nova Scotia (PHRCC 2010: 13, 17, 19). The industries that have experienced serious economic stress and restructuring in recent years, such as forestry, pulp and paper, sawmills and lumber manufacturing industries, are likely to be the source of potential workers, as will industries that compete for workers with technical skills, such as chemical manufacturing and mining.

EMPLOYMENT TRENDS IN ELECTRICITY

As noted earlier, just over 100,000 people work in the electricity industry in Canada.[16] The main demand for future employment in this sector will come from retirements, which are expected to proceed at about 5 percent per year. The industry itself is less certain about labour needs for the future than is the petroleum sector, so presents its labour needs in both low and high growth scenarios. In the low-growth labour scenario, the supply-demand gaps in the short term (by 2012) are likely to be in the trades and other nonsupport positions (2,355) and for engineers (679). In the high-growth scenario, the supply-demand gaps will be more significant at 3,466 for trades and other nonsupport positions and 1,189 for engineers (Electricity Sector Council 2008: 97–98). However, the industry is careful to note that this is a "hypothetical" gap and that employers will likely have access to employment pools, such as contractors that act as a contingent workforce for the electricity industry, to meet labour needs.

Figure 5.7 Employment Trends in the Electricity Sector in Canada

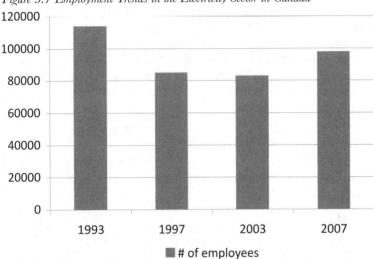

Source: Electricity Sector Council 2008: 33 (based on Statistics Canada Labour Force Survey, 2007).

Due to the existence of large, relatively stable employers in the electricity sector, employment patterns are somewhat different from the oil and gas industries (with the possible exception of natural gas distribution utilities and oil refineries). In general the electricity sector workforce is highly educated, predominantly working in full-time permanent positions, well paid, working in large organizations and has workers who are more likely to be represented by trade unions than other workers in Canada. A large proportion of workers in this sector (76 percent) have a postsecondary credential, compared with 57 percent for all workers in Canada. Earnings in the sector are 52 percent above the average in Canada. Two thirds of workers are employed at locations with one hundred or more employees, and 70 percent of all workers in the industry are employed in Ontario and Quebec (Electricity Sector Council 2007b: 12–19). A high proportion of the workers in this industry, 73 percent, are covered by collective agreements, compared with 32 percent for all workers in Canada. However, there are variations in union coverage by region with the low being in Alberta (50 percent) and the high in Manitoba (83 percent). Occupations are dominated by the trades, transport and equipment operators group, which account for 35 percent of workers in the sector. Management and administration is also large, accounting for 32 percent of the total labour force (ibid.: 18, 19). According to the Electricity Sector Council (2007b: 18), the fifteen key occupations in the electricity sector are as follows:

- electrical power line and cable workers
- power systems and power station operators
- electrical and electronics engineers
- general office clerks and utilities managers
- power system electricians
- customer service information and related clerks
- electrical and electronics engineering technologists and technicians
- construction millwrights and industrial mechanics (except textile)
- contractors and supervisors — electrical trades and telecommunications occupations
- mechanical engineers and accounting and related clerks
- secretaries (except legal and medical)
- industrial instrument technicians and mechanics, stationary engineers and auxiliary equipment operators
- operators

The electricity workforce is not one characterized by diversity, since it employs fewer women and immigrants than are represented in the Canadian workforce. In general it is largely white, male and older than average. As can be seen from Table 5.2, women constitute only 25 percent of total employment in the electricity sector, considerably less than female representation in the workforce, and most of the women in electricity are employed in traditional female administrative occupations within the sector. The sector employs about the same proportion of aboriginal persons and those from visible minorities as are represented among the employed in Canada, although it hires a considerably smaller proportion of immigrants than are represented in the workforce. The aging of the electricity sector workforce presents the largest challenge for recruitment in the near future.

Table 5.2 Electricity Sector Employment (% of total employment)

Group	Electricity Sector	Canadian Employment
Immigrants	12.8%	21%
Visible Minorities	7.9%	8%
Aboriginal	2.9%	3%
Female	25%	51%
Total Current Workforce	100%	100%

Source: Electricity Sector Council 2008: 48 (Note: Females are 51 percent of those employed, but represent 47 percent of the labour force, which includes both the employed and the unemployed.)

Figure 5.8 Occupational Groups in the Electricity Sector

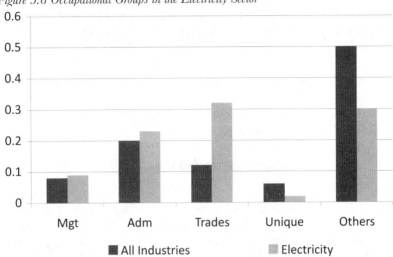

Source: Electricity Sector Council 2007b: 20 (Note: Groups in the graph include the following occupations: Mgt = Management; Adm = business, finance, administration; Trades = trades, transport and equipment operators; Unique = occupations unique to the primary sector; Others = all other occupations.)

Seventy-four percent of the electricity sector's workforce is over the age of forty and only 11 percent are between the ages of twenty-five and forty. The Canadian Electricity Association projects that between 2007 and 2012 a total of 28 percent of the sector's workforce will have retired (Electricity Sector Council 2007b: 7).

As the Electricity Council notes, workers in this sector are unlike workers in other industries in that, in addition to being largely male and older than the average Canadian workers, they also are more likely to be trade union members with considerably better wages and working conditions than the average worker. There are several reasons for this. Canada's major electrical utilities are in the public sector where the rate of unionization is much higher than in private industry. Most workers in the sector are employed by large utilities, and large employers with stable employment patterns also tend to be more highly unionized. In addition, a significant proportion of the workers in the electricity sector are skilled trades. Line workers, electricians and other related trades — even in the private sector — tend to be more highly unionized than other private sector workers.

The future labour needs in the electricity sector will be fairly consistent with past requirements for labour. As in most areas in the energy sector, specific types of occupations are in demand. "Target occupations" are as follows:

- power plant operators
- power system operators and electricians

- engineers: electrical and electronics, mechanical, civil
- stationary/substation engineers and auxiliary equipment operators
- electrical and electronics engineering technologists and technicians
- construction millwrights and industrial mechanics
- utilities managers
- contractors and supervisors
- accountants
- information systems analysts and consultants
- electrical power line and cable workers

LABOUR NEEDS IN RENEWABLE SECTORS

It is difficult to get a clear picture of the possibilities for green jobs in the energy sector in Canada for several reasons. First, there is no clear, widely accepted definition of what constitutes a green job. This issue is very important for understanding the nature of job growth in the energy sector. Second, there is a tendency to assume that the kind of job creation that has occurred in other countries with the introduction of green technology could be transferred to Canada. And third, there is a tendency for potential green projects to overestimate the total number of jobs that will be created with each project. Too often jobs in temporary construction or assembly are treated as if they constitute permanent employment.

In Canada, no standard classification exists for green industries or green occupations. Green jobs are defined in a number of different ways, ranging from any job associated with the environment to jobs dealing specifically with renewable energy. Sometimes a more strict definition is used that defines a green job as something that itself is not environmentally damaging (Renner 2008).

In Canada the most complete accounting of environmental employment is in the *Profile of Canadian Environmental Employment*, published in 2007. This report was funded by the Government of Canada's Sector Council Program and produced by ECO Canada. Its definition of environmental employment includes individuals who work in sectors of the economy related to three main areas: 1) environmental protection (air quality, water quality, land quality, waste management, restoration and reclamation, human and environmental health and safety, environmental protection management); 2) conservation and preservation of natural resources (fisheries and wildlife, forestry, agriculture, mining, energy, parks and natural reserves, natural resources management); and 3) environmental sustainability (education, research and development, policy and legislation, communications and policy awareness, management for sustainable development) (ECO Canada 2007). This is a definition that encompasses a very broad range of jobs, even those in environmentally damaging sectors (such as the oil sands), as long as it relates in some way to something as nebulous as "policy awareness" about the attempts to clean up the environment. This means that someone hired by a company in the oil sands to publicize its new environmental contributions in tree planting would be counted as an "environmental worker."[17]

According to this report, about 3.2 percent of the Canadian workforce (530,414) is engaged in either full- or part-time environment related work. The categories of this work are: trades and technology occupations (50 percent), management jobs (31 percent), administrative jobs (11 percent) and sales and service jobs (8 percent) (ECO Canada 2007: 8). The report does not specifically look at the energy sector, but does list mining and oil and gas extraction as an industry group. In this, 23 percent of the establishments have at least one environmental worker.[18] It also says that the mining, oil and gas sector is expected to have the highest growth in environmental employment, at 2.6 percent per year.

The most recent in-depth look at the employment effects of investment in the electricity sector was produced to examine the effects of the Ontario government's *Green Energy and Green Economy Act*. This research, published in *Building the Green Economy*, was sponsored by several environmental groups and specifically examines what level of investment would be necessary to meet the Ontario government's goal of creating 50,000 new green jobs. But it also examines what kinds of jobs these are likely to be (Pollin and Garrett-Peltier 2009). This report based its predictions on two levels of investment, one which is relatively modest ($18.6 billion over ten years) and would produce about 35,000 jobs per year and the other on an expanded program ($47.1 billion over ten years), which would produce about 90,000 jobs per year. These jobs include direct jobs in the targeted green activities, indirect jobs associated with supplying goods and services to the targeted green industries and induced effects, which counts the multiplier effects of the direct and indirect employment on the rest of the economy (ibid.: 6). The report makes it very clear that the 35,000 or 90,000 jobs created each year cannot be aggregated for a ten-year period. This is because these jobs are largely temporary jobs related to construction, including both trades and the service activities. So, while 35,000 jobs may be created each year, 50,000 jobs may not be created in ten years.

The more the overall level of activity is locally based, as will certainly be the case with construction but may not be the case with manufacturing or engineering services, the higher will be the employment effect. The study is careful to point out the vast majority of jobs that will be created would be in the same areas of employment where people already work. These jobs would include construction labourers, sheet metal workers, financial auditors, engineers, concrete-forming operators, secretaries, accountants, building inspectors and research scientists. Most of these jobs pay over $20 per hour.

The jobs paying less than $20 per hour are most likely to be in construction and manufacturing.

A Canada-wide estimate for employment in renewable electricity development was provided earlier in the twenty-first century by a report of the Clean Air Renewable Energy Coalition. According to this report, renewable energy generation employs on average six people per 10 MW of capacity. It also estimated that increasing the capacity by 35,600 MW by 2020 would create between 12,700 and 26,900 jobs. The major assumption behind the estimates is that all parts of manufacturing, development and construction would be filled domestically. Of the three largest contributors to potential renewable electricity generation (offshore wind, small hydro and biomass), the small hydro (or run-of-river) was predicted to be the most labour intensive per MW for pre-operational work, while biomass would be the most labour intensive in the operational phase (Clean Air Renewable Energy Coalition 2004).

The estimate of job creation by the renewable industry itself is considerably higher than those cited above. Some of this needs to be treated with skepticism. For example, in B.C. the Sustainable Energy Association claims that the province has the potential to generate 84,250 GWh of sustainable, renewable energy. This would create over 400,000 jobs over the next thirty years (BCSEA 2005). This seems to include direct, indirect and multiplier effect job creation, but even that would not explain how B.C. renewable energy creation in the electricity sector could create more jobs than exist in the entire energy sector in Canada at the moment. It is very unusual for any promise of job creation in the energy sector to be monitored to compare the promise with what actually happens. One study that did examine this (although not in the renewable sector) confirms that the anticipated job creation was vastly exaggerated, and even with a long-term approach to job creation it could have been anticipated that the promised level would not occur (Gunton 2003: 505–19).[19] The accounts of possible jobs to be created by the associations of renewable energy producers should, therefore, be treated with considerable caution.[20]

WIND

As noted earlier, wind energy is experiencing the largest growth among the renewable sector. The National Energy Board estimates that it will form 10 percent of installed capacity by 2020, although this could be difficult to achieve considering that it provides about 1 percent of capacity in 2010 (National Energy Board 2009). Employment in this sector, while very small, has grown rapidly from 1,000 in 2004 to over 4,000 in 2010. The government estimates that it will be 13,000 by 2012 (Industry Canada n.d.b). Over 430 private companies who are heavily subsidized by utilities and governments undertake all activity in this sector. Most of this production relates to project development, project operation and independent power generation. Only 16 percent of the activity is associated with manufacturing. The manufacturing firms make wind-related components such as rotor blades, control systems, turbines, inverters, nacelles, towers and meteorological towers.

The government and the industry see the wind sector as having a great potential for generating energy in the future. If this does occur, its primary job potential would be in the construction stage, but even here the numbers will be fairly small in comparison with employment in the rest of the energy sector. It should be noted, however, that wind generates more jobs per megawatt hour than coal, gas and nuclear industries (Ayee et al. 2009). If a substantial manufacturing sector were to develop, much greater job creation could be associated with the public investments in this form of renewable energy. Labour shortages exist in jobs related to operations and maintenance for wind turbines throughout North America and Europe (SQW 2008; EWEA 2009: 10–11). These are specialist jobs that require training, but again, they do not constitute a large number (Industry Canada 2010).

SOLAR

The Canadian Solar Industries Association and the Electricity Sector Council conducted a survey of employers in the industry; they estimate a total labour force of 1,524 full-time job equivalents existed in 2008 but expect this labour force to grow over 100 percent by 2011 to 3,069. This dramatic increase is based on the belief that environmentally-friendly green technologies will lead to future economic growth. The jobs expected to have the highest growth rates in the solar industries include project management (178 percent growth), installation (146 percent growth), sales (120 percent growth) and manufacturing (107 percent growth). The major constraint the industry sees to reaching these levels of growth relate to labour shortages (Electricity Sector Council 2008). Solar thermal refers to energy that is harnessed for heat and photovoltaics to convert solar energy directly into electricity. The majority of solar manufacturing jobs in Canada are concentrated in five firms whose products are primarily for export. According to one report, these firms are leading firms, internationally, but there is little Canadian demand for their products (McMonagle 2005).

BIOMASS

The major producers of biomass energy are China, Brazil, U.S. and Germany, and nearly 1.2 million are employed in biomass energy in those four countries (University of British Columbia 2009). The largest use of biomass energy for electricity is in countries where labour costs are very low. Of all of the renewable energy sources, biomass is the most labour intensive in terms of production (after the construction stage). Since the devastation of B.C. forests by the pine beetle, considerable interest has been generated in expanding the biomass industry in that province. Biomass also has government support in Saskatchewan for the production of ethanol. Biomass currently accounts for 6 percent of energy demand in Canada (Natural Resources Canada 2010), however that is not largely in a "green" form but in the still extensive practice of burning wood for fuel. It will take considerable changes in technology to convert most of this production to a clean, renewable energy source.

Clean energy biomass production employs a very small proportion of the energy sector labour force, and this probably will not change in dramatic ways in the future. Estimates of job creation from biomass, based on U.K. data, indicate that 1.27 employment/years occur per GWh of electricity produced, regardless of technology or scale of implementation (Thornley, Rogers and Huang 2008). This includes direct employment related to the bioenergy plant, agricultural production and transportation, the jobs related to development and construction of the plant, the indirect effects from upstream manufacturing and the induced economic effects from increased economic activity. On a more understandable level, a very large 25 MW plant would create jobs of about 160 full-time equivalents over the lifetime of the plant, a figure considerably higher than the twenty people who would be employed at the plant.

OTHER RENEWABLES

The largest employment in the renewable sector is with large hydro projects, although many environmental groups consider large hydro to be too environmentally damaging to be championed as a new source of renewable power in the twenty-first century. New projects are coming forward in this area in provinces that have typically had large hydro as the main supplier for electricity (such as B.C. and Quebec).

In the large hydro sector the main job creation occurs in the construction stage of the project. Smaller, microhydro (or run-of-river) projects are increasingly gaining popularity among private power producers and governments. The job creation associated with microhydro is at the construction stage, with almost no permanent direct jobs created. In Canada, there is some small tidal and geothermal electricity generation, but the technology associated with these forms of energy generation has not advanced to the stage that this type of production is likely to increase rapidly in the near future.

TWO POLICY APPROACHES: ONTARIO AND BRITISH COLUMBIA

While the diversity of provincial climate initiatives makes it challenging to summarize the large number of policy developments in every province or territory, it is worth commenting on the experience of two provinces that have adopted somewhat different approaches to incorporating labour and employment policies in their energy production initiatives: Ontario and British Columbia.

The Province of Ontario has attempted to combine its energy conservation and GHG reduction initiatives with job creation not only in the construction, or installation, of new power projects but also in the province's manufacturing sector. This reflected its view that Ontario could become a key manufacturing hub for green technology if the government took measures to ensure that the demand for renewable energy was met by its domestic industry. The cornerstone of this initiative has been the *Green Energy Act* (2009). It mandates a wide range of new environmental initiatives, including sweeping changes to Ontario's building code, energy audits for new buildings, efficiency targets for provincially-funded public sector organizations and adoption of more stringent energy saving requirements for domestic appliances, heating and air conditioning (HVAC) and other systems in the built environment that utilize energy. However, the key job creation element in the legislation was a requirement that most components for new renewable electricity generation be manufactured in Ontario.

To stimulate demand for renewable energy, the Act included a feed-in tariff (FIT) program designed to encourage new investment in renewable wind, solar, small hydro, biomass and other green energy sources. This represented an attempt to streamline its earlier Renewable Energy Standard Offer Program (RESOP), which had been the subject of complaints from prospective generators that it was too cumbersome and expensive, especially for small producers. The new Act reduced regulatory barriers that had impeded producers of renewable energy from accessing the transmission grid. It provided an expedited approvals process to encourage construction of new generation facilities and foster a more stable and predictable investment climate.

The Ontario government also established a pricing regime designed to promote the rapid expansion of wind farm and solar power projects. Initially, it set the price for solar generated electricity (PV) at 80.2 cents per KWh. This was an enormous premium over the market price for conventional electricity, which, at times, could be as low as 2.5 cents per KWh. (This price premium for solar was subsequently lowered significantly as the cost implications for the system began to be felt.) Prices for other renewable energy, from sources such as wind or biomass, which accounted for the bulk of new purchases, were considerably lower, averaging about 11 cents per KWh, but this still represented a significant premium over the prevailing market price.

The government believed that the Act would produce 50,000 new jobs, principally in the renewable energy sector during its first three years. These would be in a wide range of energy conservation areas. But the key manufacturing element was the production of components, such as solar panels, to supply the demand created by its FIT program. To further encourage domestic manufacturing, it entered into a contract with Samsung of South Korea that gave preference to that company's solar panels on condition that it build a major plant in the province — a plant large enough to supply part of North America's solar requirements. Ontario's approach in some respects copied the experience of Germany, which had built a significant renewable manufacturing industry based on using its domestic market to stimulate the development of this sector.

However, this initiative has been controversial. First Japan and subsequently the E.U. and the U.S. have challenged Ontario's domestic sourcing requirements under various provisions of WTO and NAFTA agreements. These trade challenges have yet to be resolved. Ontario believes it can shelter its policies by arguing that the way they have been implemented is sufficiently arm's-length from direct government involvement (or procurement) to circumvent the trade obligations in question. Whether this will succeed remains to be seen.

In addition to the question of whether the legislation will generate the number of manufacturing jobs the province anticipates, the policy has raised other issues. One is whether qualified electrical trades workers, such as electricians, should perform the installation work on new solar and wind farm projects. A number of the firms building these projects prefer to employ more narrowly-trained technicians who do not have a journeyperson's qualifications. These technicians would not be qualified to perform general electrical trades work, but only wind or solar installation. However, these power projects are generating electricity. They have many of the same hazards (and corresponding safety requirements) of other electrical installations. The question of whether the province should require electrical trades' certification is an ongoing policy issue, as is the question of who will be involved in training the new workers required for this program.

A second, related issue is the extent of unionization in the installation sector. While there are qualified journeypersons who are not members of the International Brotherhood of Electrical Workers (IBEW) or other construction unions, this trade is significantly unionized in Ontario. Thus, whether unionized trades workers or more narrowly trained technicians (who are unlikely to be members of the building trades unions) perform the work affects the level of unionization in the sector and the extent to which the Act promotes high wage, unionized employment.

A broader concern with the province's efforts to link its green initiatives with employment is the cost. As noted, the FIT program offers a very significant price premium for renewable energy. However, the large number of small-scale projects, all of which require connection to the main transmission grid, undermines economies of scale. Almost all are intermittent, meaning the system must also provide backup power when they are not supplying energy to the grid. Thus, even in comparison with conventional sources of energy, the high price per KWh still over-values their real contribution to fulfilling Ontario's electricity requirements.

As long as the total volume of electricity purchased under this program remained a relatively small component of the total cost of Ontario's electricity production, arguably, funding FIT was not a major issue for ratepayers. However, the share is now increasing to the point that it is beginning to put significant upward pressure on electricity rates. Whether Ontario can afford to continue to expand the program and whether the job creation aspects merit the expenditures involved are becoming significant policy issues.

These concerns are compounded by the uncertainty of whether the trade challenges by Japan, the E.U. and the U.S. result in Ontario being forced to abandon the manufacturing component of the program. If this happens, the opportunity cost in relation to other energy conservation options will be high, raising the question of whether the province can make better use of its conservation investments by supporting other initiatives.

British Columbia is another province that has publicly pursued a high profile GHG reduction strategy, through a number of policy initiatives and individual pieces of legislation. B.C.'s approach was initially formulated in the 2002 *Energy Plan* which asserted that B.C. needed to expand its production of privately-sourced renewable electricity to ensure that the province would meet the government's definition of self-sufficiency, given projections of the growth of future energy demand. To do so, the government directed its crown corporation, B.C. Hydro, to meet anticipated electricity requirements through purchasing new private power from run-of-river and other renewable projects located in B.C., while preventing the crown corporation from building any new small hydro or wind projects itself.

The 2007 *Energy Plan* accelerated this process by significantly raising the projected target for new energy. It required B.C. Hydro to be "self-sufficient" in low rainfall years by 2016 and have a surplus of 3,000 GWh of energy by 2026. This resulted in the purchase of large volumes of new private power at extremely high prices, triggering the construction of many new, small-scale run-of-river power plants. The policy was highly controversial, however. Self-sufficiency in low water years meant a major surplus in normal years — a surplus that B.C. Hydro would have to sell on the international energy market at prices far lower than it would be paying private developers for the power, forcing ratepayers to cover the losses. The 2007 *Energy Plan* included a number of other components the government believed would lower B.C.'s GHG emissions to meet a target of 6 percent below 1991 emissions by 2012. It required new electricity to be carbon neutral, effectively banning any future generation of electricity from coal-fired power plants. And it required that 50 percent of future electricity requirements be met through conservation.

This was followed in 2010 by *The Clean Energy Act*, which required that conservation account for 66 percent of new electricity demand by 2020 and that 93 percent of electricity be generated from renewable sources. It mandated an FIT and a standing offer program to purchase new small-scale private electricity. It also established more aggressive targets for GHG reductions: 18 percent lower than 2007 emissions by 2016 and 33 percent by 2020.[21]

The 2007 *Energy Plan* also included the B.C. government's principal initiatives to address labour issues in the energy sector. These have focused on identifying future labour demand for various skills and working with the federal government, private industry associations, B.C. Hydro and public educational institutions to provide appropriate training to meet this demand. Part of its strategy has also been to recruit workers internationally, to meet anticipated skills shortages in occupations such as power line technicians, electrical engineers, technologists and back office technical support staff.

Notably absent from the strategy is any reference to the role of the building trades unions as partners in the training programs or contributors to the overall skills development and employment program of the government. Also absent is any reference to the earlier approach of B.C. Hydro to train and employ B.C. trades workers through Columbia Hydro Constructors. This earlier program focused on using B.C. Hydro's capacity as an employer to train and employ members of local communities and First Nations in areas where it was building major projects. Similarly, it has not attempted to continue with previous polices that tried to use B.C. Hydro's large purchases of items such as turbines to encourage suppliers to locate some of their operations within the province and employ B.C. residents.

Thus, while the B.C. government argues that its various initiatives will create new green jobs, its approach has differed considerably from that of Ontario. It has not explicitly attempted to link its electricity policy initiatives with provincial manufacturing jobs or with a requirement to train and employ B.C. residents, where feasible. Rather, it has taken the position that the market should determine where the equipment, materials and labour should be sourced. As power projects normally do not employ significant numbers of workers once built, the government's job creation initiatives are heavily weighted to the construction phase, with few permanent positions being created. Moreover, almost all the construction work on new private power projects has been carried out by nonunion firms, and a significant part of the employment has gone to out-of-province workers.

The B.C. government's reliance on market forces rather than public policy to shape its future energy workforce has also been reflected in its decision to negotiate the Alberta–B.C. Trade, Investment and Labour Mobility Agreement (TILMA). The purpose of this agreement was to create what it viewed as a favourable investment climate by explicitly limiting the ability of government to make use of policy tools that would favour local suppliers, locally-based investors or local labour.

While the expansion of privately generated small-scale renewable electricity has been a major focus of B.C. government policy throughout the first decade of this century, the rapid growth of the province's gas industry in recent years, primarily through the introduction of new horizontal fracturing technology, is shifting the focus of its labour policy to addressing the expanding needs of this industry. The government is increasingly concerned about how to meet the new labour requirements in the context of competition for skilled workers from Alberta and Saskatchewan. Thus the growth of energy employment in B.C. will, to a significant degree, parallel developments in these two provinces in which fossil fuel extraction is the dominant source of new jobs.[22]

CONCLUDING REMARKS

The general assumption that policies that would bring about substantial reductions in carbon emissions would have a negative effect on employment in the energy industry in Canada is undoubtedly true (M.K. Jaccard & Associates 2008). However, Canada is unlike the U.S. and European countries: it is not experiencing reductions in oil and gas production as is occurring elsewhere. While Canada's conventional oil and gas production is declining, as elsewhere, its production from unconventional sources is expanding.

Canada's use of electricity is also increasing. Associated with this expanded energy production are government policies that encourage the growth of oil and gas production while doing relatively little to encourage reductions in consumption of either oil and gas or electricity. In the electricity sector a large proportion of generation comes from hydro-based systems with some provinces also heavily reliant on nuclear energy, both of which are renewable resources that do not contribute to climate-related emissions.[23]

The kinds of employment demands that have existed will continue for the foreseeable future. If government introduces substantial carbon-reduction policies, this may change, but this is not the current trajectory. New production in renewable industries like wind and solar is more labour-intensive than in existing electricity production but constitutes a very small proportion of the market so far. While these industries are likely to grow considerably by 2020, their job creation potential is relatively small. It should be noted that these industries will be competing with existing generating companies for labour, and since this is a sector where wages are high, the cost of labour may well be a barrier to continued expansion of these industries. This is because the kinds of jobs needed in the renewable energy sector are not markedly different from those required in the major energy sectors. While the labour force of the energy sector has traditionally been largely male from within Canada, the industry recognizes that labour shortages may force changes here. In virtually all areas of energy development, there are skills shortages and calls for additional training. These shortages cover a wide range of different occupations, from engineers and architects to skilled trades, equipment operators, technicians and even construction labourers. Skills shortages also vary, regionally and by energy sector.[24] Most of the shortages are for jobs in conventional energy production. However, the renewable sector is also experiencing significant shortages of qualified personnel (Robitaille and Etcheverry 2005; SQW 2008).

Other than large-scale hydro projects where several provincial governments, such as Quebec, Ontario and Manitoba, have attempted to link some of the spending with local employment or industrial offsets, public support for private green energy projects has produced fairly limited job growth outside direct construction. Even where provinces have attempted to link green energy subsidies to industrial development, their efforts have been very modest. Since most permanent jobs related to green energy are created through the manufacturing of green technology, the absence of a policy in provinces other than Ontario to increase domestic use of this technology through Canadian-based manufacturing means the loss of the employment potential of renewable energy expansion. Somewhat perversely, governments in Canada now believe that many of the policy tools associated with activist industrial strategies are "protectionist." If Canada is to realize the full job creation potential of green energy development, this view may have to change.

Notes

1.   The focus of this study is on the production of energy, not on its consumption or on Canada's energy conservation potential. The latter issues are also of critical importance in addressing GHG emissions and climate change but are outside the scope of this research. The use of energy to produce oil, gas, coal and other energy products is not the same as the resulting energy output.
2.   The terms "tar sands" and "oil sands" refer to the extraction of very heavy oil, bitumen, in Alberta. "Green bitumen" refers to the attempt to achieve emissions reductions below that of conventional crude oil (McColl 2009).
3.   In 1990, the oil and gas and electricity sector contributed about the same proportion of GHG to the Canadian total (CERI 2009: vii).
4.   Thus economic downturns in major industries, such as pulp and paper or mining, can have a very substantial impact on energy use by industrial customers.
5.   Nuclear energy production can be defined as "green" primarily because it does

not produce GHG emissions. The industry itself is the primary proponent of this definition (Timilsina et al. 2008: 13). Environmentalists tend to see the possibility of environmental destruction on a massive scale from a nuclear accident and the enormous environmental issues associated with nuclear waste as serious problems in classifying nuclear energy as "green."

6. The website also acknowledges that it is sometimes necessary to have government intervention <nrcan.gc.ca/eneene/polpol/owevue-eng.php>.

7. The Pembina Institute says federal subsidies to the industry now amount to approximately $2 billion annually (Demerse 2010).

8. Neither the federal nor the provincial governments have shown any appetite for revisiting the issue of privatizing Petro-Canada or establishing a state-run oil company similar to what many other countries, such as Norway, have done. The largest oil companies and the largest reserves throughout the world are owned by nation states (Cohen 2006: 1, 14).

9. Both Alberta and Norway have produced about the same volume of oil over the past four decades. According to the Sovereign Wealth Fund Institute, as of November, 2011, Norway had over $570 billion U.S. in its "rainy day" fund for future generations — a fund built up from its oil and gas revenues (Norges Bank Investment Management 2011: 14). In comparison, Alberta's Heritage Savings Trust Fund, which was started in 1976, had accumulated assets of $14.7 billion as of Sept 30, 2011 (Alberta Treasury Board and Finance 2012: 2).

10. Ulrike Lehr et al. (2008): 108; M. Boettcher, N.P. Nielsen and K. Petrick (2009); G. Ayee, G.M. Lowe and.G. Gereffi (2009); Ditlev Engel and Daniel Kammen (2009).

11. Over the last decade, governments have initiated various incentive programs to promote private sector green energy development. Typically, these programs provide tax abatements, or direct subsidies, such as a 1 cent per KWh payment for energy produced from new renewable projects for a fixed time period. See, for example, the $1.48 billion ecoEnergy for Renewable Power fund announced in 2010 by the federal government: ecoaction.gc.ca/ecoenergy-ecoenergie/power-electricite/index-eng.cfm.

12. British Columbia Energy Plans of 2002 and 2007 and the *Clean Energy Act* (2010), Statutes of British Columbia, Chapter 22: <bclaws.ca/EPLibraries/bclaws_new/document/ID/freeside/00_10022_01> (Province of British Columbia 2010).

13. Ontario's agreement with Samsung to build a manufacturing plant in the province as a quid pro quo for guaranteeing to purchase energy from facilities using the company's technology is an exception. However, it also reinforces Ontario's reliance on energy development through purchases from investor-owned power plants. At this juncture it is not clear how successful the initiative will be in achieving the objectives outlined by the government, nor is it clear how expensive it will end up being in the long run, given the price premium the province has offered.

14. Figures for pipeline transportation are not available after 2001, which explains the appearance of a decline in employment in that sector.

15. Synthetic and bitumen production has increased by 387 percent since 1990 (CAPP 2010: Tables 3.1b and 3.3a).

16. Canada is the third largest per person consumer in the world, after two other cold countries whose electricity largely comes from hydro: Iceland and Norway (Electricity Sector Council 2008: 41).

17. The estimates of the size of the electricity labour force range considerably, from 76,498 to 105,500 (Electricity Sector Council 2008: 31).

18. See, for example, the full-page ad in the *Globe and Mail*, May 31, 2010, which is a message from Canada's Oil Sands Producers. It features Garrett Brown of ConocoPhillips saying, "I grew up on a farm. I know what it means to have the land restored." The ad goes on to say that for years the petroleum producers have been planting grass and they are now beginning to plant trees, so that in a few years the forest will be re-established.

19. It is not possible to get information about the electricity sector from the report (ECO Canada 2007: 18).

20. Gunton's study relates to the Northeast Coal Project and compares preproject forecasts to postproject outcomes for one of the largest megaprojects ever undertaken in Canada. Less than half the expected regional employment occurred and the project's proposal greatly overestimated both direct employment and its multiplier effect. The project wound up having a negative effect on regional development.

21. This is aside from whether the jobs themselves will be good jobs. For a test of assumptions that green jobs will be good jobs, see P. Mattera (2009).

22. Other government initiatives included the Green Building Code (2007) to stimulate energy conservation in the built environment, a carbon tax with an escalating rate to make it increasingly expensive over time to purchase high carbon emitting commodities, a *Greenhouse Gas Reduction (Cap and Trade) Act* (2009) and provincial participation in the Western Climate Initiative (WCI).

23. The rapid expansion of gas production will also affect B.C.'s ability to meet earlier climate targets. The government anticipates that there will be at least three — and potentially more — large scale liquid natural gas (LNG) plants built on its northwest coastline, near Kitimat, to facilitate exports to Asia. GHG emissions from fossil fuel extraction and processing will result in the province exceeding its targets, possibly by a significant margin. Even if it builds the massive Site C dam on the Peace River to produce more hydro generated electricity, the province will still not have sufficient electricity to supply these plants. At the time of writing, it appears that two of these plants will use the energy from burning natural gas for compressing LNG.

24. As has been noted earlier, nuclear energy does have the potential to be extraordinarily damaging to the environment, and many environmentalists point to other damages that occur through large-scale hydro development.

25. Employment and Immigration (2007); A. Lorenz (2007); Electricity Sector Council (2007b); Strategic Directions Inc. (2003).

6. THE TRANSPORTATION EQUIPMENT INDUSTRY

John Holmes with Austin Hracs

There is an extensive scholarly and scientific literature on the links between transportation and greenhouse gas (GHG) emissions and on the various technologies being developed in efforts to reduce emissions from internal combustion engines. Little has been written, however, regarding the likely impacts of climate change on future employment and skill requirements in the transportation equipment industry.

The following questions guide our analysis in this chapter:

- In what ways does the transportation equipment industry contribute to climate warming, and what is the relative importance of the GHGs generated by the various sectors that comprise this industry?
- How has regulatory policy directed at the motor vehicle industry been shaped by concerns regarding climate warming, and what impact have such regulations had on the industry?
- What significant developments with regard to work and employment have occurred in the motor vehicle sector, and have these had consequences for climate warming?
- Have concerns about climate warming led to changes in automotive manufacturing processes?
- Will climate change be a more significant factor influencing the automotive sector in the future?
- What issues require more research?

In our analysis of the likely impact of climate warming on employment and jobs in the Canadian automotive sector we begin by providing our rationale for focusing on the motor vehicle segment of the transportation equipment sector and provide a contextual overview of the political economy of the motor vehicle industry in Canada. We then turn to a synthesis of both the issues raised and the silences in the existing literature on climate change and transportation.

As defined by Statistics Canada, the transportation equipment industry (North American Industry Classification System [NAICS] 336) encompasses the manufacture of aircraft, ships, rail rolling stock and motor vehicles. The production of most of these products is organized around the final assembly of a wide range of parts and components; the manufacture of the latter is also included within NAICS 336. This chapter focuses on motor vehicles and especially on automobile and light-duty motor vehicles (NAICS 3361) and motor vehicle parts (NAICS 3362) — which we will refer to collectively as the automotive or motor vehicle industry. There are two main reasons for the focus on motor vehicles. First, and even after the dramatic loss of employment during the 2007–2009 Great Recession, the automotive industry accounts for by far the largest proportion of employment in NAICS 336 (Table 1). Second, as a recent report observes, "rightly or wrongly, the auto industry has been singled out as a primary 'culprit' in climate change debates, and politicians have seized on measures affecting this industry as the centrepiece of their climate change proposals" (CAW 2007: 2).

Table 6.1 Manufacturing Employment in the Transportation Equipment Industry (NAICS 336), Canada, 2005–10.

NAICS	2005	2006	2007	2008	2009	2010
Motor vehicle manufacturing (3361)	49,523	49,204	45,587	39,343	33,002	33,851
Motor vehicle parts (3363)	95,320	89,594	80,453	63,055	50,632	56,948
Aerospace product and parts (3364)	38,132	40,126	41,269	44,157	42,413	40,488
Railroad rolling stock (3365)	6,483	5,750	4,544	4,772	3,601	3,564
Ship and boat (3366)	7,803	7,531	8,262	8,850	7,855	6,813

Source: Statistics Canada CANSIM Table 301-0006

Although the actual manufacture of transportation equipment contributes in some measure to greenhouse gas (GHG) emissions, as do virtually all manufacturing processes, it is not a major source of Canada's GHG emissions. The principal impact of transportation on GHG emissions and climate warming comes from the burning of fossil fuels to power transportation, and this impact is significant. In short, the major climate change issue associated with the automotive industry is the use of motor vehicles, not their manufacture. This distinction is important, especially in light of the extensive international trade in motor vehicles, since it means that motor vehicle-related GHG emissions in Canada depend on which cars and trucks Canadians choose to purchase and drive, not on which vehicles are produced in Canada. Of course, the emissions of vehicles produced in Canada and exported, which in recent decades have tended to be some of the larger and less fuel-efficient types of vehicle, still contribute to global climate change, irrespective of where they are driven. Transportation-related emissions are second only to electricity generation as the largest contributor to global GHG emissions. It is estimated that 14 percent of total GHG emissions worldwide is attributable to internal combustion engines in all forms of transport (vehicle, ship, air and rail) and that about one tenth of global emissions are due to passenger motor vehicles alone (WRI 2005). In Canada, it is estimated that motor vehicles account for over 80 percent of the CO_2 emissions from transportation and that over 45 percent of emissions are generated by private passenger vehicles (Table 6.2).

Table 6.2 GHG Emissions by Mode of Transportation, Canada, 1995–2009

GHG Emissions by Aggregated Transportation Mode (Mt of CO_2e)	1995	2000	2005	2009	% of Total Transportation Emissions (2009)
Private Motor Vehicles	71.3	75.4	80.4	81.6	45.8
Commercial Motor Vehicles	42.8	53.5	62.2	66.5	37.3
Air, Rail and Marine Vehicles	27.3	31.6	32.3	30.2	16.9

Source: Natural Resources Canada 2011

THE AUTOMOTIVE INDUSTRY IN CANADA

The automotive industry is viewed as a critical "national lead sector" in many industrial economies and has long been Canada's most important manufacturing industry. Historically, it has accounted for over 10 percent of Canada's manufacturing GDP, almost one-third of all manufacturing exports and has employed directly over 150,000 workers at the peak in the late 1990s. The auto industry generates a large number of spin-off jobs and is a big consumer of steel, rubber and processed aluminum as well as other commodities. Ontario, which midway through the last decade surpassed Michigan to become the leading automotive producing jurisdiction in North America, is home to all of Canada's vehicle assemblers and the majority of the country's parts producers. Later, we will discuss how the industry has been wrestling with a major crisis since the middle of the last decade, which has seen wide-spread plant closings and a loss of roughly 40 percent of direct automotive employment in Canada.

Over the past four decades, trade liberalization, beginning with the Auto

Pact between Canada and the United States in 1965 and then deepened through the Canada-U.S. Free Trade Agreement (1987) and the North American Free Trade Agreement (NAFTA) (1994), has resulted in the production and marketing of automobiles becoming fully integrated between Canada, the United States and, more recently, Mexico (Kumar and Holmes 1000, Holmes 2001). Over 05 percent of the vehicles built in Canada are exported, mainly to the United States. Thus, the economic health of the automotive industry in Canada is heavily dependent on the vehicle purchasing decisions of American consumers and also on corporate decisions by automakers regarding which models to source from their Canadian assembly facilities. For example, in the 1980s and 1990s, Canada benefited from the U.S. consumers' love affair with minivans and pickup trucks and the fact that these were precisely the models assigned to several Canadian assembly plants. Conversely, the last decade has witnessed the closing of Canadian light truck plants and one plant building full-sized automobiles, as rising fuel prices caused American consumers to move away from large cars and trucks. Similarly, over 80 percent of the vehicles sold in Canada are manufactured elsewhere. Automotive production in southern Ontario is part of a functionally highly integrated transborder production system that includes states such as Michigan, Ohio, Indiana and New York and generates an enormous volume of cross-border commercial road and rail traffic (Rutherford and Holmes 2012).

Prior to the early 1980s, motor vehicle production was centred on the Great Lakes states and Ontario and dominated by the so-called Big Three, now more generally referred to as the Detroit Three (D-3), automakers: General Motors (GM), Ford and Chrysler. Although the industry generated numbers of skilled engineering and design jobs, shop-floor production workers were traditionally male and unskilled. The assembly sector workforce was virtually 100 percent unionized, and although union density in the parts and components sector was not as high, it was still well over 50 percent. The principal unions involved in the automotive industry have been the United Automobile Workers (UAW) (and the CAW in Canada following the 1985 split from UAW), United Steel Workers (USW) and the International Association of Machinists (IAM).

Since the mid 1980s the composition and geography of North American automotive production and Canada's position within it has changed dramatically. The Canadian auto industry is now part of a globalized and highly competitive international industry in which political jurisdictions (nation states, states and provinces and more local regions) vie for investment in new assembly plant capacity and upgrades to existing capacity (Roy and Kimanyi 2007; Sturgeon et al. 2008). Governments recognize that investment in new assembly plants is frequently the catalyst for the establishment of new components production. The competition between political jurisdictions to attract new so-called "greenfield" vehicle assembly facilities has been fierce. It has become common practice for competing jurisdictions to engage in bidding wars that result in extremely lucrative incentive packages to attract new automotive industry investment to a particular state or province.

A significant number of Asian and European manufacturers — so-called new domestic automakers — have been lured to establish both vehicle assembly and parts production in North America, especially in a tier of states in the southern United States and in northern Mexico. In Ontario, Honda, Toyota and CAMI (GM-Suzuki) have established significant assembly capacity. The growth in new domestic capacity in Canada has mirrored the loss of D-3 capacity (Roy and Kimanyi 2007). These plants employ a much younger and more diverse workforce than the D-3 plants, and few, if any, are unionized.

As the new domestic segment of the industry has expanded and exacerbated the problem of North American production overcapacity, the D-3 have steadily lost market share and been forced to close many of their manufacturing facilities in the traditional automotive heartland around the lower Great Lakes. The economic consequences of this shift for communities in Michigan and southern Ontario reliant on the D-3 or their suppliers have been devastating. Once thriving communities are now rife with economic and social decay, high unemployment rates and little prospect that displaced autoworkers will find comparable alternative employment. In short, the geographical centre of gravity of the industry within North America has shifted southward and union density in the industry as a whole has fallen precipitously, particularly in the United States. By 2009, approximately 45 percent of North American vehicle production originated in non-union plants owned by new domestic automakers (Stanford 2010).

From Ford's development of the moving assembly line in the early twentieth century to the more recent advent of synchronous manufacturing and lean production, the North American automotive industry has been a leader in the development of new methods of manufacturing and work organization. There is a high degree of convergence between Canada and the United States with regard to production organization and work organization in automotive manufacturing facilities. Benchmarking has led to the standardization of global management practices in the industry. In vehicle assembly plants, shop-floor technology changes rapidly as assembly lines are rebuilt every five years or so as new models are introduced. The push for higher productivity is universal and the pressure to keep abreast of the latest refinements in production methods is constant. The organization of work, the nature of individual jobs and the skills required on the shop floor continue to evolve rapidly. This makes it difficult to single out the likely impacts on jobs and skill requirements of industry responses to climate warming. However, the strong convergence in automotive production technology and work organization between Canada and the United States noted above means that studies that focus on the changing nature of employment and jobs in the automotive industry in the U.S., especially from neighbouring states such as Michigan, may also be broadly applicable to the industry in Ontario.

An Industry in Turmoil

The present fragile state of the global economy in general and the automotive industry in particular presents a further challenge to any attempt to forecast future employment levels. After the turn of the millennium, the North American automotive industry experienced deteriorating economic conditions that culminated in a major structural crisis. Overcapacity, the rapid loss of market share by the D-3 and continued gains in labour productivity led to a steady decline in employment between 2000 and 2006 (Table 6.3). Plant closings and employment losses accelerated as the global financial crisis of 2008–2009 had a dramatic impact on the auto manufacturing industry worldwide. During 2009 alone, U.S. vehicle production fell by over one third and Canadian and Mexican output fell by almost 30 percent (Stanford 2010: 398). Two of the D-3 (General Motors and Chrysler) were forced to seek bankruptcy protection.

Table 6.3 Automotive Industry Employment, Canada 2000–2010

	2000	2002	2004	2006	2008	2009	2010
Assembly Sector	55,712	52,038	50,114	47,460	42,140	35,613	37,176
Parts Sector	98,154	96,777	97,317	92,292	79,295	61,184	60,572
Total Automotive Sector	153,866	148,815	147,431	139,752	121,435	96,797	97,748

Source: Statistics Canada, CANSIM Table 281-0024

In response to the Great Recession, and recognizing the strategic economic importance of the auto sector, governments around the world acted quickly but in different ways to address the crises faced by their respective auto industries. As Stanford notes, the North American auto rescue

> was unique in several respects. It was the only case in which governments needed to directly rescue the major automakers and ensure their corporate survival. This made the North American rescue more expensive, and more far reaching, than in other locations … [I]n contrast to other jurisdictions, which subsidized autoworker wages to forestall lay-offs, the North American rescue effort featured an attack on the compensation and conditions of autoworkers, thus undertaking a strong and deliberate challenge to the legitimacy and power of automotive trade unions. The end result, in North

America, was a unique association between "rescuing the auto industry" and "humbling the auto unions." (Stanford 2010: 383)

The government of Canada and the Ontario provincial government both participated with the U.S. in a joint rescue effort of GM and Chrysler. As a condition of their financial support, the Canadian governments demanded that the CAW agree to significant concessions on labour costs, requiring that labour costs in GM and Chrysler plants be brought down to the same level as Toyota's non-union Canadian plants. Besides providing industry-specific financial support to firms, the U.S. and Canadian governments introduced sales incentives designed to encourage new vehicle purchases. In the U.S., sales incentives were linked to the scrappage of older, more polluting vehicles (the "cash-for-clunkers" program).[1] In some instances, government financial assistance to companies was also linked to commitments from the company to invest in the development and production of environmentally "cleaner" vehicles.

At the time of writing (2012), there are signs that D-3 vehicle sales in North America have rebounded in the wake of the crisis, and the hemorrhaging of jobs has stopped. Ironically the D-3, which lost 2.5 million units of capacity through plant closings during the crisis, now find their productive capacity stretched to meet recovering demand.

The Automotive Industry Labour Force in Canada

According to a 2008 report produced by the federally funded Council for Automotive Human Resources (CAHR), women represent only approximately 10 percent of the total workforce in motor vehicle assembly in Canada but represent over one quarter of the total workforce in motor vehicle parts manufacturing (CAHR 2008: 90). Among parts manufacturers, there is considerable variation in gender employment patterns. With only one exception, all manufacturers surveyed for the CAHR report employed more men than women. In both the assembly and parts sectors, females are consistently under-represented in the skilled trades and over-represented in office and administrative positions. With regard to the age profile of the workforce, the CAHR report estimated that approximately one third of the workforce in motor vehicle and parts manufacturing is under the age of thirty-five and about 10 percent is over the age of fifty-five. If disaggregated by job classification, with only one exception (skilled trades, which has a larger number of people over fifty-five), each classification has more employees under the age of thirty-five than fifty-five or older (CAHR 2008: 95). Although the automotive industry's labour force is composed predominantly of white, Canadian-born workers, some segments of the automotive parts industry employ a large number of recent immigrants (Yates and Vrankulji 2006). A significant number of recent immigrants also occupy supervisory staff positions in some vehicle assembly plants.

MOTOR VEHICLES AND CLIMATE WARMING

The Manufacture of Motor Vehicles

Earlier in this chapter, we noted that the major climate change issue associated with the auto industry is the use of motor vehicles, not their manufacture. However, some issues related to the manufacturing process are worth noting, and automakers are making efforts to reduce GHGs associated with their manufacturing processes.

Efforts to reduce energy needs and GHG emissions from vehicle assembly plants has been driven both by economic considerations and by criteria attached to government financial aid provided to the automakers. For example, the Program for Strategic Industrial Projects (PSIP) was created in October 2005 by the Canadian federal government as a "special purpose program" to support the development of new technologies as well as to promote the long-term stability of the auto assembly sector and, by extension, the Canadian auto parts sector. There were three key projects supported under PSIP: the renovation of Ford's Oakville assembly complex, renovation of GM's Oshawa assembly complex and Toyota's construction of a new greenfield assembly plant in Woodstock, Ontario (Shiell and Somerville 2012). Although the primary objective of the assistance was to strengthen the Canadian auto industry through support for the implementation of flexible manufacturing capacity at Canadian assembly plants, the reduction of both energy consumption and GHGs were integral elements in each project.

Besides energy consumption, one of the main contributors to climate warming associated with vehicle assembly plants is the release of volatile organic compounds (VOCs) from the paint shops. This is also a significant issue in plants that produce large volumes of plastic based automotive parts and components. All three PSIP-funded projects included investment in new paint shop technologies to reduce VOC emissions. For example, as part of its PSIP renovation in Oakville, Ford's Fumes to Fuel Project captures the fumes from the new paint booths, filters out the particulates and then super-concentrates the solvent VOCs in fluidized bed carbon concentrators to recover high-octane fuel. The high-octane fuel is then used to generate electricity for use in the plant with an internal combustion engine generator and to power a large hydrogen-based fuel cell. The project reduces GHG emissions from the manufacturing plant and reduces the plant's reliance on the electrical grid.[2] Ford is exploring the strong potential of a hydrogen-powered future by developing hydrogen-based technologies not only for its new vehicles but also for its manufacturing facilities. Hydrogen produces near zero emissions, delivers higher fuel economy and can be used either in fuel cells or internal combustion engines.

The PSIP-supported GM Beacon Project and the more recent federal financial support to assist in the GM Canada bankruptcy restructuring included commitments from GM to invest in the development of more fuel-efficient internal combustion engines (ICEs) and the design of vehicles powered by alternative cleaner fuel technologies. Toyota's new state-of-the-art flexible assembly plant in Woodstock uses the latest Toyota manufacturing and environmental systems. The PSIP federal funds were used to support preproduction and environmental technologies in the Toyota plant and paint shop.

One element of the broader move toward lean production in the automotive industry (and in many other sectors of manufacturing) is the outsourcing of parts and use of just-in-time delivery (JIT). While this has improved manufacturing efficiency and lowered costs, it has increased the volume of GHG emissions as a result of the increased frequency of deliveries of parts to assembly plants by transport trailers operated by third-party logistics firms. This is graphically illustrated by the road congestion experienced in the Greater Toronto Area (GTA) and at the Windsor–Detroit border. It is unlikely that this trend will be reversed in the foreseeable future at the intracontinental scale or within the southern Ontario–Great Lakes region. There is evidence, however, that increased fuel costs are having an impact on longer distance global sourcing patterns. For example, in the first half of the last decade there was a dramatic reduction in automotive parts production in Mexico as firms moved their operations to East Asia, and especially China, in search of lower labour costs. More recently, however, this trend has been reversed due to rising transportation costs.

Some attention in the literature has focused on introducing end-of-life recycling regulations aimed at reducing the total environmental footprint of passenger vehicles (MacLean and Lave 1998; Bellmann and Khare 1999; Smith and Crotty 2008). Such regulations have been more fully developed in Europe than in North America and potentially could lead to a growth in jobs associated with the disassembly and recycling of vehicles.

The Use of Motor Vehicles

Notwithstanding the importance of the automotive sector as an economic driver, the fact remains that motor vehicle usage is a major contributor to GHG emissions and climate warming. It is clear that serious efforts to combat climate warming must include changes in transportation and logistics industries. There are two broad ways in which the aggregate GHGs associated with motor vehicles can be reduced: a reduction in the total number of vehicles in use; and reducing the GHGs emitted from each individual vehicle. Obviously, one way to cut GHG emissions would be to drastically reduce private motor vehicle usage. Certainly, in high-density urban settings it makes sense to encourage a shift to mass public transit. This could result in some automotive manufacturing plants being converted to produce mass transit vehicles. Many municipalities are moving to rethink planning and zoning regulations with the goal of intensifying land use and increasing residential densities within existing urban boundaries to prevent further low-density urban sprawl, but it will take decades before benefits flowing from these policies begin to be realized. Thus, given the existing built environment in North America, which for decades has been shaped by the individual automobility afforded by the privately owned motor vehicle, it is likely that the need and demand for private motor vehicles will continue well into the future. Recent studies emphasize that even in major urban areas people living in the suburban and outer fringes of regions such as the GTA have much larger carbon footprints than those living in the inner city because of the difficulty in servicing these lower density areas with public transportation and the consequent continued reliance on the private automobile.

The most immediate issue before policymakers, therefore, is how best to shape regulations to reduce GHG emissions from individual motor vehicles. The challenge for the motor vehicle industry lies in developing new technologies that will reduce the environmental footprint of individual passenger vehicles by improving fuel efficiency and developing alternative fuel/power technologies that produce zero or at least much lower GHG emissions than conventional ICEs (see Maxton and Wormald 2004).

Government Regulation of Vehicle Emissions and Fuel Efficiency
Since 1995, governmental regulatory practice involving the automotive industry has evolved to reflect growing concerns with regard to global climate change. Vehicles produced today are certainly significantly cleaner and more fuel-efficient than those produced fifteen years ago.

The regulatory environment in which the Canadian automotive sector operates has undergone substantive changes. Many of these changes are linked to the *Canadian Environmental Protection Act 1999* (CEPA), which included provisions for federal regulations limiting emissions from new cars and light trucks. In 2001, the federal government set out a number of policy measures designed to bring Canadian emission standards for engines and standards for fuel efficiency in line with the U.S. Environmental Protection Agency's (EPA) requirements and to replace standards contained in Canada's *Motor Safety Vehicle Act* of 1993. By 2004, Canadian emissions and fuel standards were harmonized with the U.S. federal EPA requirements, including the U.S. Tier 2 program for new light-duty vehicles, light-duty trucks and medium-duty passenger vehicles.

In short, the Tier 2 program was designed to minimize vehicle emissions that negatively affect the ozone. These emissions include particulate matter, nitrogen oxides, non-methane organic gases (consisting primarily of hydrocarbons) and volatile organic compounds. Unlike previous regulations, the Tier 2 program applied the same set of standards to all passenger cars, light trucks and medium-duty passenger vehicles (National Academy of Sciences 2002). According to the EPA, "The program thus ensures that essentially all vehicles designed for passenger use in the future will be very clean vehicles" (EPA 1999: iii). The complete Tier 2 program was phased in between 2004 and 2010. To help ensure compliance with these standards, both Canadian and U.S. fuel standards have been modified. Sulphur levels in both gasoline and diesel fuels have been reduced as a result of Canada's Sulphur in Gasoline Regulations, which came into effect in 2002. By 2007, the Canadian national average sulphur content in gasoline was determined to be 18 mg/kg, a considerable reduction from the more than 300 mg/kg recorded in 2000 (Environment Canada 2009).

Besides making automobiles cleaner, regulations have forced automakers to improve fuel efficiency, thus reducing carbon dioxide emissions. Once again, Canadian standards have been harmonized with those of the United States' Corporate Average Fuel Economy (CAFE) standard (National Academy of Sciences 2002). By the 2011 model year, the U.S. industry-wide average fuel economy of new cars and light trucks was scheduled to be 27.3 miles per gallon (11.61 kilometres per litre).

In North America, the State of California has been a leader in using regulation to induce the automotive industry to produce cleaner and more efficient vehicles. To combat smog in Los Angeles, California started regulating vehicle pollution before the U.S. *Federal Clean Air Act* was passed in 1970 (Brown 2004). Subsequently, EPA rules were written to allow California to impose stricter standards for vehicle pollutants but not for fuel economy (which remained governed by the federal CAFE standards). They also permitted other U.S. states to voluntarily adopt California's pollution standards but prohibited the creation of their own. The stricter California standards caused significant logistical problems for the industry, as only a portion of any model line required additional modification to meet the more stringent California standards. As of 2008, fourteen American states, including New York, Florida and Pennsylvania, had either adopted or were in the process of adopting California's strict emissions standards. In the same year, Quebec and British Columbia moved to enact legislation that would mirror California's emission standards (*Vancouver Sun* April 2, 2008). The size of California's market, along with the integrated nature of the auto industry, has meant that California's standards have become the precursors to U.S. national standards and by extension, North American standards.

In April 2010, the U.S. and Canada jointly announced new rules for greenhouse gas emissions from automobiles and boosted fuel efficiency standards. The new rules require cars and light trucks to get on average 35.5 miles per gallon (15 kilometres per litre) by 2016 (Gardner 2010). This represents an approximate 25 percent increase over the current standards. The new rules also mandate that the average vehicle emissions will be limited to 250 grams of carbon dioxide per mile by 2016, down approximately 15 percent from 2012. Speaking about the new standards, Canada's former Environment Minister Jim Prentice reiterated the importance of joint common standards given the highly integrated nature of the North American auto industry.

The 2010 Canada and U.S. greenhouse gas emission rules for automobiles eliminated the need for separate California standards. It is estimated that the new standards have increased new vehicle prices on average by approximately $1,000. According to David Mondragon, President of Ford Canada, the new standards represent an improvement not only for the consumer, who will have better and cleaner cars, but also for the automotive industry that will no longer need to navigate a patchwork of competing federal and state based regulations. Commentators have also speculated that in the same way that the increasingly strict standards of the 1990s spurred technological advancements, these new and much tougher rules will force automakers to continue to invest in developing new automotive technologies.

Automotive Technologies for Reducing
GHG Emissions and Improving Fuel Efficiency

Incremental improvements in fuel efficiency can be achieved from existing gasoline fired internal combustion engine technology through the use of lighter materials, the development of more efficient engines and transmissions and advanced electrical systems. A range of alternative fuels and fuel systems that emit fewer GHG are also being developed, including: clean diesel engines; biofuels (such as ethanol); hybrid power systems that combine an electric motor with a gasoline engine; all-electric vehicles; and hydrogen-based fuel cells (that convert hydrogen into electric power while producing virtually no pollution).

Media discussions of fuel efficiency gains usually focus on the hybrids, but wider adoption of more mundane clean technology packages will be critical in efforts to reduce GHGs. Many of these, such as variable speed transmissions and clean diesel, are already available and in widespread use in Europe and Japan. Despite the fact that some diesel powered vehicles boast average fuel economies that rival some electric hybrids, penetration of diesel powered vehicles into the North American market has been limited because average diesel engine emissions, particularly of nitrogen oxides, fail to meet North American emission standards (CAR 2004).

Electric hybrid vehicles are becoming increasingly popular in the North American market and are now firmly entrenched into major manufacturers' product lines. Broadly speaking, hybrids enhance fuel economy in at least three ways. First, with the addition of the secondary power source, consisting of the battery pack and electric motor, these vehicles rely less on the ICE. Second, with the power offered by the battery pack, the ICE can be turned off when idling. Third, hybrids utilize regenerative braking that captures and stores a significant portion of the energy otherwise lost while braking (ibid.). Depending on the technologies and vehicle configurations, hybrids may be categorized as micro, mild, parallel non-plug-in, parallel plug-in or series (Center for Education and Research in Environmental Strategies 2008; CAR 2004). Hybrid technologies offer the possibility of significant fuel economy and emissions enhancements; however, these improvements also come with a significant price premium from $5,000 to $10,000 above the cost of a conventionally powered identical model.

Other Alternative Fuel Technologies
In addition to hybrid technologies, a range of other alternative fuel technologies are poised to potentially reshape the entire automotive sector. In the longer term, for example, hydrogen or zinc air powered fuel cells (Table 6.4) may constitute the future of the industry and the future of new jobs in the industry (Molot 2008; Molot and Mytelka 2007). Other alternative fuel technologies such as full electric, propane, biofuel or flex fuel represent near term and current options for carmakers and consumers (Table 6.5). Biofuel — most commonly ethanol, which is made by fermenting the sugar components of plant materials — is viewed as a potential alternative to gasoline.

Table 6.4 Longer Term Alternative Fuel Technologies

Technology	Advantages of the technology	Drawbacks or challenges with the technology
Hydrogen Fuel Cell	The consumption of hydrogen in a fuel cell releases water vapour rather than carbon dioxide	Hydrogen is currently derived from natural gas or coal, with an associated release of greenhouse gases to the atmosphere Hydrogen is highly unstable and volatile in nature, which is problematic for the storage and distribution Would require a complete new network of refueling stations
Zinc Air Fuel Cell	Twice as efficient as a traditional ICE Superior range; can travel 400–550 km before needing to be refueled Quick refuel times (ten minutes) Zinc used in process this 100% recyclable	Commercial costs are very high Zinc recovery equipment is also inherently inexpensive Thus far applications have been reserved for the military

Source: Derived from Centre for Education and Research in Environmental Strategies [CERES] (2008) and Clark et al. (2003)

Both biofuel and electric powered vehicles are popular because they offer a significant reduction in carbon emissions. However, studies have shown that the potential for these alternative fuels to reduce greenhouse gas emissions is particularly sensitive to the source of energy used to produce either electricity or the alternative fuels. Therefore, it is important to consider the carbon footprint of the entire life cycle of the vehicle. For example, if the electricity used to charge a vehicle's batteries is derived from hydroelectric or nuclear power then its total emission reduction potential is high. If the electricity is generated by burning fossil fuels such as coal, then its overall emission reduction potential is low (Dupressoir et al. 2007b). Similarly, in the case of ethanol biofuel, if the ethanol is produced using biofuel to generate the steam for breaking down the foodstock then the ethanol will ultimately produce less greenhouse gases than traditional gasoline. However, if fossil based electricity is used in ethanol production, gasoline is likely more climate friendly. Moreover, biofuel feedstock cultivation is also a greenhouse gas contributor. Here, the emissions are due mostly to nitrogen, methane and carbon dioxide released during the production of fertilizers and pesticides.

Changing Nature of Employment and Jobs in the Automotive Industry

How has work and employment in the automotive industry changed since 1995, and how might employment levels and job design change in the future, especially as the industry responds to the challenges posed by global climate warming? There are few recent studies of changing patterns of employment and skill requirements in the North American automotive industry. Of these studies, only three are worth highlighting and two of those only very tan-

Table 6.5 Current or Near Term Alternative Fuel Technologies

Technology	Positive features of the technology	Drawbacks or challenges with the technology
Lithium-ion Electric Battery	Zero carbon emissions emitted from vehicle Easily recharged from common electric outlets Electric engines exhibit excellent acceleration and performance	Limited range Source of electricity may be produced by burning fossil fuels More expensive than traditional ICES
Biofuel, generally in the form of ethanol	Made from biomass Can have a lower carbon footprint than traditional fuels Potentially renewable source of fuel Competitively priced	May have higher carbon footprint than traditional fuels since vehicles need proportionally more biofuel than gasoline to produce the same combustion levels Vehicles still emit CO_2
Motor Fuel Propane (Liquefied Petroleum Gas)	Lower vehicle maintenance costs Lower emissions than vehicles using traditional fuels Competitively priced	Vehicles need proportionally more propane than gasoline to produce the same combustion levels Vehicles still emit CO_2
Flex fuel engines	Vehicles can use entirely ethanol or gasoline as fuel without engine modification Ethanol-Diesel engines are also available	Vehicles still emit CO_2

Source: Derived from Fu et al. (2003) and CAR (2004)

gentially address the issue of climate change and work. The Canadian study, *Competing Without a Net*, was commissioned by the Council for Automotive Human Resources (CAHR) with the primary objective of identifying human resource challenges facing the automotive manufacturing sector in Canada (Council for Automotive Human Resources 2008). The second study, *Beyond the Big Leave*, was produced by the Centre for Automotive Research (CAR) to assess the future prospects for the automotive industry in the state of Michigan and especially, the impending challenges related to automotive human resources (Dziczek et al. 2008). A more recent 2011 study from CAR, *Driving Workforce Change*, does focus explicitly on the regional (Michigan, Ohio and Indiana) impacts of the transformation of the automotive industry to a green economy. Although focused on the U.S. Great Lakes states, the two CAR reports underscore the changing labour needs in the North American automotive sector in general. For reasons outlined earlier, the issues facing the industry in Ontario are likely to be very similar to those encountered in states such as Michigan and Ohio (also see Rutherford and Holmes 2012).

All five major automakers who participated in the 2008 CAR study reported that they did not expect there to be major changes in the nature of automotive work in the near future. In other words, they did not expect the way that motor vehicles are presently manufactured to change in a fundamental way. This is not to say that production processes and work organization remain static. Over the last decade, the industry's traditional distinction between "skilled" and "nonskilled" work has become increasingly blurred. No longer can any job in a modern automotive assembly or parts facility be considered "unskilled." The incorporation of lean production practices has increased the responsibilities of employees on the shop floor, with production workers assuming more and more responsibility for "... organizing their own work teams, monitoring their own product quality, performing routine maintenance and managing the business case for the work they do" (Dziczek et al. 2008: 37).

The continuing trend toward higher levels of automation in the production process has certainly changed the demands on production workers by reducing the physical aspects of jobs (manual dexterity and physical strength) and increasing the technological content of the work. Proficiency with computer based automation and manufacturing related software packages is currently a requirement for select auto production workers but in the future is expected to be a requirement for all workers since "the ability for workers to troubleshoot software problems is going to be key ... and this will continue to intensify the need for ... computer skills and technical literacy in the workforce" (CAR 2008: 48). The positions occupied by skilled trades workers and maintenance associates are undergoing considerable change. Technological change in the industry is driving the D-3 automakers to reduce skilled job demarcations by increasing cross-training and shifting toward combined mechanical and electrical training.

CAR's 2011 study notes that when the study began there was "only limited understanding of the specific nature of the transformation of skills relevant to efficient and renewable vehicle technologies and other career opportunities in the green economy," (CAR 2011. 1). The study suggests that while the region (Michigan, Ohio, Indiana and we might add Ontario) has been home to the production of traditional vehicle engine production, it is quite possible that new green vehicle propulsion systems will be produced outside the region. Furthermore, advanced technologies could well require fewer workers to produce the same volume of propulsion systems. Automakers interviewed for the study stated that green products and production techniques will have a more profound effect on engineering and technical staff requirements than on production and tradesworker skill sets in the automotive industry. A major focus of the study is the issue of how to facilitate the transition of displaced workers into other sectors of an emerging green economy since many autoworkers who have lost their jobs due to industry restructuring during the Great Recession will never be hired back into the auto industry, and many of them have only limited formal education.

The Impact of Climate Warming on Work and Employment in the Transportation Equipment Industry: What Do We Need to Know?

In sum, very little has been written regarding the likely impacts of climate change on employment and skills requirements in the transportation equipment industry. At best, what is available provides only broad-brush estimates of employment change (see, for example, Dupressoir et al. 2007b; Baum and Luria 2010). Although few in number, these reports reflect a consensus that neither incremental efficiency improvements nor longer-term technological changes in response to climate change concerns threaten the viability of the motor vehicle industry for the foreseeable future. In this context, whilst climate warming is clearly the principal driver of technological change in vehicle design, and especially powertrain design and engineering, it is not seen as fundamentally changing the way in which motor vehicles are built.

Moreover, the reports argue that compliance with government regulations that mandate improvements in fuel efficiency and reductions in GHG emissions will involve

> greater labor content per vehicle and higher employment across the fleet. This will include new investment in a host of incremental improvements to conventional gasoline powered internal combustion engines, from new controls for valves and timing, to variable speed transmissions and advanced electronics. It will also include entirely

new systems like hybrid drive trains and advanced diesel engines. (Baum and Luria 2010: 3)

In short, responding to climate change concerns will add more content and value to automotive production — content which, in turn, should require more engineers and workers to design, manufacture and assemble and, other things being equal, should create more rather than fewer automotive jobs. Of course, all other things are never equal. For example, during the 1990s, substantial increases in labour productivity in the automotive industry greatly increased output with only modest increases in employment. As one study concluded,

> re-engineering the U.S. automobile fleet to use energy more efficiently will require new investments in advanced technology, increasing the demand for skilled labor. Instead of presenting a threat to the auto industry, reigning [*sic*] in reliance on oil and cutting pollution from fossil fuels can demonstrably create jobs, accelerate innovation and increase demand for advanced manufacturing. (Baum and Luria 2010: 6)

In general, it seems likely that, at least for the foreseeable future, factors such as the perennial tendency toward industry overcapacity and instability in the global capitalist economy will have a more significant impact on overall employment levels in the industry than will climate warming.

Even if one accepts the argument that improving the fuel economy and reducing vehicle GHG emissions may create more jobs, much more detailed research is required to assess the impact of green policies on employment trends and skill requirements in the automotive industry. For example:

- Will government regulations on fuel efficiency and emissions and longer-term changes in urban planning regulations lead to a modal shift from private vehicles to public transportation and reduced demand for automobiles?
- What will be the impact on employment trends in the automotive industry of meeting the new 2016 fuel economy and emissions standards?
- What specific new engineering and manufacturing skills are required to develop and work with some of the more radical new automotive powertrain technologies such as all electric or hydrogen fuel cells?
- How do these skill requirements mesh with other skill needs associated with a shift toward increased integration of mechanical, electrical and software engineering?

Given the global nature of the automotive industry, another important and currently unknown employment related question is: Which nations and/

or regions will most likely capture the jobs and economic benefits associated with the shift to a more fuel-efficient North American vehicle fleet? For example, although the technology for lithium ion batteries used in plug-in hybrids and electric vehicles was largely developed in North America, battery production is currently dominated by Japan, China and Korea. Similarly,

> both Europe and Japan have substantial leads in hybrids, diesels, DDI [diesel direct injection] and turbochargers. Most of these technologies have high value-to-weight ratios, making them eminently shippable. Nearly all of the key components in Nissan, Honda, Toyota, Ford and Mercury hybrids sold in the United States are made in Japan. (Baum and Luria 2010: 6)

Baum and Luria, however, go on to note that while Europe and Japan have a lead in a number of these new powertrain technologies, their focus is on applications of the technologies in small cars, rather than the larger vehicles that dominate the North American market. The same report underscores a concern from a Canadian perspective. Today, most of North America's high volume engine and transmission plants are located in the United States. This is even truer for advanced vehicle R & D and testing capacity. Thus, it will be a challenge for Canada to secure a share of the new jobs created in the industry as a result of meeting the new 2016 fuel economy and emissions standards.

In conclusion, there is little extant literature that explicitly addresses the nexus between climate warming and employment and jobs in the automotive industry. Research is required to provide much more precise forecasts of employment trends and specific skill requirements, not only in response to the development of new green technologies but also with regard to broader changes in the industry. These include shifting workforce demographics, changing skill requirements in response to other technological changes (such as the rise of mechatronics) and the "big question" regarding the likely future size of the industry in Canada. As a 2007 CAW discussion paper observed,

> We need to carefully analyze how proposed measures (such as regulated improvements in vehicle fuel efficiency) will affect Canada's auto industry and seek ways of supporting and strengthening the fight against climate change that also strengthen (rather than undermine) this crucial sector of our economy. (CAW 2007: 2)

Notes

1. Given the enormous improvements in fuel efficiency and "cleaner" engines achieved over the last couple of decades, removing older vehicles from the road can make a significant contribution to the reduction of GHG emissions.

For example, federal emission regulations in 1970 required cars to produce no more than 4.2 grams of hydrocarbons, 39.6 grams of CO_2 and 4.1 grams of NOx (nitrous oxide) per mile. Equivalent standards for 2010 model year cars are 0.055 grams, 2.1 grams and 0.07 grams respectively.

2. The energy savings are projected to be significant. With production volumes equal to those in 2001, it was estimated that per unit consumption of electricity and natural gas would be reduced by 18 percent and 28 percent respectively, which would reduce CO_2 emissions on a per unit basis by 24 percent compared to 2001. Of course, because of the recent and ongoing global economic situation, production volumes have remained significantly (30%+) below 2001 levels.

7. THE FORESTRY INDUSTRY

John Holmes

Historically, the forest products industry has been one of Canada's leading manufacturing sectors and its largest net exporter. It has been a major component of the industrial structure and employment base in regions across the country but especially in Quebec, northern Ontario and British Columbia. In 2010, according to the Forest Products Association of Canada (FPAC), it accounted for 12 percent of manufacturing GDP, exports of $26 billion and direct employment of 236,700 (Forest Products Association of Canada 2011). In close to two hundred communities across Canada, more than 50 percent of workers are directly dependent on forest products for their livelihood.

The forest sector consists of several well recognized subsectors: primary forestry activities including harvesting (logging) (NAICS 113); woodlot management and silviculture (NAICS 115); solid wood processing in sawmills to produce lumber, shakes and shingles, wood chips and pulp-related materials (NAICS 3211); the pulp and paper subsector producing products such as pulp, newsprint, printing papers, packaging papers and paperboard as well as value added paper products like tissue, napkins and other consumer paper products (NAICS 322); and the manufactured wood products subsector producing commodities such as dimensioned lumber and panels (NAICS 3212) as well as higher value added engineered products such as doors, windows, kitchen cabinets, manufactured housing and flooring (NAICS 3219). This chapter focuses primarily on the impact of climate warming on the logging, solid wood processing and pulp and paper subsectors.

The challenge of assessing the impact of climate warming on the industry is compounded by the fact that Canada's forest products sector has undergone major structural change since 2004. Factors driving the restructuring include: a general downturn in demand for structural lumber; the persistent high value of the Canadian dollar against the U.S. dollar, which has made Canadian forest products less competitive in one of their principal markets; increased competition from overseas producers; and the impact of the "Great Recession" of 2008–11, which saw the collapse of U.S. housing starts and therefore the demand for lumber and a significant decline in the demand for paper used in advertising. In fact, the impact of the Great Recession on the Canadian forest sector has been catastrophic. During the first half of 2009, British Columbia, for example, witnessed a 26.3 percent decline in lumber production, a 14 percent decline in pulp shipments and a 26.6 percent decline in newsprint shipments. Forest products exports for the province in the first half of 2009 were down by 27.1 percent for solid wood products and down by 25.8 percent for pulp and paper products compared to the same period in 2008 (R.A. Malatest and Associates 2010: 12).

Overall, Canada's forest products workforce has been significantly downsized, losing in excess of 100,000 jobs between 2004 and 2009 (Tables 7.1 and 7.2). In sharp contrast to the automotive industry, the Canadian forestry sector has received little assistance, especially financial assistance, from the federal and provincial governments to facilitate restructuring and help the industry respond to the crisis. Although there are now some signs of recovery in the solid wood sector, research suggests that a significant number of the most recent layoffs are likely permanent, as the industry continues to restructure. Thus, transitioning displaced workers from an aging workforce is currently the foremost human resource challenge confronting the industry (R.A. Malatest and Associates 2010).

Forests and climate warming are intimately connected. At different times and depending upon external conditions, forests may act as either a carbon sink or a carbon source; as such, forests are a key element in the global carbon cycle that helps to regulate climate. As a sink, forests store large amounts of carbon in the trees and soil by removing carbon dioxide, the major greenhouse gas (GHG), from the air and storing the carbon as biomass (wood, leaves and roots). Canada's 400 million hectares of forest represent an enormous carbon sink,[1] absorbing up to twenty times Canada's total annual CO_2 emissions from the burning of fossil fuels (Humphreys et al. 2006). As forests are logged, burned or simply decay, however, they switch from being a significant carbon sink to a carbon source. When trees are harvested, some carbon is released through soil disturbance and the decay of waste left on logging sites. Pest attacks or diseases that kill large numbers of trees both increase the stock of dead trees that release CO_2 as they decay and elevate the risk that such forests may burn and release carbon into the atmosphere. Climate warming is widely expected to accelerate both pest infestations and the risk of forest fires. Harvested trees that are converted into solid wood products continue to store carbon until such time as the wood products are burned or decay. This is an important point that we will return to shortly.

In analyzing the likely impact of climate warming on employment and jobs in the Canadian forestry sector, we reviewed a large number of sources written in the period since 1995. Given the major role played by forests in determining carbon balances, it is not surprising that there is a very extensive

Table 7.1 Forestry Employment by Region, 2004–2009 (in thousands)

Employment	Region					
	Atlantic	Quebec	Ontario	Prairies	BC	Canada
2004	29.8	84.1	45.8	23.6	72.3	255.6
2005	28.2	76.3	44.1	21.2	70.4	240.1
2006	22.6	67.5	39.2	18.5	70.0	217.8
2007	23.3	53.5	33.8	18.5	72.3	201.4
2008	21.1	52.6	32.7	21.0	53.7	181.1
2009(estimate)	15.1	52.3	27.5	17.4	40.4	152.7
% change from 2004	-49.3	-37.8	-40.0	-26.3	-44.1	-40.6

Source: R.A. Malatest and Associates (2010: 17) (based on Statistics Canada Labour Force Survey)

Table 7.2 Forestry Employment by Sub-sector, 2004–2009 (in thousands)

Employment	Sector			
	Primary Forestry and Logging	Primary Wood Manufacturing	Pulp and Paper	Total
2004	72.1	114.4	69.2	255.7
2005	69.5	106.3	64.3	240.1
2006	63.0	92.7	62.2	217.9
2007	60.5	87.7	53.3	201.5
2008	54.1	67.1	59.8	181.0
2009 (estimate)	44.3	54.0	53.7	151.9

Source: R.A. Malatest and Associates (2010: 16) (based on Statistics Canada Labour Force Survey)

scholarly and scientific literature on the links between forests, GHG emissions and climate change. From a social science perspective, there are studies that focus on assessing the broader vulnerability of forest-based communities to climate change and a few recent studies of the major labour market adjustment challenges facing the Canadian forestry industry due to the current deep structural crisis within the industry. However, even the few existing studies that focus on the forest industry labour market make only scant reference to the likely impact that measures designed to mitigate climate warming will have on the future of employment and jobs in the industry (for example, Wood Manufacturing Council 2005; R.A. Malatest and Associates 2010).

The following questions guided our review and analysis of the literature: What role do forests play in the global carbon cycle and climate warming? What are the implications of this for the forest products industries? How has government policy directed at the forestry industry been shaped by concerns regarding climate warming, and what impact has such policy had on the industry? Have concerns about climate warming led to changes in forestry practices and manufacturing processes? What are the implications of these changes for skills development and training? Will climate change be a more significant factor influencing the forestry sector in the future? What issues require more research?

Before turning to these questions, we begin with a brief contextual overview of the political economy of the forestry industry in Canada.[2]

THE FORESTRY INDUSTRY IN CANADA

The forestry industry is an extractive resource based industry that traditionally has relied on local sources for its basic resource input: raw wood, usually in the form of harvested logs. Wood is a low value, high volume commodity that incurs substantial transportation costs. Consequently, wood typically was logged from regions with abundant natural forests, and the early stages of processing, such as the production of sawn lumber or wood pulp for paper, was located close to the wood supply. Since historically large areas of Canada were covered by natural forests, several regions of the country became major producers of forest products, with many small communities in relatively remote locations dependent upon the local sawmill or pulp mill.

Canada's forest products workforce is characterized by older workers. Based on the 2006 census, 45.4 percent of forest products workers were forty-five years of age or older, compared to 39.7 percent of the overall Canadian labour force. The workforce in both logging activities and the mills is predominantly male and reflects a wide range of education and skill levels from hard physical manual labour involved in logging operations, through the highly valued tacit knowledge and skill of paper machine operators and the formal trades skills of maintenance workers, to the highly educated production managers and forestry professionals (R.A. Malatest and Associates 2010: 4). In British Columbia it is estimated that six out of ten people working in forestry are in occupations unique to primary industries, such as operators of logging machinery, chainsaws and skidders and silviculture and forestry workers.

The industry in Canada has traditionally been highly unionized with a complex history of regionally based unions, U.S. based international unions, union breakaways and subsequent mergers (Hak 2007; Sweeney 2010). Some of the principal unions involved in the industry over the last quarter century have been: the Canadian Paperworkers Union (CPU); the Pulp, Paper and Woodworkers of Canada (PPWC) centred primarily in British Columbia; the Fédération des travailleurs et des travailleuses du papier et de la forêt (FTPF-CSN) representing a segment of forestry workers in Quebec; and the International Woodworkers of America (IWA-Canada), now merged into the United Steelworkers union (USW), which represents sawmill workers in western Canada. The CPU was formed in 1974 when Canadian workers broke away from the U.S. based United Paperworkers International

Union (UPIU). The CPU later merged with other Canadian unions to form the Communication, Energy and Paperworkers union (CEP), which today represents many pulp and paper workers in Canada. The relatively high union density in the industry, especially in the mills, produced production jobs that are relatively well paid in comparison to many other manufacturing jobs. Prior to the 2008–11 Great Recession, some mills in the B.C. interior were finding it difficult to attract new young workers due to competition from the high wages being generated in the oil and gas industry in northern B.C. and Alberta.

Much of the forest products labour force is located in small- to medium-sized communities far removed from larger urban centres and heavily dependent on forestry-related industries as their primary source of economic activity. This raises a number of labour market issues. For example, if a mill is downsized or closed it is very difficult for mill production workers to find alternative employment within the community, and certainly finding employment with comparable pay and benefits is virtually impossible. The isolated nature of many of these communities usually precludes the option of commuting to another job in a different location. For the same reason, accessing training and education is also a challenge.

In recent decades, forest-based industries in North America have experienced profound changes due to economic globalization and technological change (Bael and Sedjo 2006; Sedjo and Bael 2007). Beginning in the 1980s, traditional North American regions of production such as Quebec, Maine, the Great Lakes and Cascadia (B.C., Washington, Oregon) began to experience restructuring, job losses and mill closures due to growing international competition and falling commodity prices. These regions' proportion of global production decreased as both existing and new entrant firms sought lower labour and raw material costs elsewhere. Most new investment in the forest products industry since 1980, and especially in the pulp and paper sector, has been concentrated in the southeast United States, the Iberian Peninsula, Brazil, Chile and Southeast Asia, regions that enjoy competitive advantages due to lower labour costs, lower tax rates and cheaper sources of wood fibre produced in plantation forests (Marchak 1997).

Biotechnology has been applied to produce trees that grow and can be harvested more rapidly and that yield wood with the desired characteristics for industrial products. Innovations in silviculture have reduced the reliance on existing natural forests such that today, intensively managed, planted forests have become a major source of harvested wood. Technological developments in pulping technology have allowed the use of different tree species. As a consequence, the traditional ties between forest processing industries and regions with abundant natural forests have been eroded. For example, in the United States there has been a dramatic shift in forestland ownership and production locations, with major U.S. based forest corporations in the past twenty-five years divesting themselves of almost 50 percent of their U.S. holdings of timber rights whilst at the same time purchasing offshore forest assets (Sedjo and Bael 2007). Within North America, there has been a significant shift in the production of forest products away from the old-growth forests of the Pacific Northwest toward new managed timber resources in the southern United States. This shift had a significant negative impact on forestry in British Columbia since several U.S. based forestry companies divested themselves of their assets in B.C. to concentrate production in the southern U.S.

Sedjo and Bael (2007) suggest that globalization has had a greater impact on the pulp industry than on the structural wood industry in North America. Until the recent collapse of the U.S. housing market, companies whose major products were solid and structural wood (with pulp and paper as secondary products) thrived on the strong U.S. housing market, and their principal products were less impacted by globalization. On the other hand, North American companies focused on pulp and paper have been forced to restructure their assets due to the pressures of globalization. The restructuring has been characterized by a number of trends including a rapid and extensive change in ownership patterns in the industry (Sweeney 2010).

Historically, many of the large players in the North American forestry industry, such as Weyerheuser, MacMillan Bloedel and Crown Zellerbach, were highly integrated across a number of the forestry subsectors. Their own logging crews would harvest the wood, and waste from their solid wood mills would be used as feedstock for their pulp and paper operations. This provided firms with supply chain security and allowed them to shift fibre resources across their operations in response to counter-cyclical movements in lumber and pulp commodity prices. Over the last two decades, however, this kind of vertical integration has given way to horizontal integration and a shift from integrated firms to separate specialized firms engaged in each subsector of the broader forestry industry. Within each subsector, consolidation has occurred through an almost continuous process of mergers and buyouts. Many of the formerly large players in the solid wood and pulp sectors have divested their timberland holdings, especially in the United States (Sweeney 2010). Other recent challenges to the profitability and sustainability of the Canadian forest products industry include: the amplification of commodity price cycles; trade disputes over softwood lumber with the United States; and pressures from environmental lobbies both at home and abroad for government policy to preserve the dwindling supply of old-growth forests.

FORESTS AND CLIMATE CHANGE

Forests, GHGs and the Carbon Cycle

As noted earlier, forests are a key element in the global carbon cycle that helps to regulate climate. As a carbon sink, trees remove carbon dioxide from the atmosphere and convert it to wood, leaves and roots. As a source, they release stored carbon into the atmosphere when they decompose or burn. The soils and wetlands in Canada's boreal forest also store significant amounts of carbon. As trees decay, carbon is emitted slowly back into the atmosphere. Forest fires cause rapid and significant emissions of carbon dioxide and also release other and more potent GHGs such as methane and nitrous oxide. The area burned by forest fires in Canada varies considerably from year to year, but the GHGs released by fires can be very significant and can exceed removals of carbon by forest growth. For example, "in extreme fire years, like 1995, direct emissions from wildfires in the managed forest have represented up to 45% of Canada's total greenhouse gas emissions" (Natural Resources Canada n.d.b).

These removals and emissions are not determined solely by natural processes — forest management activities such as harvesting, tree planting and efforts to fight fires and insects all have a significant impact. When trees are harvested, some carbon is released through soil disturbance and the decay of waste left on logging sites; however, if the woody biomass is captured in solid wood products, the latter not only continue to store carbon but also generate far fewer GHGs in their production than do other common building materials like concrete, brick, glass and steel. A recent report noted that wood products manufacturing has the lowest GHG intensity of nine primary material processing sectors (Statistics Canada 2009d). Only when wood products are incinerated or decompose do they release their carbon into the atmosphere.

Changes in forest carbon balances, whether from human or natural processes, contribute to climate change by altering the amount of carbon dioxide in the atmosphere. In turn, a changing climate will affect forest carbon storage as a consequence of changes in forest productivity, decomposition, regeneration and succession, as well as changes to species, species communities and their geographical distributions. The eventual net outcome is not immediately obvious. On the one hand, for example, a warmer climate can increase the rate of carbon sequestration by speeding up the growth of vegetation, while on the other hand the same climate warming is likely to significantly reduce carbon storage by accelerating decomposition and increasing the risk of forest fires and insect infestations.

As a result of mild winters over the last decade it is estimated that the severe mountain pine beetle infestation in central British Columbia has killed almost 1 billion m^3 of lodgepole pine (Konkin and Hopkins 2009). Unless rapidly logged for use in sawmills, chipped to feed pulp mills or used as fuel for new bioenergy projects, these dead pine trees represent a huge source of future GHG emissions since much of their stored carbon will be released back into the atmosphere as they decay. Besides general climate warming, another concern regarding contemporary climate change is an increase in extreme weather events, and Canadian forests may well become subject to more frequent severe storms and wind damage.

Impact of Forest Industries on Net Carbon Balances in Canada

Are Canadian forests a net sink or a source of carbon on balance? What is the contribution of logging and forestry-related activities in Canada to GHG emissions? The scientific evidence is mixed and estimates of forestry-related GHG emissions vary significantly. Two major, independent modelling exercises of Canada's forest carbon balance demonstrate that the source/sink balance of Canada's forests has fluctuated over time (Henschel and Gray 2007). The CBM-CFS3 model developed by the Canadian Forest Service (CFS) estimates that Canada's managed forest has been a sink for most of the past seventy years and that between 1990 and 2005 it was an overall sink in all but five years (Natural Resources Canada n.d.a) The recent trend toward a more negative carbon balance is thought to be mainly the result of a recent upswing in fire and insect disturbances combined with increased temperatures and an aging forest. The forest area harvested by logging each year remained fairly stable during the 1990–2005 period; therefore, it is unlikely that timber harvesting was a cause of the higher incidence of annual negative carbon balances.

The independently developed Integrated Terrestrial Ecosystem C-budget (InTEC) model has been used to model carbon balances in Canada over the past one hundred years. The InTEC analysis suggests that Canada's forests as a whole were a small carbon source in the period 1895–1905 due to large disturbances near the end of the nineteenth century; a large carbon sink in the period 1930–1970 due to forest regrowth in previously burnt-over areas; and a moderate carbon sink in the period 1980–1996 (Chen et al. 2000). Both models point to significant regional variation in carbon balances across Canada. For example, forest areas in the Prairie provinces have become a large carbon source due to recent fire activity; a large forest sink exists in eastern Ontario/western Quebec due to a mid aged forest; while, in recent years, large areas of British Columbia's forests have been carbon neutral (it is too early yet for the trees killed by the pine beetle to begin to decay and release carbon) (Chen 2007).

Natural Resources Canada (NRCan) estimates that from 1990 to 2005, harvesting in Canada's managed forests resulted in an average of about 43 million tonnes per year of biomass carbon in branches, roots and leaves being left in the forest, and about 41 million tonnes of biomass carbon being transferred from the forest ecosystem to the forest products sector each year (Natural Resources Canada n.d.a).

Some authors equate the GHG emissions from logging in Canada with those from cars and trucks. For example, Stewart Elgie is quoted in a 2007 interview as stating that

> logging in Canada releases more than 150 million tonnes of carbon per year; by comparison all of Canada's cars and trucks emit about 145 million tonnes. In other words, logging is as serious a culprit in releasing carbon as all of the country's cars and trucks, at least in the short term. (Rushton 2007)

However, as Natural Resources Canada points out,

> the timing of the biomass carbon emissions is quite different than that of the car and truck emissions, which occur immediately. The biomass left in the forest decomposes slowly, while the biomass carbon that is transferred out of the forest (equivalent to about 150 million tonnes of carbon dioxide each year) is emitted over time according to the use made of the wood. From 1990 to 2005, biomass carbon equivalent to about 65–75 million tonnes of carbon dioxide was stored in products that last for decades, such as lumber used in housing, while an amount equivalent to about 35-45 million tonnes of carbon dioxide was stored in less durable products (including paper) and was emitted to the atmosphere in the first few years after harvest. Much of the remaining carbon was released shortly after harvest from the burning of wood waste or biofuel as a renewable source of energy. (Natural Resources Canada n.d.a)

NRCan argues that reducing timber harvesting would not have a large impact on CO_2 emissions from Canadian forests because sustainable forest management practices result in a harvest of less than 0.5 percent of the managed forest in any given year. Furthermore, the harvested areas regenerate to forest so that, in any year, there is renewed sequestration of carbon occurring on the previously logged areas. Finally, a significant proportion of the carbon removed from the forest continues to be stored in durable forest products such as lumber (NRCan n.d.).

The length of time that forest products remain a source of carbon storage depends on a number of factors including the efficiency with which the logged trees are converted into forest products, the longevity of the product and how it is ultimately disposed of (e.g., incinerated, recycled and landfilled). For example, only about 50 percent of the harvested log is converted into dimensioned lumber (although much of the waste is either chipped and used as pulp feedstock or burned as biofuel), while the harvested wood-to-product ratio is estimated to be 85 percent for pulp and paper. Research suggests that wood carbon stored in landfills has a much larger residence time than tree biomass in a forest.

This underscores the importance of analyzing greenhouse gas emissions over the full life cycle of forest products. The Heinz Center, with several industry partners, produced a comprehensive study of GHG emissions over the entire supply chain from forest harvest to waste disposal and product decomposition for two magazine chains and a dimensional lumber chain (Gower 2006). Consistent with other studies, the Heinz Center study found that forest management operations accounted for less than 1 percent of total greenhouse gas emissions from the supply chain. In the magazine supply chain, the highest percentage (61–77 percent, depending on the mills) of greenhouse gas emissions came from paper manufacturing at pulp and paper mills, with transportation being the second highest contributor of GHG emissions (between 5–9 percent). Thus, the study concluded that the potential to significantly reduce GHG emissions for the magazine supply chain lies with improving energy efficiencies in the pulp and paper manufacturing process. In fact, the pulp and paper industry has made significant progress in reducing GHG emissions from mills (see Forest Products Association of Canada 2009). Since 94 percent of the GHG emissions associated with the dimensional lumber supply chain was generated by the transportation of the lumber from the sawmill to the retail outlets, the real opportunity for reducing GHG emissions in this supply chain lay with the use of more fuel-efficient transportation modes. The study also emphasized that the final disposal method for unrecovered magazines and waste dimensional lumber (landfilled, incinerated or recycled) can potentially have a large effect on the carbon footprint of the magazine and dimensional lumber chains.

At present, a significant volume of logs is exported from Canada to the United States and Asia to be processed into solid wood products. A recent pamphlet (USW 2010) argues that in the overall value chain, the amount of carbon generated when logs are exported for processing rather than being processed domestically rises by over 50 percent due to the GHGs generated by the extra transportation required.

Potential Growth Areas for Forest Products:
Engineered Wood Building Products, Wood-Fired Energy Generation and Biofuel Refining

With increasing concern regarding GHG emissions and climate warming, attention has turned to increasing the use of wood as a building material and for wood-fired energy generation. The Intergovernmental Panel on Climate Change has identified changes in the design, construction and operation of buildings as one strategy to significantly reduce GHG emissions. Although lumber has long been used as a framing material in the construction of single family homes in Canada, its use in the construction of multistorey residential and commercial buildings has been very limited, in part, by building codes. British Columbia, in an effort to assist the province's beleaguered forest industry, moved in January 2009 to raise the limit on wood frame construction from four to six storeys. The speed skating oval for the 2010 Winter Olympics near Vancouver was used as a showcase example of building with wood. One million board feet of sawn wood, mostly from beetle-killed trees, was used in the construction of the 2.6 ha roof. In Quebec City, the new headquarters building for the Confédération des Syndicats Nationaux (CSN) was completed with all the structural elements made from wood rather than steel or concrete.

Not only is wood a product that stores carbon and is durable, it also requires significantly less fossil fuel to produce than other building materials. Parfitt, for example, reports that it takes "2.9 times more fossil fuel energy to produce the equivalent amount of concrete slabs, 3.1 times more energy to produce the equivalent amount of clay bricks and 17.3 times more energy to produce the equivalent amount of steel studs as it does softwood lumber" (Parfitt 2010a). More research is now being directed to the development of a wider and more sophisticated range of engineered wood products to be used in building construction in order to reduce the life cycle carbon footprints of buildings.

Many forest product mills already have cogeneration projects that burn waste wood fibre to produce both heat and electricity for use in the mill. There are now planned projects to build large wood-fired electrical generating plants in B.C. and to build biorefineries to produce bioethanol and synthetic biodiesel from wood in Quebec. Williams Lake, B.C., already has one of the largest wood-fired electrical generating facilities in North America. Owned by EPCOR, the facility initially used sawdust and wood chips from sawmills in the Williams Lake region to burn and spin turbines to produce 66 megawatts of electricity. Much of the over 600,000 tonnes of wood that is now fed into the EPCOR plant comes from dead lodgepole pine killed by the mountain pine beetle. Although burning the wood for power generation releases GHGs, if left to decompose in the forest the dead pine trees would also release greenhouse gases over time.

Wood-fired bioenergy provides an alternative revenue stream for beleaguered forest industry firms and is also promoted as so-called green energy. Although GHGs are released when wood is converted to energy, it is argued that if new trees are planted, eventually the carbon sequestered by the new trees will offset such emissions. However, industry watchers have urged caution before moving to large-scale energy generation from biomass (Parfitt 2010a). The call for green power projects issued by BC Hydro in March 2009 focused on wood as an energy source but also implied that logging on new forest tenures could be used to directly support electrical power generation. As Parfitt observes,

> this marked a radical departure from the norm, wherein the "fallout" or byproduct from sawmills — wood chips and sawdust — became the feedstock for the pulp and paper industry, wood pellet producers, wood boilers and the occasional wood-fired electrical generating facility. It raised the alarm of the province's pulp and paper industry, which worried about increased competition for finite wood supplies. (Parfitt 2010a: 21)

In Quebec, a province that has suffered a large loss of employment in the pulp and paper sector, a company recently announced that it planned to build five large-scale wood-fired biorefineries, each at a cost of $1.2 billion and each capable of producing 630 million litres of biodiesel fuel per year (Yakabuski 2009). When burned, the biodiesel would produce 90 percent fewer CO_2 emissions than conventional diesel. Parfitt raises a number of questions regarding this project, however, noting that

> there is no mention of the number of trees that would be required to produce so much "green" fuel. What would the CO_2 emissions associated with converting all those trees to fuel be? How long would it take a new generation of trees to sequester the carbon stored in the first batch of trees? (ibid.: 23)

FORESTRY AND CARBON CREDITS

The broader question is, what role can Canadian forests play in helping Canada reach its GHG emission reduction targets and in carbon credit trading schemes? When the Kyoto Protocol was being negotiated, Canada pushed hard to ensure that countries who signed on to the protocol could elect to include forest management in their calculations when accounting for GHG emissions and removals. It was argued that this would provide an incentive for countries to adopt sustainable forest management practices designed to reduce GHG emissions and increase carbon sequestration in forests. At the time, it was also thought likely that this would work to the benefit of Canada with its huge area of managed forests. Although this option was built into the Kyoto Protocol, Canada ultimately elected not to include forest management in Canada's carbon accounting. This was because a subsequent study conducted by the Canadian Forest Service (CFS) indicated that although Canada's managed forests have usually been a carbon sink in the past, there was a greater than nine in ten chance that they would be a net source of

GHGs in the period 2008–12, due in part to fire, insect damage and the age of the forests (NRCan n.d.).

The Western Climate Initiative was launched in 2007 by a partnership between British Columbia, California and a number of western U.S. states and subsequently expanded to include Manitoba, Ontario and Quebec. A key element in the initiative is to increase the planting of trees in order to sell their carbon storing capacity later in a market for tradable carbon credits (a so-called cap and trade system). Once a market is created for carbon, Elgie argues that

> in many places the carbon values will begin to approach or even exceed the timber values in our northern [Boreal] forests — and that's at a price of $15 per tonne of carbon. As the global warming problem becomes more pressing and demand for carbon storage rises, most experts think we will see carbon trading at $30 to $50 per tonne within a decade. If carbon gets up to that price, many of our northern forests will be worth far more for carbon [credits] than for timber. (quoted in Rushton 2007)

However, many technical questions regarding carbon trading markets remain. There is a continuing debate regarding the development of a comprehensive accounting system for forest credits in such a future market (Parfitt 2010a: 26).

THE IMPACT OF CLIMATE WARMING ON WORK AND EMPLOYMENT IN THE FOREST PRODUCTS INDUSTRY: WHAT DO WE NEED TO KNOW?

As noted earlier, literature that addresses the likely impacts of climate warming on employment and jobs in the forestry sector is, at best, sparse. Understandably, recent writing on human resource issues in the industry has focused on the sharp contraction in employment experienced over the last few years and how best to respond to the needs of laid-off forest workers. Furthermore, a recent report emphasizes that

> the kinds of structural changes that are predicted to result from climate change will occur alongside a host of other changes that are simultaneously affecting markets for forest products. Technological changes, trade disputes, changes in exchange rates, interest-rate changes, and changes in consumer tastes and preferences are just a few examples of the changes that will be occurring at the same time as the market effects of climate change. It may, therefore, be difficult to isolate the effects of climate change from other market influences, and it may be difficult to develop and implement specific

adaptation measures in response solely to the market impacts of climate change. (Williamson et al. 2009: 46)

We conjecture that there are at least two major ways in which climate warming will impact employment. First, and over the longer term, climatic changes could lead to a shift in the geographical range of different forest species and hence the location of commercially viable wood harvesting and processing (Perez-Garcia et al. 2002; Aitken et al. 2008). Parfitt notes that

> an increasing number of scientists [are focusing] on how certain trees will fare in the face of higher temperatures and dramatically altered precipitation patterns. Some tree types will adapt better, and continue to occupy their ecological niches. Others will "migrate" — move south to north or from lower to higher altitudes. And still others will be extirpated, or face localized extinctions. (Parfitt 2010a: 12)

Over time it is expected that the boreal forest in Canada will advance northward into the tundra and that its southern limit may also shift as a result of drier and warmer conditions.

Climate warming is likely to lead to increased risks of forest fires and insect infestations that could also have a significant impact on the distribution of commercially viable supplies of wood fibre for the industry. It will also impact logging operations (Williamson et al. 2009). A significant portion of the forest harvest in Canada occurs in the winter when the ground is frozen. This allows for access to wetlands, reduces soil disturbance and decreases the costs of delivered wood. In short, climate warming could change the geographical distribution of jobs in the sector, lead to the establishment of new forest-based communities further north and the economic demise of some more southerly mill-based communities. While there is a climate science literature that seeks to model likely regional shifts in the geographical range of different forest species (see Williamson et al. 2009), the literature is silent on the impacts of such shifts on future patterns of employment in the forest products industry.

The second major way in which climate warming may impact employment relates to jobs and skill requirements. Although the production of traditional wood and paper products will remain important for the foreseeable future, emergent new wood based products, production methods and processes associated with the shift to a greener economy have the potential to transform the forest products sector and have a significant impact on jobs and skill requirements. Currently, the forest products sector employs people in a wide range of skilled occupations and professions including machinists, mechanics, electricians, carpenters, steam engineers, millwrights, foresters, forest technicians and technologists, chemists, engineers, biologists, economists, administrators and marketers (R.A. Malatest and Associates 2010: 4). These jobs will continue to be required in the continued and traditional processing and manufacturing of lumber, panels and pulp and paper products. However, the introduction of new wood products and processes will generate new skilled employment opportunities. The development of more sophisticated engineered wood products for building construction, the use of wood as an input for bioenergy generation (either wood-fired heat and electricity generation or production of biofuels such as ethanol) and the use of cellulose fibre in a range of new products will all have consequences for training and skill development in the industry.

> The transition currently underway on the manufacturing side of the industry will have a significant impact on the skill sets required by the forest industry of tomorrow. As the focus on emerging technologies in areas such as bioenergy, bioproducts and building systems increases, the industry will require highly trained individuals with the appropriate skills to process this next generation of forest products. (NRCan 2007)

At the same time, the further introduction of computer based technologies into all aspects of the forest industries — from the use of GPS technology in forest management, through the use of laser guided technology to optimize dimensional lumber and minimize the waste in saw mills, to computer controls on paper machines — continues to transform the content of many traditional jobs and to replace formerly low skilled manual work with more skilled work.[3] The 2007 *Annual Report on The State of Canada's Forests*, issued just prior to the onset of the Great Recession, noted that the sector faced "the problem of an aging worker population and a high demand for skilled workers within the forestry sector and other sectors" (NRCan 2007:18–20). Also, there were not enough skilled workers graduating from university forestry programs. The report argued that the forest industry must work to overcome the hurdle of a negative image that dissuades young, skilled workers from wanting to work in the sector. The technological and innovative advancements made in the forest industry — viewed as a low tech, dying sector with minimal opportunities and with minimal concern for environmental issues — are often overlooked. A more recent study stressed that "clearly the key challenge to the sector is going to be in striking a balance between the need to lay-off its workforce during these trying economic times, while remaining a viable option as a career choice for skilled workers" (R.A. Malatest and Associates 2010: 28).[4]

Recognition has been growing of the potential importance of well managed forests to act as net carbon sinks, which in turn represent potential carbon credits that could be used in a cap and trade system. In Canada, and especially in British Columbia, there is increased pressure from alliances of environmental activists and unionized workers in the logging, pulp and paper and solid wood processing industries for a new model of forest management based around management techniques that maximize carbon storage both in the forests and in forest products. In May 2010 a landmark Canadian Boreal Forest Agreement was cosigned by firms represented by the Forest Products Association of Canada (FPAC) and a number of environmental groups. Under the Agreement, FPAC members "commit to the highest environmental standards of forest management" and conservation groups "commit to global recognition and support for FPAC member efforts." Logging is suspended on nearly 29 million hectares of boreal forest to allow development of conservation plans, and the "do not buy" campaigns waged by environmental activist groups will be suspended (Canadian Boreal Forest Agreement Secretariat 2010).

Sound management models could go a considerable way to offsetting GHG emissions elsewhere in the economy, and at the same time, capturing the value of CO_2 in the forest sector could create a stronger, more diversified and more sustainable forest economy. As a recent report from the Canadian Centre for Policy Analysis (CCPA) concluded, "where logging does occur, it is vital that society gets the best possible environmental and economic returns. From a climate change perspective, that means placing carbon storage at the forefront of forest product use" (Parfitt 2010b). Moving to such a model will require much more sophisticated forest management techniques and likely increased employment in silviculture and forest management. The increased focus on forest management could also help offset the negative image of the industry held by younger workers. R.A. Malatest and Associates quote an industry stakeholder as follows:

> Youth are less interested in jobs in the forest products sector. Intensive information campaigning in the 1980s and 1990s portraying the forest products sector as a clear-cutting, environmentally destructive industry has tainted the image of the industry in the eyes of young Canadians. However, the current reality of the forest products industry in Canada is one of ever-greener practices and increasing environmental stewardship. New, innovative practices and products such as biomass products and bio-energy are providing green, carbon neutral, forest-based alternatives to traditional carbon-positive fossil fuel-based energy and forestry stakeholders are looking at ways to expand the interest of the sector in these new directions. This reality needs to be communicated to young Canadians. (R.A. Malatest and Associates 2010: 29)

In summary, there is virtually no existing research that focuses on the potential impact that climate warming will have on employment and jobs in the Canadian forest products industry. Recent labour market research that focuses on the forest products industry has been preoccupied with managing the consequences of the serious contraction that has occurred in the industry since 2005. Research is urgently required to identify the impact of the move toward a greener economy on employment trends and skill requirements in the forest products industry. Areas in which research is required include:

- What will be the impact of the move toward greening in the various subsectors of the forestry products industry (forest management, logging, solid wood processing, pulp and paper and manufactured wood products) on both employment levels and skill requirements, province by province?
- Can such impacts be easily differentiated from changes in employment due to other political economic transformation?
- Can models developed in the climate science literature to predict regional shifts in the geographical range of different forest species be used to estimate the impacts of such shifts on future regional patterns of employment in the forest products industry?
- What examples of best practice exist in Canada and internationally concerning the funding, implementation and outcomes of greening skills requirements in the sectors of the forestry products industry?
- What international and Canadian examples exist for aiding forestry communities in adapting to the restructuring of the industry?

Notes

1. In total, Canada's forests cover 402 million hectares and represent 10 percent of the world's total forest cover, including about 30 percent of the world's boreal forest and more than 25 percent of its temperate rainforest. For carbon accounting purposes, Canada's managed forest is defined as covering 236 million hectares (Natural Resources Canada n.d.b).
2. Although some are now a little dated, there are a number of excellent analyses of the political economy of forestry in Canada, especially of the industry in British Columbia. See, for example, Marchak (1983), Howlett (2001), Hayter (2000) and Barnes and Hayter (1997).
3. For an early discussion of the transformation of work within pulp and paper and the replacement of workers' tacit knowledge with more codified technical knowledge, see Zuboff (1988).
4. On this point, see also the 2008 document, "A Workforce Strategy For Alberta's Forest Industry" (Edmonton: Alberta Employment and Immigration).

8. TOURISM, CLIMATE CHANGE AND THE MISSING WORKER

Uneven Impacts, Institutions and Response

Steven Tufts

For over two decades, researchers have examined the issue of climate change and its present and future impacts on tourism related activity. Tourism researchers based in Canada, especially a group from the University of Waterloo, have been at the forefront of international studies on the implications for tourism as climate change inevitably affects tourist receiving and generating regions, as well as the modes of travel between places (Scott 2008; Wall et al. 1986; Wall and Badke 1994; Scott and Beckman 2010). Researchers have also examined the contribution of tourism activity to global warming. It is now estimated that tourism activity is responsible for approximately 5 percent of global greenhouse gas (GHG) emissions, but such emissions are increasing as air travel expands in emerging markets (see UNWTO-UNEP 2008).

This chapter reviews recent literature on the impact of climate change mitigation and adaptation on tourism related employment and work in Canada. Statistics Canada estimates that tourism generates over 600,000 jobs in the country and remains a growth sector (Table 8.1). While Canada is commonly believed to be a substantial "winner" as climate change affects the global tourism market, the case is much more complex and contradictory than a simple benefit from extended warm seasons might suggest (Deutsche Bank Research 2008; Hamilton et al. 2005; Scott et al. 2004). The impacts of climate change will be experienced differently from region to region depending not only on local variations in climate change but also on changing competitive contexts. Of particular interest is the wide range of possible impacts climate change will have on employment in this diverse sector. I begin with a brief outline of the sources used and the research questions framing the chapter, followed by a brief discussion of tourism related industries and the present competitive environment. I then offer a detailed assessment of the research on the effects of climate change on tourism related employment and the response by labour to these changes.

Despite the range of potential impacts on employment and long-established research linking tourism activity to the environment, workers have largely been absent from analysis as active agents of climate change mitigation and adaptation. This is the case in several "state of the research" pieces in articles and books. For example, Dubois and Ceron's (2006) attempt to set an agenda for research on climate change and tourism completely neglects any role for workers as stakeholders and does not include the lack of knowledge of employment impacts among several of the identified research gaps. Similarly, Scott and Beckman (2010) do not mention employment impacts beyond nonquantified job losses and wage reductions. A recent (and perhaps most comprehensive) treatment of climate change and tourism to date largely leaves any mitigation responsibilities for behavioural change to managerial innovation, new technologies and consumer education (Gossling 2011). Workers and their institutions are conspicuously absent from the discussions.

This is disappointing given the importance of tourism related employment to postindustrial economic development and developing economies in the Global South (often stated a priori as justification for research on the impacts of climate change). Further, there is no clear indication of whether a "high road" or "low road" will be followed as labour markets adjust. The chapter concludes with a call to put workers at the centre of the development of tourism policy in responding to climate change.

TOURISM RELATED WORK AND CLIMATE CHANGE: NEW QUESTIONS

The link between tourism and the environment has been studied for over a century, dating back to the earliest recognition of the importance of specific "climatic assets" that draw people toward destinations (e.g., alpine regions, warm climate seasides). Not until the postwar period, however, did researchers begin to link tourism to broader processes of environmental change. In Canada, researchers have noted the impacts of recreational activities on natural ecosystems since the 1970s. In the 1980s, the positive and negative environmental impacts of tourism were studied, paving the way for research on sustainable tourism practices and "ecotourism" development in the 1990s. By the early 2000s, however, the impacts of global environmental change — including but not limited to climate change — on tourism became a major focus (for a complete discussion see Gossling and Hall 2006). In the specific case of climate change and tourism research, Daniel Scott and colleagues classify the scholarly evolution of the English language literature into four stages: a "formative stage" in the 1960s and 1970s when only a few reports focused on the need for accurate climate data to assist recreational planning and development; a period of "stagnation" in the early 1980s as the focus shifted to other areas of environmental concern (e.g., air pollution); the "emergence" of research in the late 1980s and 1990s that predated the formation of the Intergovernmental Panel on Climate Change (IPCC); and lastly a recent "maturation" period of more detailed research over the last decade "advancing understanding" between climate change research and the complex vulnerabilities in the sector (Scott et al. 2005). Despite the progress made in the literature, it is interesting to note the lack of attention to employment impacts.

In order to assess the links between tourism employment and climate change, the literature examined for this chapter included over two hundred English language references with some relationship to three primary research questions:

1. What are the present and future impacts of climate change on tourism related employment in Canada in terms of overall job growth and geographical variations in employment?
2. What are the present and future impacts of climate change on tourism related work in terms of changing labour processes, work organization, skill and training requirements and labour market support?
3. What has been the present response by employers and workers to the risks and challenges of climate change for tourism?

The above questions were used to guide the review and analysis. Overall, the research is a rich inventory of the existing and future challenges climate change poses to tourism, but there is a paucity of research detailing the impacts of employment and work and the responses of labour. Given the lack of research addressing the specific questions, several of the findings emerge as speculative and call for future research.

TOURISM AND TOURISM EMPLOYMENT DEFINED

A major barrier to analysis of the impacts of climate change on tourism related employment is the chaotic conceptualization of what actually constitutes the sector. Given the diverse inputs required to support tourism, ranging from fuel production for air travel to foodstuffs for restaurants and linens for hotels, direct and indirect tourism employment is substantial. Further, induced employment (e.g., jobs created through multiplier effects) can also be vital to tourism dependent communities and regional economies (Frechtling and Horvath 1999). As a result, it is perhaps too complex to quantify accurately the full impact of climate change on *all* tourism employment, especially given the multiple scenarios of locally variable temperature and precipitation changes. This discussion is therefore limited to the impacts on major tourism related sectors as identified in a range of quantitative measures, such as

Tourism Satellite Accounts, an occasional Statistics Canada report on trends in the Canadian tourism industry. The major sectors are transportation, accommodation, food services and travel services. Other tourism related industries that depend on both tourists and residents (e.g., recreation and cultural services) are not a primary focus here. Some indirect and induced tourism related employment is covered in other chapters in this book (i.e., construction, transportation).

In terms of tourism employment, it is also important to differentiate between tourism generated employment, which measures employment in a sector resulting directly from tourism (international and domestic) and tourism related employment, which quantifies all employment in sectors servicing tourists and residents (Wall and Mathieson 2006; Lieper 1999). For example, tourism generated accommodation and food and beverage services employment in Canada is reported to be approximately 300,000 while total employment in these two sectors is now over 1 million (see Table 8.1).

Table 8.1 Tourism Generated Employment in Canada (2004)

Tourism Related Sector	Employment (000s)	% Total Employment
Transportation	73.3	12.0
Accommodation	161.6	26.5
Food and Beverage Services	145.3	23.8
Other Tourism Industries[a]	110.0	18.0
Other Non-Tourism Industries[b]	120.5	19.7
Total	610.6	100.0

[a] *Other tourism industries include recreational and entertainment services, travel services, etc.*
[b] *Includes industries where employment is generated by tourism activity (e.g., motor vehicle parts, retail groceries, etc.*
Source: Statistics Canada 2009a

Tourism Sector Profile

Climate change adaptation and mitigation are processes that are dependent upon several contingent factors that vary among tourism related industries and geographical locations with different competitive contexts. For example, tourism agencies are less vulnerable to climate change as they can continue to book travel away from vulnerable areas, while hotels located in such areas are not mobile (see Simpson et al. 2008). Overall, tourism in Canada continues to contribute significantly to economic activity. Using data from Tourism Satellite Accounts, the World Travel and Tourism Council forecasts that tourism activity in Canada for 2022 will directly and indirectly contribute over $100 billion to the economy, approximately 4.4 percent of Canada's gross domestic product (GDP) and will directly generate 320,000 jobs in 2022, approximately 1.8 percent of total employment (WTTC 2012). Presently,

Canadians spend more abroad than they receive from tourists, creating consistent travel deficits. Canada's travel deficit has been over $6 billion annually since the middle of the last decade. In 2004, Canada dropped out of the top ten international tourist destinations as U.S. tourists stayed at home. Between 1998 and 2007, day trippers from the U.S. decreased by almost 50 percent and vehicle entries declined by 40 percent between 2003 and 2007, largely due to border congestion and the high dollar (TIAC 2009). Declining numbers of international visitors to Canada (who largely come from the U.S.) are a concern as tourism is an important export industry.

While overall growth is expected for the sector, there are several challenges in the current competitive environment in Canada. A full discussion is beyond the scope of the chapter, but there are some broad challenges that are directly linked to the issue of climate change. The first broad challenge lies in the way many tourism experiences are "packaged." Mass package holidays (resorts, cruises) are still a significant part of many tourist experiences and will continue to cater to aging tourists in Western markets, but contemporary tourists travel less to the same destination, resulting in fewer return visits. Ecotourism continues to be one of the most contradictory forms of tourism, particularly in those cases where it offers a "sustainable" tourism experience that is still dependent upon GHG emitting air travel (see Nowicka 2007). And then there are mega-events such as the 2010 Winter Olympics in Vancouver. While these are mass tourism events, there is pressure by tourists and residents to make such large-scale projects environmentally responsible.

The second broad challenge is external "negative events" that have also limited growth in Canada. International travel was reduced in Canada following 9/11, and in 2003, Toronto was devastated by the issue of a World Travel Organization travel warning in the midst of the SARS outbreak (Tufts 2009). While these events are not related to climate change, the resulting "shocks" serve as test cases for tourism economies that are vulnerable to extreme weather events associated with climate change.

A third competitive challenge is a number of state regulations that are the subject of industry lobbying efforts. First of these is that, despite the growth of GHG emissions from air travel, tourism industry associations claim that air ticket prices in Canada are too high, largely due to structural costs (airport fees, excise fuel taxes, security charges, etc.) (TIAC 2008b). There is also pressure on the federal government to continue to expand the number of Open Skies agreements with the E.U. and other regions to increase air passenger travel. The Tourism Industry Association of Canada (TIAC) also claims that there needs to be significant improvements in intermodal transportation in Canada, including large investments in high speed rail (ibid.: iv). And finally, the state's climate change policy poses a challenge to the "branding" of Canada's international image to tourists abroad. As TIAC notes, Canada's international image remains very much associated with the pristine outdoors and natural landscapes. Canada's reputation as being openly hostile to global agreements aimed at reducing GHG emissions (e.g., Kyoto) and the development of "dirty oil" in Alberta's tar sands contradict efforts to "position Canada as a green and sustainable tourism destination" promoting parks and green industry certifications (ibid: 19–20).

Snapshot of Tourism Workers in Canada

Despite these limitations, employment in key tourism related sectors continues to grow, and the industry expects labour shortages (even in the midst of a global recession) for certain segments of the tourism sector (CTHRC 2009b; see Figure 8.1 and Table 8.2). TIAC and other industry associations (Canadian Restaurant and Foodservice Association [CRFA] and the Hotel Association of Canada [HAC]) also continue to lobby aggressively for expansion of Canada's Temporary Foreign Workers (TFW) Program and to "streamline" the TFW program and the labour market approval process to expedite applications (NTTC 2010: 44). A brief statistical profile of the five major tourism related sectors and major occupations portrays a diverse, complex and segmented workforce (Table 8.3). In terms of gender segmentation, women dominate accommodation and food services but are less likely to be employed in transportation services, which are dominated by males. Similarly, recreation and entertainment services employ relatively low numbers of females and persons born outside Canada. Younger workers are concentrated in food and beverage services where the average hourly wages are lowest and the prevalence of part-time work highest.

Figure 8.1 Tourism Related Sector Employment in Canada, 1997–2006 (in thousands)

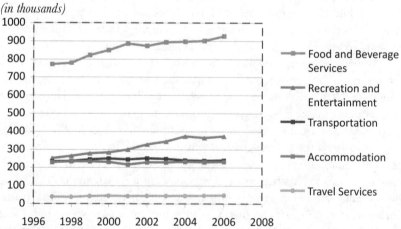

Source: Statistics Canada 2008

Table 8.2 Forecast of Labour Demand 2025

Sector	Potential Labour Demand 2025	Project Labour Shortage 2025
Tourism Sector	2,200,228	256,669
Accommodation	293,559	17,091
Food and Beverage Services	1,162,484	172,258
Recreation and Entertainment Services	386,745	42,795
Transportation Services	300,677	24,828
Travel Services	56,763	-231

Sources: CTHRC 2008 and 2009a

Table 8.3 Profile of Selected Tourism Related Sectoral Employment by Employee Characteristics, Canada, 2006

	% Female	Age group ratio 15–44/ 45+	% Born in Canada	% visible minority	% full-time	Average hourly wage (2006)	% change in hourly wage since 1997	% union member employ-ees[a]
Total tourism industry	54.6	2.9	79.6	18.8	61.4	17.95	29.2	11.5
Transportation	29.5	1.1	79.5	17.4	82.2	31.61	25.1	32.9
Accommodation	62.5	1.9	77.4	19.0	71.9	17.21	48.5	16.3
Food and beverage services	60.1	4.8	78.3	22.7	51.1	12.48	33.7	2.6
Recreation and Entertainment	48.5	2.7	87.2	10.9	61.1	20.58	20.2	13.1
Travel Services	68.2	2.0	65.8	22.9	80.1	21.56	34.3	5.0

Sources: Statistics Canada 2008; CTHRC 2009 (Note: Census Data does not include unionization data. This data is taken from the Statistics Canada Labour Force Survey.)

Differences also exist in terms of the largest occupational groups (Table 8.4). The occupations with the highest percentage of female workers are cashiers and light-duty cleaners, while only 6.7 percent of taxi drivers are women. Taxi drivers and light-duty cleaners are, however, more likely to be a visible minority and born outside Canada. There are also differences in education levels by occupation. A taxi driver is almost three times more likely to have a university degree than a bus driver. There are also several occupations where a high percentage of workers are attending school, especially those occupations employing younger workers.

Table 8.4 Demographic Characteristics of Main Tourism Related Occupations, 2006

Occupation (NAIC)	No. of workers	% of tourism-related occupations	% female	% visible minority	% born outside Canada	% university certificate or degree	% attending school
Food counter attendants, kitchen helpers and related occupations	225,535	13.6%	62.2	22.1	22.0	4.5	53.7
Food and beverage servers	177,880	10.7%	79.5	15.1	25.2	9.0	41.7
Cooks	140,370	8.5%	37.4	26.1	29.6	3.5	30.6
Restaurant and food service managers	91,105	5.5%	47.2	26.6	36.1	14.8	9.1
Bus drivers and subway and other transit operators	66,930	4.0%	36.4	10.3	18.9	5.5	5.3
Cashiers	57,770	3.5%	83.4	31	27.6	5.5	52.8
Light duty cleaners	47,160	2.8%	80.2	28.5	64.6	5.6	17.2
Program leaders and instructors in recreation, sport and fitness	41,725	2.5%	61.3	9.3	12.1	19.3	52.1
Taxi and limousine drivers and chauffeurs	38,735	2.3%	6.7	48.8	58.3	14.3	6.3
Bartenders	36,185	2.2%	65.2	7.7	10.2	8.7	31.8

Source: CTHRC 2009

Last, there are important differences in the percentage of workers who are union members. While the transportation sector has a higher percentage than the Canadian average, all other sectors have far less union presence, with food and beverage services (the largest sector) having minimal representation. The lack of organized labour is an important factor in the ability of workers to voice concerns in labour market policy, resist specific employer adaptation initiatives and advance worker developed alternatives.

High Roads and Low Roads: Response and Organizational Change in the Sector

Overall, tourism related employment outperforms job growth in most industries. In terms of response to a rapidly changing competitive context, there are a range of actions by firms and local communities that have a direct impact on employment and work in the sector. In a recent review of human resources in the U.K., these responses were characterized as polarized, with some evidence of increased professionalization of tourism work and skills training. At the same time, the competitive global pressures have seen the emergence of marginalized labour (often undocumented) in hotels and a deprofessionalization of some occupations such as airline stewards in low cost carriers (Baum 2007).

Here we see parallels with competing high and low road strategies in North America's hospitality sector. *Industry at a Crossroads*, a 2006 report produced by a task force commissioned by UNITE HERE Local 75, detailed the union's vision for Toronto's hospitality workers. The report was commissioned following the 2003 SARS outbreak, which displaced thousands of precarious hospitality workers (Tufts 2009; UNITE HERE 2006). The vision was largely inspired by the study of hotel work by the Working for America Institute (WAI), which similarly called for a high road model that builds "an economy based on skills, innovation, opportunity, sustainability and equitably shared prosperity rather than on low-road practices that lower living and working standards and weaken communities" (WAI 2003; Tufts 2010). Major recommendations of the Toronto study included: living wages and benefits for all hotel workers; desegregation of ethnically segmented labour markets; the right to union protection; comprehensive training opportunities; reasonable workloads; work-family life balance; and adequate social supports such as affordable housing and access to public transit.

Few employers, however, are close to implementing these goals. Most tourism related industries face structural impediments and competitive pressures that limit their ability to adopt this model (Riley et al. 2002). For example, many small and medium sized enterprises (SMEs) in the sector (e.g., restaurants, bed and breakfast operations, local tour guides) do not have the capacity to provide training. Relative ease of entry into the market also creates significant competition, lowering wages. While industry and government associations are active in providing minimal training tools for employers, a primary lobbying focus seems to be on increasing the labour supply through temporary foreign workers rather than investments in skills and productivity improvements. The status quo for most of the industry seems to be some skills building capacity with a continued dependence on marginalized segments of the labour market (i.e., immigrants, grey labour, young workers, etc.).

CLIMATE CHANGE AND TOURISM: IMPACTS AND RESPONSES

Despite the regional specificity of climate change, economists have attempted to model the impacts of climate change on tourism flows and the national GDP, using advanced economic equilibrium models (Berrittella et al. 2006; Biganon et al. 2008). There is agreement that Canada (and other high latitude, developed economies) will perform well under different climate change scenarios. In fact, a map produced by the World Tourism Organization (UNWTO) depicting the regions most vulnerable to climate change does not highlight Canada at all (Simpson et al. 2008). But this depiction of Canada as winner in the case of climate change and tourism is limited to national scale analysis. A simple review of studies and recent developments indicates several regional hotspots where tourism is threatened, even if tourism flows increase overall. These hotspots include communities facing pine beetle infestations in northern British Columbia, rural areas facing a decline in snow covered hill and mountain slopes for skiing, and large urban destinations experiencing a higher frequency of heat waves in the peak tourist season. Tourism related industries will be able to exercise some capacity to adapt even in those areas that are considered the most vulnerable. For example, it is argued that technological advances in snowmaking will compensate for reduced snow in even the most severe climate change scenarios, mediating the impacts (Scott et al. 2008). Similarly, golf courses and other summer attractions developed near ski hills will benefit from lengthened seasons but may be stressed by competition for scarce water and increased pestilence (Scott and Jones 2007).

While there has been significant and increasingly sophisticated research on the effects of climate change on communities, there are too many complex and contradictory trends to make generalized statements for the entire country. Researchers, however, are confident that climate change will bring significant and localized change to tourism economies. While this makes any definitive statement on the implications for employment and work impossible, it does provide a framework for discussing the range of employment impacts. Further, the responses to these changes can follow different trajectories, some being high road and others low road as discussed in greater detail later in the chapter.

The impacts of climate change on tourism can be divided into three categories: first order impacts are those changes that directly affect tourism activity (e.g., warmer winters); second order impacts are those that result from mitigation and adaptation strategies that are directly related to tourism (e.g., increase in air travel taxation); and third order impacts are those broad aspects of climate change that affect all economic activity (e.g., declines in overall economic output reducing travel expenditures). The possible high and low road responses to these impacts are discussed below. While most of these responses are presently conjectural, there are a few precedents that may be relevant to future action.

First Order Impacts

First order impacts are those changes to the climate that will directly affect tourism activities. In many cases, they will be real changes, but it is important to recognize that mere perceptual changes can be just as important, such as the belief that skiing has declined in a region when the case may be very different (Bicknell and McManus 2006).

Warmer and Shorter Winter Seasons

Impacts of shorter winter tourism seasons are dependent firstly on the severity of the climate change scenario. Dan Scott and his colleagues have examined the potential impacts on days available for seasonal activities (skiing, water boating, golf and hiking) under a variety of climate change scenarios (Scott and McBoyle 2007). At the most obvious level, just as specific tourism activity is correlated to the length of the season, so is the amount of labour required to deliver the required services. The quantitative amount of labour is, however, only one consideration, as there will also be shifts in the types of jobs and skill requirements. For example, in the case of winter skiing in Canada, snowmaking may become increasingly important and in some cases, new north facing slopes may need to be developed in resorts. There will also be great regional variations in these impacts, as ski hills in Quebec and Ontario will be affected at different rates than larger high altitude resorts in Western Canada (which may receive more tourists arriving by air from northeastern North America and Europe). This will require new skills ranging from mechanics to service snowmaking machines to persons with expertise in cloud seeding. There may also be shifts in the services provided at resorts as they turn to the summer season for greater revenue. Any instability will inevitably put pressure on wage rates and demand even greater flexibility from an already largely precarious workforce.

Longer, Hotter and Wetter Peak Seasons

Naturally, shorter winters mean a lengthened summer season. As stated above, this can lead to greater labour demand for services such as golf courses and many other recreational activities. Longer seasons may also benefit aboriginal communities, which have increasingly engaged in tourism related development. However, there are many other counter trends related to hotter and, in some regions, wetter summers. In hot areas with decreased precipitation, reduced water levels and water quality has significant implications for boating and other water related activities, reducing the demand for marine based service labour. Other effects such as urban heat waves may also shift tourists to inside activities. If temperature changes make cities less desired locations for tourists and residents, demand for tourism related workers will likely decrease.

In areas with decreased water levels, new skills will be required, such as groundskeepers able to care for plants requiring less water. Water conservation in resorts will require training and education of workers as to appropriate water saving strategies and awareness about water quality issues.

Extreme Weather Events

After the experience of SARS, the vulnerability of Canada's tourism industry to negative events became readily apparent (Tufts 2003). Different regions are vulnerable to different kinds of extreme weather — for example, the drought and forest fire prone areas such as Kelowna in Western Canada. Large forest fire events can threaten infrastructure and lead to longer-term decline in demand. Similarly, increased floods or coastal erosion due to greater storm events will have an impact even in a largely continental climate. In severe cases, extreme events can displace an entire community's tourist industry and workforce, not only from their jobs but their homes as well. The impact of Hurricane Katrina on New Orleans' low wage service workers resulted in UNITE HERE establishing a relief fund to assist displaced hospitality workers.

Of particular concern is the ability of low wage workers to weather storms without adequate state support. It is unlikely that tourism related employers will be able to employ workers in a disaster environment, and unemployment insurance may be inadequate if significant rebuilding of industry related infrastructure is required. Over the longer term, there is also the concern that financial pressures on firms due to increased insurance premiums in specific destinations will force employers to reduce other costs such as labour.

Changes in Flora and Fauna

As climates change there will undoubtedly be shifts in plant and animal life. Invasive species thriving in warmer climates can have a significant impact on natural parks and other outdoor tourist destinations. The mountain pine beetle infestation in B.C. is an extreme example that has affected parks in Canada. While infested areas may be less attractive to tourists, in some cases it may also be necessary to restrict areas to tourists in order to prevent the spread or manage the infestation through controlled burns. However, as part of the economic recovery strategy, the federal government has invested in economic diversification programs that are turning to enhanced local tourism to absorb displaced forest workers in towns such as Fraser Lake and Quesnel (Western Economic Diversification Canada 2008).

Changes in local wildlife will also impact tourism activity. While the threats of polar bear and whale extinction are of concern to wildlife watching industries, wildlife may become more abundant in some regions. Increased productivity of fish stocks in northern Ontario, for example, may lead to increased angling. In a discussion of the impacts of climate change in northern Ontario, Browne and Hunt (2007) note the potential for increased fish productivity while stocks in southern Ontario are less certain to benefit. Infectious disease spread by insect migrations may also impact tourists and tourist workers. The continuing threat of the West Nile virus is one example (Ceron and Dubois 2005). Tourism workers exposed to tourists may be particularly vulnerable to such diseases.

Second Order Impacts

Second order impacts are those arising from mitigation and adaptive responses that affect tourism workers. It is here that regulatory processes (mandatory
and voluntary) are engaged. While reduction of GHGs is perhaps most often
discussed in terms of reduced air travel and consequent decrease in tourism
demand, this is only one of a range of second order impacts.

Reduction of Air Travel CO_2 Emissions

Internationally, air transport is responsible for approximately 12 percent of
all transport related GHG emissions, less than 2 percent of all GHGs (Stern
2007). Emissions related to air travel are, however, the fastest growing tourism related emissions, despite claims of significant technological advances
in fuel efficiency (Scott et al. 2010).

For air transportation workers, changes in air travel regulation and practices will undoubtedly affect work and employment. First, there are immediate
questions around strategies that would reduce demand and/or access to air
travel. It is important to recognize, however, that air travel is predicted to
increase on the next thirty years, especially from regional emerging markets
such as South East Asia.

Surcharges and taxation would slightly decrease demand as will mandatory carbon offsets. Proposals such as the International Air Passenger
Adaptation Levy (IAPAL) — emerging as a means of collecting revenues
from airline ticket purchases to be distributed to climate change vulnerable
regions — may increase the costs of flying but are unlikely to reduce demand
significantly if implemented. Similarly, even if largely voluntary carbon
sequestering programs (e.g., carbon offsets) were regulated, it is unclear
whether they would lower demand significantly, especially if airlines were
able to continue their existing process of deprofessionalizing the industry,
shifting it toward a low cost model.

More radical proposals such as air travel rationing (e.g., limited number of
air miles per person or region) and shifts to alternative modes of travel are less
likely. First, rationing alternatives would themselves become commodified as a
market for flight rations developed. As for other alternatives (e.g., transoceanic
ships, high speed rail and even airships), there are simply no adequate sub-
stitutes in terms of speed, costs or fuel efficiency at this time (Monbiot 2006).

The likely efforts to reduce emissions will focus on fuel and logistic
efficiencies. Air fleet renewal and the development of new fuels will be involved, but there are technological limits to such gains. If the international
air travel industry is to meet its aspirational carbon reduction targets, airports
themselves will also have to find ways to gain air traffic efficiency to increase
load factors (Scott et al. 2010). Beside the downward pressure on wages to
compensate for increased climate change charges, airline and airport workers
may see further intensification in their work.

Reduction of Ground and Water Transport CO_2 Emissions
While air travel is estimated to become the largest source of tourism related GHGs, cars are the primary source of tourism related emissions at present. Day trips and extended travel in cars will undoubtedly continue. Again, fuel and energy efficiencies are held to be the primary means of reducing emissions not only for cars but for cruise ships as well. However, real reductions in GHGs will require intermodal shifts to other forms of transit. Specifically, TIAC advocates the development of high speed rail in the main urban corridors and greater development of mass public transit in cities as key components of a sustainable tourism that reduces emissions and insulates tourism demand from external fluctuations in gas prices. The implications for workers are again related to broader sectoral shifts away from private to public transit systems.

Increased Energy Efficiencies in the Accommodation Sector
Accommodation services and other facilities are major consumers of energy. A significant strategy for greening the accommodation sector is the refurbishment of existing properties and the development of new properties with the most recent energy efficient systems. These range from LEED-certified building standards to "smart rooms," which reduce energy consumption through features such as reducing lighting when no motion is detected. Such refurbishment has implications for job creation in the construction and engineering sectors.

There are, however, contradictory processes in hospitality and other services. These consumer spaces are becoming increasingly luxurious as tourism service providers seek to give tourists an experience that is qualitatively different from the functional bedroom in the home (Gossling 2011; Scott et al. 2010). Large screen TVs and sheets with a high thread count that require more energy to clean will consume greater amounts of energy. In fact, the impact of such luxuries (termed "amenity creep" by hotel workers' unions) has already proven to increase the workload of room attendants.

Green(wash)ing and Rebranding the Tourism Industry
The greening of the tourism industry has a long history. The emergence of ecotourism itself as an entire market segment in the 1990s is a response to demands for environmentally and socially sustainable experiences. The long debate about what actually constitutes ecotourism and the contradictory nature of the term continues in recent research on climate change (Nowicka 2007; Scott and Beckman 2010). Prior to now-popular certification practices, hotels adopted energy saving programs such as requests to multinight guests to forego the daily changing of sheets. While this would have saved the firm money and labour, there is no evidence that any savings were passed on to workers in terms of absolute workload reduction.

Presently, there is significant pressure on tourism firms to pursue some sort of environmental certification. Green certification processes remain uneven and the impacts on the labour process unclear. For example, the Hotel Association of Canada (HAC) has recently endorsed the Green Key certification system (HAC 2009). Green Key is a significant certification process but is completely voluntary and privately run. Furthermore, Green Key's tiered rating is granted after a short self-assessment by the property and the submission of an annual membership fee. Eco certification processes by second party assessors (let alone independent third parties) are less common. Such systems will inevitably leave the industry open to accusations of greenwashing their product. While calls are made for national or even international regulatory systems, they have not yet been developed. At the same time, there is job creation in environmental industries administering these voluntary offsets for travel, which must be considered as part of climate change's creative destruction process in labour markets.

On a larger scale, the greening of the industry is related to rebranding efforts to see Canada as a green destination and to capitalize on decades of iconography of Canada as a natural location with pristine environments. It is difficult to shift the established image to one of urbanism. Failure to maintain some sense of nature in the popular image of Canada is argued to be harmful to the industry and its job creation potential.

Third Order Impacts
Broad political and economic impacts of climate change will also affect tourism in Canada. These impacts include overall declines in economic output in Canada and abroad as well as political unrest that impedes tourism flows.

Economic Contraction
Overall economic contraction will inevitably reduce incomes and tourism expenditures inside and outside of Canada. If resources are shifted toward food production or imports in emerging markets, there will be limits on the growth of global tourism demand. While state transfers to depressed regions may limit some of these effects, large-scale economic decline will limit their effectiveness. Massive wealth transfers from rich to poor countries in order to assist vulnerable nations are also unlikely under current political and economic systems. The result may be increased competition for a smaller than anticipated tourism market. Increased competition will also lead employers to pursue low cost labour.

Political Instability and Climate Change Migration
It is argued that the conflict in the Sudan may be the first climate change war, given that decreased availability of water is leading to migration. If anticipated growth in climate change refugees in the Global South occurs,

there could be greater pressure to regulate borders. Any restrictions in travel will decrease the flow of tourists. Furthermore, any restrictions in the flow of migrants threatens the tourism sector's current strategy as a major employer of migrant workers.

HIGH ROAD OR LOW ROAD RESPONSE TO CLIMATE CHANGE?

Given the silences in the tourism/climate change literature, the above analysis of the impact of climate change on employment and work in tourism related industries highlights the research that has yet to be done. It is difficult to examine the response by labour market actors when so little has been studied or conceptualized. UNITE HERE, the largest hospitality workers' union in North America, has yet to formulate a position on climate change. Other industrial (general) unions with a presence in the sector have limited most of their policy to their core sectors (i.e., manufacturing and green industrial production). For example, the Canadian Auto Workers (CAW) represents workers in many sectors including transit and air travel, but they simply call for airlines to invest in more fuel-efficient aircraft, improved logistics and shifts to mass public transit (CAW 2007).

Whether the sector experiences systemic instability because of climate change or the processes of adaptation to climate change create their own instability, labour market adjustment is unavoidable in the sector and indeed is underway. A low road approach will simply rely on creative destruction in markets, with firms and workers exiting and entering to meet new demands (e.g., closures of ski hills and the expansion of golf courses). Even short periods of adjustment require some support for workers, and the current employment insurance system in Canada simply is not geared to low wage service workers who qualify for lower benefits and are forced to find new employment quickly (Tufts 2009). A high road path, which would reintegrate tourism workers into new jobs, would involve increased income supports and subsidies for training to acquire new tourism related skills such as snowmaking or even skills for non tourism related sectors.

It is possible to engage in an exercise that examines juxtaposed trajectories for the response to the challenges and impact of climate change on tourism related work. Here, we compare low road responses, mostly associated with "business as usual" and the status quo, and high road responses, which require both higher levels of state and institutional stimulus and regulation and new sites for creative intervention on the part of the labour market actors (Table 8.5).

A low road approach will continue to rely on increased flexibility in a sector with already highly flexible and precarious employment relationships, given the seasonal nature of tourism. Tourism sector employers are actually positioned to weather storms and economic contractions related to

Table 8.5 High Road versus Low Road Response to Climate Change Impacts on Work

Climate Change and...	Low Road Response	High Road Response
Wage levels	Precarious low wage service work model High levels of anti-union firm behaviour	Living wage for tourism workers Employer neutrality in unionization campaigns Changes in state regulations to allow increased union density
Employment relationship and working conditions	Hyper flexibility in labour markets Intensification of work to meet "green" standards	Employment security within sector Limit impacts of "greening" on job levels and labour processes
Dependence on foreign workers	Increase reliance on temporary/undocumented migrants Persistent labour market segmentation	Pathways to normalized status for immigrant workers Equity in hiring and promotion practices Hiring halls for (re)entry of older tourism workers into the labour market and local youth training strategies
Skills development and "greening" of tourism work and workers	Minimal instruction in low-emission work practices Labour-industry partnership and reliance on Reliance on third party private providers of "green" training and curriculum Voluntary self-assessment certification (e.g., Green-Key Global) Individualization of action and selection of workplace "eco champions"	Advanced understanding climate change and its impacts on work for all workers Partnerships with labour-management and public post-secondary institutions Development of international standards versus voluntary CSR green labour standards Joint labour-management "green committees" assessing skills needs and programs
Labour market adjustment	Unmanaged "creative destruction" in tourism-related industries Limited EI support and programs skills upgrading programs	Income supports for displaced tourism workers Subsidized training for "new" tourism activities and exit from the sector
Social investment and support for workers	Increased privatization of transit expansion Workplace commuting allowances	Increased subsidization of public transit for all workers/tourists Transferable workplace benefits

climate change because they are not burdened with pension legacies or other longer-term commitments to workers. Presently, tourism related services have integrated global low wage supplies of labour into their human resources practices and have increasingly lobbied to increase labour supply through temporary foreign worker programs. This practice will likely intensify labour market segmentation by race and gender.

The greening of the sector will undoubtedly continue to be pursued, but the impact of employer directed strategies on workers will vary. At present, the high degree of self-assessed greenwashing and minimal instruction in sustainable environmental practices provided by third party services and industry associations will not greatly improve the skills base of the workforce (TIAC 2008a). Human resource strategies that simply select "eco champions" in management to implement top down strategies and identify better practices are also less likely to find long-lasting success. There is, however, some evidence that a higher road may be taken in response to climate change. In terms of wage levels, pressures to reduce labour costs as a means of adaptation will be countered only by changes in labour supply and collective bargaining. While union density is lower than the Canadian average in all tourism related sectors except transportation, some sectors such as accommodation have been targeted by unions, and standards have likely been improved through recent union campaigns.

Overall, however, unions have a weak presence in the sector and will have to increase their power and presence to play a significant role in climate change adaptation and mitigation. Living wage campaigns and the expansion of neutrality agreements (i.e., agreements that limit employer resistance to organizing) at national and global scales may allow this but only in the medium to long-term without change to existing labour regulations (see Tufts 2007).

Here, it is apparent that state intervention will be required to restructure current immigration policy and establish greater equity in hiring practices. Regulation of labour markets through the establishment of hiring halls that can place dislocated workers with new employers and training centres for young workers will also require greater union and state involvement to break the existing patterns and practices.

State involvement in providing public infrastructure and social supports will also be central to the adoption of a high road model. Shifts to public transit could continue to expand with higher fares and lower subsidies or enhanced state support. The Tourism Industry Association of Canada (2008a) has suggested that employers give employees flexible commuting allowances, which reward carpoolers and workers who take public transit to work. In Toronto, UNITE HERE Local 75 has negotiated a subsidized transit pass program for workers. While this program is successful, it does potentially challenge transit systems as they can lead to greater ridership with lower revenues (as employers purchase passes for workers at bulk rates). A high road approach by the state, however, would include increased subsidies for public transit for all workers and tourists.

Given the flexible nature of the sector, the state could also increase the transferability of social benefits. For example, eligibility for extended employment insurance benefits in times of crisis would benefit workers in the sector and allow employees to upgrade their skills during economic downturns, resulting in higher productivity upon return.

There are also some promising avenues to integrate green skills development into high-road strategies. For example, many unions in the sector in Canada (e.g., UNITE HERE and United Food and Commercial Workers Canada [UFCW]) have negotiated education and training funds that can be allocated to climate change education. UNITE HERE Local 75 in Toronto is also establishing a union administered hospitality training centre that could provide labour and management approved climate change education (Tufts 2010). Here, there is potential to form partnerships with colleges and universities already providing climate change education dealing with tourism at academic and applied levels. Not only is sustainable tourism taught at the university level, but there are also several applied adventure, recreational and ecotourism programs in the Canadian college system. (See Gossling 2011 for more on the link between students and climate change mitigation in tourism related industries.) As for certification and audits, there are opportunities for joint labour-management initiatives to move away from self-assessment models toward more rigorous and legitimate forms of international "gold standard" certifications (British Columbia Ministry of Tourism, Sport and the Arts 2008).

The extent to which the high road model is adopted in different communities will depend on union power and state intervention. A low road model in response to climate change will lead to greater instability. Raising standards and retaining workers in the sector is a reasonable strategy in the face of labour shortages due to demographic changes. Unfortunately, employers will be tempted to rely on the margins of global labour markets, especially if climate change displaces greater numbers in the Global South and increases the supply of migrant labour to the North. Climate change is only one driver of change in this large and complex sector, but it does have the capacity to reproduce existing low road practices without significant intervention. The high road will continue to be uphill.

CONCLUSION: CENTRING WORKERS IN CLIMATE CHANGE AND TOURISM RESEARCH

This discussion is shaped by the lack of research on work and workers, but there are several key points that must be noted and that may be useful in informing future research on climate change and tourism related work and employment. First, despite an increasingly sophisticated literature on the impact of climate change on tourism, impacts on workers are neglected and work remains an a priori consideration with little nuance. The limits to knowledge on local variability and vulnerabilities in climate change make generalized models problematic, especially with the range of climate change scenarios and community capacities. Not surprisingly, these limitations are applicable to discussions of climate change and work and employment. However, climate change will have first, second and third order impacts on tourism work and workers, with complex interactions.

Second, these impacts will inevitably involve different degrees of creative destruction in tourism related labour markets. We require much more sophisticated models that are able to translate the impact of climate change to local levels of tourism related and tourism generated employment. This will be a challenge as there is barely adequate cooperation among physical and social sciences in tourism related research and there are as yet limited resources for research into broader questions of climate change and tourism (Hall and Higham 2005).

Third, it is too early to determine whether there will be a high or low road response to various impacts, but high road initiatives will require greater labour market intervention by unions and government. We need in-depth qualitative research linking mitigation and adaptation practices to changes in labour processes and a better understanding of the specific role tourism related workers and their organizations play (positive) and can play (normative) in climate change mitigation and adaptation. There are, however, two barriers. First, intellectual trends in tourism studies have shifted away from political economy approaches toward culturalist understandings of the phenomena biasing consumer behaviour at the expense of service providers. More importantly, the uneven institutional capacities among labour market actors in the tourism sector impede developing research that can be turned into strategic action. Specifically, the relatively weak presence of organized labour giving voice to workers and how they might shape the response to climate change is a primary concern.

Lastly, an employment centred framework is required to understand the specific role tourism related workers and their organizations do play and can play in climate change mitigation and adaptation. Before we can begin to imagine a greater role for workers in these processes, we must centre labour in discussions of adaptation and mitigation in the tourism sector. Specifically, we can look at how workers in destinations, areas of origins and the spaces of travel between are affected by and shape climate change processes. This must, however, be done with consideration of existing competitive contexts and labour markets. The focus should then turn to look at not only how industry and government responses to climate change impact workers, but also how workers' actions and workplace knowledge can shape employer and state understanding of what is to be done. Clearly, this involves a shift away from approaches that tend to focus solely on the responses and power of capital and the state.

9. CLIMATE CHANGE AND WORK AND EMPLOYMENT IN THE CANADIAN POSTAL AND COURIER SECTOR

Meg Gingrich, Sarah Ryan and Geoff Bickerton

In this chapter, we examine the relationship between climate and postal work, including mail transport, energy use in postal facilities and paper production. Because the postal sector is a crucial economic sector providing jobs and indispensable services to Canadians, it is essential to analyze these connected concerns.

The following questions have guided our work:

- What significant developments have occurred within the postal and courier sector with respect to work and employment?
- How do the effects of and perceptions surrounding climate change influence the demand for and the use of postal and courier services in Canada?
- Have concerns regarding climate change inspired changes in the practices of suppliers, customers and service providers?
- Is it possible to separate the effects of climate change from other drivers of change?
- Will climate change be a more significant factor influencing the sector in the future?
- What issues require more research?

This chapter, based on a thorough review of the literature since 1995, examines the impact of climate change on work and employment in the Canadian postal and courier sector, which is a subset of the transportation sector and includes the processing and delivery of letters, ad mail (direct mail) and packets and parcels to residences, businesses and public enterprises. The sector encompasses the postal service (Canada Post Corporation), major overnight courier companies, same-day car and bicycle couriers and local messenger and delivery firms. Although it is impossible to isolate precisely the impact of climate change on work and employment in the Canadian postal and courier sector from other social, economic and technological developments that have occurred within the sector over the past two decades, there can be no doubt that climate change will increasingly affect the industry. For example, it will influence the decisions of major service providers with respect to the equipment, choice of vehicles and procurement and design of facilities. Further, it will shape the decisions of larger corporate customers with respect to the type of paper and packaging materials used in mailings and deliveries. Finally, it will continue to define the decisions of individual postal users, potentially leading to a shift toward the use of electronic communications as an alternative to paper as a means to convey information. It is yet to be determined if environmental concerns will have a major impact on delivery modes, the production process, work schedules and organization of the industry.

SNAPSHOT OF THE SECTOR

The postal and courier sector comprises the processing and delivery of four major products: letter mail, ad mail (direct mail), periodicals and parcels and packages. Letter mail, including transaction mail (formerly known as first-class mail), and addressed advertising mail are handled almost exclusively by Canada Post Corporation (CPC) due to federal legislation providing CPC with an exclusive privilege over these services. Direct mail or unaddressed advertising mail is delivered by Canada Post in conjunction with letter mail delivery, by many major daily and community newspapers as inserts and by a host of small delivery companies. Periodicals are not covered by the CPC exclusive privilege, but are delivered almost exclusively by Canada Post. Parcels and packages, or courier products, are delivered by large overnight courier companies and smaller same-day couriers. This analysis will focus on the activities of Canada Post and the courier companies and will not attempt to evaluate the contribution made by newspaper inserts or independent ad mail delivery agents with respect to employment or product volumes.

THE POSTAL AND COURIER MARKET: ORGANIZATION OF THE INDUSTRY

In Canada, the delivery of letters in both rural and urban areas is completely dominated by Canada Post Corporation due to the provisions of the *Canada Post Corporation Act* that provide CPC with an exclusive privilege to deliver all but letters of an urgent nature. In addition to letter mail, CPC also operates its own parcel delivery service in direct competition to the private sector. In downtown, high-density areas, CPC uses a dedicated parcel delivery workforce of approximately 2,300 employees equipped with step vans to pick up and deliver parcels and transport other types of mail. In suburban and rural areas, CPC uses motorized letter carriers and rural and suburban mail carriers to deliver both letters and parcels. Beginning in 2011, Canada Post began to reorganize its delivery network in urban areas by motorizing letter carriers and integrating parcel delivery with letter mail. In addition to its in-house parcel operations, CPC also owns 90 percent of Purolator, Canada's largest overnight courier company. Together, CPC and Purolator operate the largest fleet of vehicles in the country.

The Canadian courier industry is estimated to be worth $8 billion in sales and until the recent recession was growing at 2.6 percent in volume and approximately 6 percent in revenue annually. The courier industry is divided into two major segments. First, there are courier companies that provide overnight and later-day delivery and have a national and international scope of delivery. These companies make approximately 90 percent of the deliveries. The core companies in this segment are UPS (United Postal Service of America), Purolator, Canada Post Corporation and Federal Express (FedEx). These companies have extensive transportation networks and sophisticated delivery sequencing techniques. Their use of technology and economies of scale enable them to compete effectively on the basis of price and quality of service.

The other segment of the industry is comprised of small and mostly inefficient same-day local delivery companies. This segment of the industry includes a wide variety of operations, ranging from individual owner-operators and "mom and pop" operations employing one to five messengers, to large multinationals such as Dynamex, the nation's largest provider of same-day local market services (Canadian Centre for Policy Alternatives 2005). From an environmental perspective, the organization of the same-day courier segment can be characterized as a complete disaster. There is little if any attempt to use technology to sequence deliveries to maximize delivery density. In contrast to the practices of the large parcel delivery companies, including CPC, numerous drivers and delivery companies frequently criss-cross cities delivering in entirely different areas during a single day. These practices result in an unnecessary use of nonrenewable resources and contribute to increased greenhouse gas emissions (GHGs), air pollution and traffic congestion.

Although there is fierce competition within the courier and ad mail (direct mail) industries, there is also a considerable interrelationship between the operations of many of the enterprises. It is common for most major private sector couriers to contract with local courier and messenger services to perform the final delivery in small towns. Many smaller companies use Canada Post to deliver in remote rural areas.

Recently, Canada Post and FedEx have reached an agreement to have CPC perform the final delivery of FedEx parcels in rural and low density areas. Many community newspapers rely on Canada Post to deliver their publications and the ad mail inserts to subscribers in small towns and rural areas where independent delivery is not feasible.

Concerning the economic aspects of the industry, the major core companies in the postal sector have been consistently profitable. Despite postage rates that are among the lowest in the industrialized world, Canada Post has been profitable each year between 1996 and 2011. UPS and FedEx do not report separate financial statements for their Canadian operations, but their international operations remained profitable throughout the 2009 recession. Purolator continues to be profitable.

EMPLOYMENT PATTERNS

Canada Post Corporation is the most significant employer of postal and courier workers in Canada. In 2011 CPC employed approximately 75,000 workers. According to CPC's 2010 *Social Responsibility Report*, 50.5 percent of employees were women; First Nations peoples accounted for 2.3 percent; persons with disabilities 4.7 percent; and visible minorities 12.3 percent. These numbers do not include temporary, casual or term employees, whereas the overall employment numbers do (Canada Post Corporation 2010). Overall, CPC is Canada's sixth largest employer.

Whereas employment in Canada Post has been declining due to reduction in letter volumes, employment in the courier sector has been increasing in response to the growth of the demand for parcel delivery. In 2010 approximately 50,000 workers were employed by 2,016 companies. The industry is sharply divided by the size and technological sophistication of the employers. Fully 65 percent of employers, mainly same-day, local companies, report having four employees or less. Only fifteen companies, providing delivery to national and regional markets, have five hundred or more employees. In the overnight/later market segment, four companies (Purolator, Canada Post, UPS and FedEx) account for the majority of the couriers employed.

A study by the Canadian Centre for Policy Alternatives (CCPA) of courier workers in Winnipeg found that across the country, approximately 80 percent of all couriers in this market segment are employed as "employees" (also referred to as the "core" segment) with the rest being designated as independent contractors. The study notes that classification as "employees" gives courier workers access to legislative protections and benefits, including workers compensation coverage and employer contributions to both the Canada Pension Plan (CPP) and Employment Insurance (EI). Employment in this core segment of the industry is characterized by low turnover. In most of the overnight segment, drivers are full-time employees and receive wages and benefits equal to or slightly superior to the average of industrial workers. Workers in sorting facilities are generally part-time, receive wages below that of the drivers and often are not entitled to benefits.

The exception to this model is Canada Post, where part-time employees are entitled to the same wages and benefits as full-time employees. At Canada Post, there was a steady trend toward greater use of part-time and casual employment during the period 1984 to 2000. However, as a result of contractual changes negotiated in 2000 — including a staffing ratio of full-time hours — the number of regular full-time employees increased and remained somewhat constant until the recession of 2009.

The same-day local delivery companies are at the other end of the scale. Since there is no need for large distribution networks and expensive technology, there are virtually no barriers to entry into the market. The CCPA report states "essentially anyone who can walk, has a bike, or has access to a vehicle, can participate" (CCPA 2005: 4). Because owner-operator agreements carry no fixed labour costs for the courier company, there are no economic incentives for courier companies to place caps on hiring. This has flooded the market with an abundance of messengers, many of whom must compete on cost alone. Frequently, employees are misled about their legal entitlements. Not surprisingly, labour turnover is very high, wages are low and benefits are virtually nonexistent. Due to the highly competitive nature of the industry with easy entry and exit, the rate of unionization is very low, although the Canadian Union of Postal Workers (CUPW) has had some recent success in organizing car and bicycle couriers and is committed to continue organizing in this sector.

CHALLENGES AND CHANGES IN THE INDUSTRY

Almost every business and the vast majority of individual citizens receive or send mail on a daily basis. Likewise, industries such as financial institutions, law firms and pharmaceutical distributors use courier services on a daily basis, and almost every business uses courier or local messenger services at some time or another. Thus, for much of the post World War II period, the Canadian postal and courier sector has served as a barometer of the economic health of the nation, as volumes have been indicative of levels of economic activity.

In addition to the effects of economic fluctuations, the postal and courier sector has also evolved in large part due to technological transformations and changes in delivery practices. The effects of various changes are diverse and have been both positive and negative. For instance, the courier industry has benefited considerably from the trend of both large and small businesses of adopting "just in time" inventory practices. This has increased the demand for overnight and same-day services dramatically and shifted the emphasis of the industry to providing fast service for businesses instead of the less time sensitive service for residential customers. To meet the new demand for fast overnight delivery, several courier companies established their own fleet of cargo aircraft.

Over time, volumes of letter mail and parcels have ebbed and flowed. The volume of parcel deliveries has increased enormously during the past fifteen years, while letter volumes grew considerably from 1995 onward, levelling off in 2008 and declining since then. Presently, the outlook for letter mail is uncertain. During the last two decades, several factors — including the proliferation of facsimile machines in the 1980s and the widespread use of email in the 1990s — have provided individuals and businesses with fast, low cost alternatives that could negatively impact letter mail volumes. In contrast, the volume of other types of mail, such as addressed and unaddressed ad mail, continues to increase.

Rapid technological developments in e-commerce and electronic communications present the industry with both new challenges and business opportunities. For example, the gradual acceptance of electronically signed documents and the use of encryption methods for electronic mail will likely reduce the number of deliveries of legal documents. In all probability, this loss of paper based products will be more than offset by the steady and rapid double digit growth of parcel and package deliveries generated by electronic retail shopping through the Internet.

THE CARBON FOOTPRINT OF THE POSTAL AND COURIER SECTOR

Worldwide, national postal services employ more than five million people and operate a global network of more than 600,000 post offices and almost one million postal vehicles. This represents the planet's largest physical distribution network (Universal Postal Union 2006). To date, there is no standardized methodology used to measure the carbon footprint of postal and courier work.

One common measurement used is life cycle assessment, which quantifies the amount of energy used and waste generated at every stage of the mail cycle (including aspects such as the extraction of raw materials, product manufacturing, distribution and final disposal) (Lee and Xu 2005). Researchers have used life cycle analysis (an abbreviated version of the life cycle assessment) to measure carbon emissions of the United States Postal Service (USPS) ground transport, finding that electricity consumption at mail/distribution facilities was one of the greatest factors influencing emissions totals (Mangmeechai and Matthews 2007). There are drawbacks to these methodologies, such as the lack of a mechanism to weight various parts of the mail cycle to achieve a more comprehensive and accurate understanding of which aspects of the cycle have the greatest carbon impact.

In addition to life cycle analysis, the Universal Postal Union (UPU), the United Nations' specialized agency for postal service, is currently working to develop a harmonized methodology that will be available to all 191 UPU countries to measure greenhouse gas emissions. Despite problems with harmonized methodologies, various entities have made estimates of the carbon footprint of the postal and courier industry. UPU estimates that posts generated at least 26 million tons of CO_2 in 2008 through the operation of postal vehicles and buildings alone (Universal Postal Union 2010). This represents approximately 0.07 percent of the total 38 billion tons of greenhouse gas emissions that the United Nations Environment Programme estimates are generated annually. This estimate is similar to the conclusions reached in a comprehensive study of the energy consumption, waste generation and pollutant emissions associated with mail in the United States. It found that the four major mail classes of USPS (letters, ad mail, periodicals and packages) comprise 0.47 percent of the national total of CO_2 equivalent emissions and 0.6 percent of the nation's energy consumption (SLS Consulting 2008).

In addition to problems with standardized methodologies, there are also no standardized systems for assessing environmental strategies to deal with the carbon footprint of the sector. In response to this, a new reporting framework for the postal industry, called the Environmental Measurement and Monitoring System (EMMS), was introduced in 2008. Led by the International Post Corporation (IPC), EMMS will act as a common reporting framework within which postal companies can declare their environmental management strategies and performance.

In Canada it is difficult to determine the actual success of companies such as Canada Post Corporation in reducing GHG emissions, due to CPC's habit of constantly restating the results provided in previous reports. In 2010, by restating previous numbers, CPC was able to declare success in meeting its objectives even though the amount of GHG emissions per letter delivered actually increased over 2008 levels. In its 2010 *Social Responsibility Report*, Canada Post Corporation reports that it was responsible for 181 kilotonnes of GHG emissions in 2010, a reduction of 4 percent from its 2008 emissions. However, during the same period, mail volumes declined by 8 percent so that the rate of emissions per letter actually increased. In its 2010 report, CPC revised sharply upward all of the previously reported levels of GHG emissions. For instance, while CPC had previously reported 107 kilotonnes of emissions for buildings for 2002, the 2010 report states that emissions for buildings in 2002 were actually 120.4 kilotonnes. Since CPC's target was to achieve a 14 percent reduction in CO_2 emissions between 2002 and 2012, it was able to claim success by restating upwards the levels reported for 2002.

There are no comparable figures for the global courier industry. Major corporations such as FedEx and UPS publish comprehensive social responsibility reports, but their operations are very different than many of the smaller local and regional courier companies. However, the study conducted by SLS Consulting for the United States Postal Service (USPS) indicated that the greenhouse gas emissions associated with parcel delivery are fourteen times greater than those associated with first-class letters and seven times greater than delivery of addressed ad mail. The American study also found that the greenhouse gas emissions reported by UPS in its *Corporate Sustainability Report* were higher by factor of 3.6 on a per parcel basis than those reported by the U.S. Postal Service (SLS Consulting 2008). This is most likely due to the more extensive use of air transportation required to meet their compressed delivery standards and the greater efficiency achieved by USPS by integrating parcel and letter delivery within the same delivery vehicles. It is likely that the overall greenhouse gas emissions of the courier industry are equal to or greater than that of postal administrations.

INDUSTRY RESPONSE: TINKERING AT THE MARGINS

Reading the relentless optimism generated in social responsibility reports and annual statements of postal and courier companies, one might be tempted to think that concern regarding climate change is transforming the practices of the industry. While there are some changes occurring in the practices of suppliers, customers and service providers, it is not clear whether most of the initiatives are designed more to enhance profits and serve as advertising gimmicks rather than to reduce GHG emissions.

It is clear that none of the major players in the industry are at all interested in discussing an overall reform in the organization of the industry or even modest regulatory reform as a means of significantly reducing GHG emissions produced by the industry. Even slight organizational changes, such as reorganizing "call for" items so that residents could go to the nearest postal or courier outlet to pick up their parcel or package, are never considered, despite their obvious environmental advantages. At every step of the way, the dictates of capitalist competition trumps environmental sustainability.

Indeed, even publicly owned enterprises such as Canada Post Corporation appear more interested in using the environment as a public relations prop than actually addressing the issue of environmental degradation of the planet. An example of the negative approach to environmental concerns can be found in the 2008 CPC *Annual Report*, which portrays environmental issues as more of a threat to business than legitimate problems that must be dealt with to safeguard the health of the planet. Instead of examining major changes in the organization of the industry that might result in significant improvements in delivery density and corresponding reductions in GHG emissions, Canada Post and most other service providers have restricted their emission reduction activities to taking some actions to lower the GHG emissions associated with their vehicles, facilities, packaging materials and modes of transportation of products. Not surprisingly, these actions are also designed to cut costs and increase profits.

In recent years, almost all postal administrations and major courier companies have taken action to reduce the fuel consumption of their vehicle fleets and are in the process of either introducing or testing the introduction of hybrid or electric vehicles. In Canada, Purolator continues to be an industry leader with respect to investment in hybrid electric vehicles (HEVs) in its curbside delivery fleet. More than one third of UPS-Canada's fleet of

2,000 delivery vehicles now runs on low carbon fuel, mainly propane.

Postal administrations and courier companies have also been reducing the GHG footprint resulting from the operation of their facilities. FedEx has now opened three solar powered distribution centres in California, and more are planned in the future (FedEx Corporation 2008). Likewise, New Zealand Post uses solar energy and has built new buildings that let in natural light throughout the day. The United States Postal Service (USPS) plans to reduce its petroleum use by replacing its older vehicles with newer, more fuel-efficient vehicles and has inaugurated a green roof on one of its main buildings in New York (GAO 2008). The roof is expected to reduce the amount of contaminants in stormwater runoff and generate lower heating and air-conditioning bills. In 2007 Canada Post made a commitment that all new facilities would be LEED-certified. Since then it has registered eight buildings across the country for LEED certification, including a new mail processing plant in Winnipeg and letter carrier depots in Alberta, Ontario and Quebec.

In addition to CPC, both FedEx and UPS are purchasing new planes to help reach their targets for the reduction in GHG emissions caused by their fleet of aircraft. DHL, a component in the Deutsche Post DHL Group, one of the biggest mail, transport and logistics corporations in the world, is testing a deep-sea cargo ship equipped with a giant sail to transport freight between Germany and Venezuela. Depending on the wind's force, fuel costs could be cut by 10–35 percent.

Not only have various postal services tried to reduce GHG emissions through changes to their fleets and buildings, but some posts have also adopted green purchasing policies. In 2009, in response to new legislation designed to reduce landfill waste, Royal Mail in the United Kingdom introduced a discount for green mail of 2 percent for products made from recycled paper and 4.7 percent for products that are recyclable.

Most posts are taking further steps by making efforts to reduce the amount of undeliverable mail, which constitutes approximately 3 percent of total volume. A recent study by Pitney Bowes indicates that consumers re-evaluate their negative opinions of direct marketers if they actively try to be more eco-friendly by taking measures such as eliminating the delivery of undeliverable mail (Quenqua 2007). Ironically, Canada Post continues to require letter carriers to deliver undeliverable mail to the address even if they know the addressee no longer resides there. Changing this practice would have a positive environmental effect, as fewer nonrenewable resources would be used unnecessarily. All of the posts and major courier companies have introduced very impressive targets, but most, like FedEx's 20/20 plan (20 percent reduction in CO_2 emissions by the year 2020) are safely distant into the future.

CANADA POST: CLIMATE CHANGE AND DELIVERY MODES

One issue that requires much more analysis is the impact of the delivery mode of the post on both CO_2 emissions and employment. In 1982, CPC discontinued its practice of providing door-to-door delivery to all communities with 2,000 or more residences. Instead of delivery to the door, CPC began to introduce community mailboxes and postal kiosks where residents pick up their mail. More recently CPC has commenced a review of the location of all rural mailboxes with the result that many roadside mailboxes have been moved from the lot line of the residence and moved to community mailboxes. In many cases the new locations are beyond easy walking distance from the residence.

This change from residential delivery to community mailbox pickup has considerable implications with respect to employment levels of letter carriers and rural route mail carriers within Canada Post. It has also occurred without any consideration or analysis of the environmental consequences of relocating the delivery point to a location that frequently causes the mail recipient to drive to the community mailbox to obtain their mail. Nor has there been any life cycle assessment of the energy required and waste produced as a result of the production, location and maintenance (including the energy requirements of snow clearing, lock changes, etc.) of the community mailboxes.

This issue was directly addressed in the report of the advisory panel of the strategic review of Canada Post Corporation in December 2008. The advisory panel recommended that Canada Post specifically include in its annual report an overview on the delivery methods it uses, indicating the number of addresses served by each delivery method and the financial costs and environmental impact of each on a per unit basis. It also recommended that the planning, approval and implementation of Canada Post's modernization plan be informed by the expectation that it will reduce Canada Post's environmental footprint and that this approach should inform existing initiatives. Further, it should be formulated as part of the modernization plan upon which benchmarks should be set and against which the board of directors should report progress through its annual report (Transport Canada 2008).

CANADA POST, CLIMATE CHANGE AND AD MAIL

There are some areas where environmental concerns may have significant impact on employment levels at Canada Post. Throughout the world, there is a growing concern over the amount of CO_2 emissions and waste disposal issues associated with direct mail, or ad mail. This concern has manifested itself in a broad based movement to create the establishment of "do-not-mail" lists and even to have unsolicited ad mail banned altogether, which could threaten the volumes and revenues of postal administrations. In the United Kingdom, as an example, the report of the Independent Review of the U.K. postal services sector, chaired by Richard Hooper, estimated that mail market revenues could be reduced by a total of 350 million pounds by 2011–12 if customers switched to other media because of environmental concerns (Hooper, Hutton and Smith 2008). This issue was also addressed in the *Report of the Advisory Panel of the Strategic Review of Canada Post Corporation* in December 2008. It noted that a number of submissions expressed the views that Canada Post has an environmental responsibility, that ad mail is a misuse of paper and forest products and that Canada Post needs to confront this issue in an environmental way.

A DM News/Pitney Bowes survey on direct mail and the environment shows that consumers greatly overestimate the negative effects of direct mail on the environment. Approximately 48 percent of respondents thought that advertising mail from U.S. households counted for more than half of the country's municipal waste when it is actually responsible for 2 percent. Respondents also greatly overestimated the amount of carbon emitted through the delivery of advertising mail. When asked to rate the emissions from seven activities, respondents chose direct mail as the third largest emitter when it actually emitted the least.

Similar concerns are gaining traction among the public, as evidenced in a 2008 study conducted by CPC with Harris/Decima that resulted in a white paper called *The New Environmentalism*. More than 60 percent of Canadian respondents said they always or often think about the environmental impact of mail and catalogues, and participants said they recycle 85 percent of their advertising mail. The survey also revealed that, in many cases, consumers are willing to pay more for environmentally-friendly products as long as those costs are considered reasonable. Consumers state that environmentally-friendly products are typically 10–20 percent more expensive than their rivals and many, especially baby boomers, are willing to pay that extra amount (Harris/Decima and Canada Post Corporation 2008).

There is evidence that good environmental behaviour by ad mailers and postal administrations will be rewarded. According to the DM/Pitney Bowes survey, 68 percent of respondents said they would have a higher impression of direct mailers if they used recycled paper and cardboard. Approximately 67 percent would think more highly of mailers if they planted trees to offset paper production. Regarding certification, 53 percent said their opinion of unsolicited mail would be better if an agency green seal of approval were awarded and 67 percent said the same thing if a third party issued a similar green label (Quenqua 2007).

The direct mail industry is responding to these environmental concerns. The United Kingdom national standards body, the British Standards Institute, has launched a new assessment and certification scheme that aims to get marketing companies to reduce waste paper and increase the recycling of direct mail. This initiative is known as the PAS 2020 Direct Marketing Environmental Performance. It is the first independent assessment and certification scheme to be launched for the marketing sector that provides environmental best practice standards (Direct Marketing Association U.K. 2009). PAS 2020 has been developed in partnership with the Direct Marketing Association (DMA). Similar initiatives are likely to follow in North America (ibid.).

POSITION OF THE UNIONS

The Canadian Union of Postal Workers (CUPW) represents approximately 55,000 people, with urban operations accounting for 48,000 employees and rural/suburban operations constituting 6,600 employees. CUPW includes all of the operational workers at Canada Post as well as couriers and sorters at approximately fifteen private sector courier companies. It contends that the federal government should sponsor a thorough examination of the overall environmental impact of all postal and courier services, including an environmental assessment of the different delivery modes such as door-to-door delivery and community mailboxes. The union also believes that such a review should examine how the industry could be re-organized to operate in a more environmentally-friendly manner. In addition, CUPW has called upon CPC to conduct an environmental audit to identify measures that can be taken to reduce its carbon footprint.

CUPW believes that greater competition in letter delivery, as advocated by various right wing think tanks, would create more environmental problems. There is a direct and inverse relationship between increased delivery density and environmental impact, and the decreased delivery density created by competition would lead to an increased use of fossil fuels, pollution and traffic. According to the union, from an environmental perspective, it not only makes sense to maintain the letter monopoly but also to extend it to the parcel delivery market. Moreover, the union asserts that the postal service can and should be used to develop and test environmental practices that could be extended to other industries. CUPW believes this can be achieved much more easily by a publicly run corporation, for it is easier to regulate and focus on diverse goals when profit making is not the sole concern of the corporation. At its 2011 National Convention the union adopted a comprehensive policy on the environment, calling on its members to work with environmental activists and to address the GHG footprint in the postal sector.

In addition to CUPW, the Public Service Alliance of Canada (PSAC) represents the nonmanagerial white-collar workers at Canada Post and workers at Purolator in British Columbia. PSAC argued to the Strategic Review of Canada Post Corporation that CPC should include environmental protection criteria in all of its policy objectives. Union Network International (UNI) is the international global union that represents postal and courier workers.

It argues that postal administrations must recognize that workers must be consulted and included in the changes the industry faces regarding climate change. It also encourages unions to be involved in company approaches to climate change.

EVALUATING WHAT WE KNOW

There are many issues that require much more analysis to further our understanding of the relationship between climate change and work and employment in the postal sector. Academic publications have addressed changing patterns in mail demand, emissions from the magazine production process, union responses to the economic and climate change crises, the segmentation of overnight and same-day courier delivery and one section of the USPS attempts to approach environmental issues. Despite all of this, there is an absence of research on the effect of climate change on jobs in the postal sector. Is the number of jobs changing? How are the types of jobs changing? Is this related to climate change or other factors? What type of training is needed to adapt to new types of jobs? This type of rigorous analysis would be helpful to understand more fully the impact of climate change on work. The studies on changes in mail demand and mail volumes fail to engage fully with the qualitative changes that are occurring in how people communicate. Econometric models fail to explain the changes that are taking place.

Academic publications do not address how regulation or proposed regulation might impact the postal sector, even though this may be a driver in how companies respond to the climate change crisis. The research fails to evaluate the multiple forms of compliance programs, self-regulation and greenwashed marketing that are occurring in the postal sector. Furthermore, little research has looked at how unions are responding to climate change or how they can respond. Discussions about the differences in types of technology — some eliminate jobs while others reduce carbon emissions — show how complicated issues like technological change can be, as specific changes determine whether there is a positive or negative impact on employment.

Government agencies recognize that climate change plays a role in the postal sector either implicitly or explicitly. However, they do not analyze the impacts of the environment and environmental change on mail volumes or whether this is linked to a substitution of electronic mail for environmental reasons. Nor do they analyze the response of postal operators, the impact on jobs and whether governments are regulating the impact of climate change. While the Universal Postal Union, for example, acknowledges that training is needed in the context of industry changes related to climate change, it fails to address more concretely how the work is changing and what kinds of training are specifically needed. Throughout the research to date, there is little evaluation of the causes of shrinking mail volumes or the role of technological change in environmental impact and jobs. There is little discussion of route optimization, the environmental impacts of multiple postal operators or of parcel and mail delivery to the same address, which is integrally linked to postal liberalization and the parcel market.

The actors in the postal and courier industry — postal agencies and their unions — have produced analysis that incorporates environmental reporting and concerns. Many postal companies are including environmental concerns in their annual reports in terms of risks, challenges, products and opportunities. These reports discuss the macro-trends in the postal industry, and some incorporate climate regulation into their analysis — especially those companies operating in the E.U. However, they tend not to quantify or explore how important the environment is as a factor in electronic substitution of physical mail.

Most postal companies have recently started releasing Corporate Social Responsibility reports outlining their CO_2 emissions linked to different aspects of their production chain. Though these reports tend to include a section on employees, they fail to link responses to climate change with employees' jobs. Furthermore, the reports all use different baselines so the emissions data is not comparable.

Industry associations — such as the Canadian Marketing Association, the U.K. Direct Marketing Association, the Envelope Manufacturers Foundation, PostEurop or the Magazine Publishers Association — have dealt with a range of issues including the importance of the universal service obligation, the number of jobs linked to the industry or the economic significance of the industry. The associations provide guides for their members explaining the environmental impact of different aspects of the production chain. Furthermore, some companies are offering tools to measure the emissions associated with campaigns or environmental certification schemes.

On the whole, it has been the labour market organizations that have produced the most information on climate change and the postal system. However, much of this information is geared toward the perspective of industry, minimizing the risk of negative publicity or planning for or avoiding future environmental regulation. Virtually no research has been conducted on the environmental impact of major changes that also have a significant impact on employment and work in the postal sector — specifically the impact of postal deregulation. Similarly, there has been no examination of the impact on energy use and GHG emissions of changing the delivery modes from door-to-door delivery to centralized community mailboxes and kiosks.

A FUTURE RESEARCH AGENDA: WHAT DO WE NEED TO KNOW?

In order to fully understand the relationship of climate change and work and employment in the postal sector, it is necessary to go beyond an examination of the GHG emissions caused by the current work organization of the sector. Instead, we need to examine the environmental consequences of the operational changes that have been or may be introduced into the production processes by employers. We also need to consider the impact of changes that may result from a reorganization of the sector, either as a result of greater cooperation between service providers, or legislative changes such as deregulation of the posts or the introduction of new regulations in the courier sector.

Some future areas of investigation could include the examination of

- the environmental impact of various types of delivery services such as door-to-door delivery, centralized delivery to community mailboxes and picking up mail at post offices in both suburban and rural settings. This would include a life cycle assessment of community mailboxes;
- the environmental consequences of postal deregulation;
- the environmental consequences of regulating the same-day courier industry to promote greater delivery density;
- the potential to use the tax system to provide incentives for courier companies to adopt more environmentally-friendly practices in the processing and transportation of parcels;
- the environmental consequences of establishing a monopoly in the final destination delivery of packages and parcels to provide greater efficiency and delivery densities;
- the environmental consequences of adopting a new work organization involving the integration of letter delivery with parcels, packages and pickups performed by motorized letter carriers;
- the potential for postal and courier companies to use price incentives to require more environmental practices on the part of customers and suppliers;
- the environmental consequences of offering additional financial and government services and Internet and printing access in postal facilities in rural communities;
- the relative use of energy in producing, delivering and disposing of catalogues as compared to the savings of energy due to online or telephone shopping and delivery by the post or courier;
- a life cycle assessment of the energy requirements and waste produced by all postal and courier products through the entire product cycle, including extraction of raw materials, product manufacturing, distribution, use, maintenance/repair and disposal; and
- the environmental and employment consequences of service providers pooling their resources to enable residents to obtain "call for" items at the nearest possible postal or courier facility.

CONCLUSION

In an industry that has experienced a strong growth record with respect to overall volumes and employment it is difficult to isolate the impact of climate change on employment and work. While there has been some analysis of environmental impact of postal work, specifically as it regards the carbon footprint of the mail chain, we lack analysis of the relationship between climate change and employment in the sector.

However, it is clear that public opinion, governmental measures designed to reduce climate change, industry changes and actions taken by trade unions will have a direct impact upon employment levels, the work process and the organization of the postal sector in the future. Trade unions and academic partners must play a valuable role in analyzing the relationship between work, employment and climate change within the postal and courier sector.

REFERENCES

Aitken, S.N. et al. 2008. "Adaptation, Migration or Extirpation: Climate Change Outcomes for Tree Populations." *Evolutionary Applications* 1.

Alberta Employment and Immigration. 2007. *Building and Educating Tomorrow's Workforce: Workforce Strategy for Alberta's Energy Sector*. Edmonton: Alberta Employment and Immigration.

Alberta Treasury Board and Finance. 2012. *Alberta Heritage Trust Fund 2011–2012 Second Quarter Report For the Six Months Ending September 30, 2011*. Edmonton: Alberta Treasury Board and Finance.

Ayee, G., M. Lowe and G. Gereffi. 2009. "Wind Power: Generating Electricity and Employment." In *Manufacturing Climate Solutions: Carbon-Reducing Technologies and U.S. Jobs*. Durham, NC: Duke University, Center on Globalization Governance and Competitiveness.

Bael, D., and R. Sedjo. 2006. *Toward Globalization of the Forest Products Industry: Some Trends*. Working Paper 06-35. Washington, DC: Resources for the Future. <rff. org/Publications/Pages/PublicationDetails.aspx?PublicationID=17461>.

Ball, David P. 2012. "Government Pipeline Rhetoric Reminiscent of Cold War, McCarthyism." *Vancouver Observer*, January 11.

Balstad, Roberta. 2010. "The Interdisciplinary Challenges of Climate Change Research." In *UNESCO World Social Science Report 2010*. Paris: UNESCO and the International Social Science Council.

Barnes, T., and R. Hayter (eds.). 1997. *Troubles in the Rainforest: British Columbia's Forest Economy in Transition*. Victoria, BC: Western Geographical Press.

Barrett, J.P., J.A. Hoerner, S. Bernow and B. Dougherty. 2002. *Clean Energy and Jobs: A Comprehensive Approach to Climate Change and Energy Policy*. Washington, DC: Economic Policy Institute; Center for a Sustainable Economy.

Baum, A., and D. Luria. 2010. *Driving Growth: How Clean Cars and Climate Policy Can Create Jobs*. Natural Resources Defense Council; United Auto Workers; Center for American Progress.

Baum, T. 2007. "Human Resources in Tourism: Still Waiting for Change." *Tourism Management* 28, 6.

Bauman, Zygmunt. 2011. *Collateral Damage: Social Inequalities in a Global Age*. Cambridge: Polity Press.

BCSEA (B.C. Sustainable Energy Association). 2005. *Sustainable Energy Solutions for B.C.: A Contribution by the B.C. Sustainable Energy Association to the Alternative Energy & Power Technology Task Force*. Victoria: BCSEA.

Belèn-Sanchez, A., and P. Poschen. 2009. *The Social and Decent Work Dimensions of a New Agreement on Climate Change*. Geneva, Switzerland: International Labour Organization.

Bellmann, K., and A. Khare. 1999. "European Response to Issues in Recycling Car Plastics." *Technovation* 19, 12.

Berrittella, M., Andrea Bigano, Roberto Roson, and Richard S.J. Tol. 2006. "A General Equilibrium Analysis of Climate Change Impacts on Tourism." *Tourism Management* 27, 5.

Bicknell, S., and P. McManus. 2006. "The Canary in the Coalmine: Australian Ski Resorts and Their Response to Climate Change." *Geographical Research* 44, 3.

Bigano, Andrea, Roberto Roson, Francesco Bosello, and Richard S.J. Toll. 2008. "Economy-Wide Impacts of Climate Change: A Joint Analysis for Sea Level Rise and Tourism." *Mitigation and Adaptation Strategies for Global Change* 13, 8.

Blackwell, R. 2010. "Japan Takes Issue with Ontario's Green Energy Plan." *Globe and Mail*, September 13.

Blue Green Canada 2012. *Amicus Submission to the World Trade Organisation Regarding Disputes WT/DS412 and WT/DS426*, May. <canadians.org/trade/documents/WTO/submission-WT-DS412-0512.pdf>.

Boettcher, M., N.P. Nielsen and K. Petrick. 2009. *Employment Opportunities and Challenges in the Context of Rapid Industry Growth: A Closer Look at the Development of Wind, Wave & Tidal Energy in the U.K.* Munich: Bain and Company. <bwea.com/pdf/publications/Bain%20Brief_Wind%20Energy%202008_FINAL.pdf>.

Borenstein, Seth. 2012. "This Summer Is 'What Global Warming Looks Like.'" Associated Press online, July 3. <bigstory.ap.org/article/us-summer-what-global-warming-looks>.

Bourdon, C.C., and R.E. Levitt. 1980. *Union and Open-Shop Construction: Compensation, Work Practices and Labor Markets*. Lexington, MA: Lexington Books.

Bowen, Alex, and Nicholas Stern. 2010. "Environmental Policy and the Economic Downturn." *Oxford Review of Economic Policy* 26, 2.

Bridges Weekly. Published online by the International Centre for Trade and Sustainable Development. <ictsd.org/news/bridgesweekly>.

Brigham, Mike. 2009. "OPA-FIT Analysis, Part 3." Toronto: Green Energy Act Alliance. <fit.powerauthority.on.ca/Storage/10265_OPA-FIT-Analysis-Part3.pdf>.

British Columbia Ministry of Tourism, Sport and the Arts. 2008. *Green Tourism Forum II Report*. Vancouver: Ministry of Tourism Sport and the Arts, Tourism British Columbia, and the Council of Tourism Associations of British Columbia. <tca.gov.bc.ca/tourism/docs/Green_Tourism_Forum_II_Report.pdf>.

Brown, S.F. 2004. "California Rocks the Auto Industry: How a State Agency Ruling on Climate Change May Force Detroit to Spend $33 billion." *Fortune* 9.

Browne, S.A., and L.M. Hunt. 2007. *Climate Change and Nature-Based Tourism, Outdoor Recreation, and Forestry in Ontario: Potential Effects and Adaptation Strategies*. Thunder Bay, ON: Ontario Ministry of Natural Resources and the Icarus Foundation.

Burda, Cherise. 2011a. "New Analysis Compares Ontario Election Promise on Clean Energy, Climate Action and Sustainable Transportation." Media release, September 20. Drayton Valley, Alberta: Pembina Institute. <pembina.org/media-release/2271>.

___. 2011b. "Fact: Green Energy Is Good for Ontario." Blog, October 3. Drayton Valley, Alberta: Pembina Institute. <pembina.org/blog/578>.

Burton, I., S. Huq, B. Lim, O. Pilifosova, and E. Schipper. 2002. "From Impacts Assessment to Adaptation Priorities: The Shaping of Adaptation Policy." *Climate Policy* 2, 2.

Busby, Peter. 2009. *Canadian Architect* 18.

___. 2002. "Building Kyoto: The Design Professions and the Construction Industry Have Much to Contribute to Meeting Canada's Kyoto Commitments." *Canadian Architect* July. <canadianarchitect.com/issues/story.aspx?aid=1000116244>.

Butler, Don. 2011. "Anti-Turbine Forces Turned Election Tide; Liberals Lost 10 Seats Targeted by Coalition Group Wind Concerns Ontario." *Ottawa Citizen*, October 9.

Buzzetti, Hélène. 2011a. "Ressources Humaines — Ottawa Coupe en Catimini." *Le*

Devoir, July 19.

___. 2011b. "Ressources Humaines — les Conseils Sectoriels n'étaient pas Efficaces, Dit le Ministère." *Le Devoir*, July 21.

Calvert, John. 2007. *Liquid Gold: Energy Privatization in B.C.* Halifax and Winnipeg: Fernwood Press.

Campaign Against Climate Change. 2010. *One Million Climate Jobs: Solutions to the Economic and Environmental Crises.* London: Campaign Against Climate Change, in conjunction with the Communication Workers Union, Public and Commercial Services Union, Transport Salaried Staffs Association and the University and College Union.

Canada Green Building Council. n.d. "Database of LEED certified Projects." <cagbc. org/leed/leed_projects/index.php>.

Canada Post Corporation. 2010. *Social Responsibility Report: Our Environment.* Ottawa: Canada Post. <canadapost.ca/cpo/mc/aboutus/corporate/socialresponsibility/ default.jsf>.

___. 2008. *Making the Connection: 2008 Annual Report.* Ottawa: Canada Post.

Canadian Boreal Forest Agreement Secretariat. 2010. "Canadian Boreal Forest Agreement." <canadianborealforestagreement.com/index.php/en/>.

Canadian Centre for Policy Alternatives. 2005. *Straddling the World of Traditional and Precarious Employment: A Case Study of the Courier Industry in Winnipeg.* Winnipeg: Canadian Centre for Policy Alternatives. <policyalternatives.ca/documents/ Manitoba_Pubs/2005/Courier_Industry.pdf>.

CAPP (Canadian Association of Petroleum Producers). 2010. *Statistical Handbook for Canada's Upstream Petroleum Industry (2009 data).* Calgary and St. John's: CAPP.

___. September 2009. *Oil Sands: An Important Asset Generating Benefits across Canada.* Calgary and St. John's: CAPP.

Canadian Urban Institute. 2008. *Sustainable Building: Canada on the Move.* Toronto: Canadian Urban Institute.

CAR (Center for Automotive Research). 2011. *Driving Workforce Change: Regional Impact and Implications of Auto Industry Transformation to a Green Economy.* Ann Arbor, MI: Center for Automotive Research.

___. 2008. *Beyond the Big Leave: The Future of U.S. Automotive Human Resources.* Ann Arbor, MI: Center for Automotive Research.

___. 2004. *The Advanced Power Technology Dilemma: From Hydrocarbons to Hydrogen.* Ann Arbor, MI: Center for Automotive Research.

CAW (Canadian Auto Workers). 2007. *Climate Change and Our Jobs: Finding the Right Balance. Discussion paper for the CAW Canada–Quebec Joint Council. St. John's Nfld. August 2007.* Toronto: CAW. <caw.ca/en/3532.htm>.

CEA (Canadian Electricity Association). 2004. *Keeping the Future Bright: 2004 Canadian Electricity Human Resource Sector Study.* Ottawa: CEA.

CEC (Commission for Environmental Cooperation). 2008. *Green Building in North America: Opportunities and Challenges. Secretariat Report to Council under Article 13 of the North American Agreement on Environmental Cooperation.* Montreal: CEC. <cec.org/files/ PDF//GB_Report_EN.pdf>.

Centre for Civic Governance. 2011. *This Green House: Building Fast Action for Climate Change and Green Jobs.* Vancouver: Columbia Institute. <civicgovernance.ca/sites/ default/files/publications/This%20Green%20House_Report.pdf>.

Centre for Economic Policy Research. n.d. *Global Trade Alert.* London: Centre for

Economic Policy Research. <globaltradealert.org/>.

CEP (Communications, Energy and Paperworkers Union of Canada). 2009. *Energy Policy # 917*. Ottawa: CEP. <cep.ca/docs/en/policy-917-e.pdf>.

CERES (Centre for Education and Research in Environmental Strategies). 2008. *Submission to the Review of Australia's Automotive Industry: Battery Electric Vehicles (BEVs)*. Brunswick East, Australia: CERES.

CERI (Canadian Energy Research Institute). 2009. *The Impacts of Canadian Oil Sands Development on the United States' Economy: Final report*. Calgary: CERI.

Ceron, J., and G. Dubois. 2005. "The Potential Impacts of Climate Change on French Tourism." *Current Issues in Tourism* 8, 2–3.

Charlton, Andrew. 2011. "Man-Made World Choosing Between Progress and Planet." *Quarterly Essay* 44.

Chen, Jing Ming. 2007. "Convergence of Current Estimates for the Carbon Sink in Canada's Forests and Remaining Challenges." Workshop on Reducing Greenhouse Gas Emissions by Conserving Forests: Approaches to Stimulate Action, sponsored by David Suzuki Foundation and Nongovernment Organizations, Toronto, June 13–14.

Chen, W., Jing Chen, Jane Liu and Josef Cihlar. 2000. "Annual Carbon Balance of Canada's Forests during 1895–1996." *Global Biogeochemical Cycles* 14, 3.

Clark II, W.W., E. Paolucci and J. Cooper. 2003. "Commercial Development of Energy — Environmentally Sound Technologies for the Auto-industry: The Case of Fuel Cells." *Journal of Cleaner Production* 11, 4.

Clarke, T. 2008. *Tar Sands Showdown: Canada and the New Politics of Oil in an Age of Climate Change*. Toronto: James Lorimer.

Clean Air Renewable Energy Coalition. 2004. "Canadian Renewable Electricity Development: Employment Impacts." A paper prepared for the Clean Air Renewable Energy Coalition by the Pembina Institute. <cleanairrenewableenergycoalition.com/documents/Employment-Predictions.pdf>.

Cohen, Marjorie. 2006. "Why Canada Needs a National Energy Plan." *CCPA Monitor* 12, 8.

Construction Sector Council. n.d. <constructionsectorforecasts.ca>.

Cosbey, Aaron. 2011. "Renewable Energy Subsidies and the WTO: The Wrong Law and the Wrong Venue." *Global Subsidies Initiative Blog*, June 21. <iisd.org/gsi/news/renewable-energy-subsidies-and-wto-wrong-law-and-wrong-venue>.

Council for Automotive Human Resources. 2008. *Competing Without a Net: The Future of the Canadian Automotive Industry, Full Report and Addendum*. Toronto: The Council.

CTHRC (Canadian Tourism Human Resources Council). 2009a. *Who's Working for You? A Demographic Profile of Tourism Sector Employees*. Ottawa: CTHRC. <cthrc.ca/en/research_publications/labour_market_information/total_tourism_sector_employment.aspx>.

___. 2009b. *The Future of Canada's Tourism Sector: Labour Shortages to Re-emerge as Economy Recovers*. Ottawa: CTHRC.

___. 2008. *The Future of Canada's Tourism Sector: Long On Prospects … Short On People*. Ottawa: Conference Board of Canada. <otec.org/PDF/Supply-Demand%20Compilation%20Report_ENG.pdf>.

D. Parsons & Associates. 2009. *Greening the Economy: Transitioning to New Careers*. Toronto: Peel Halton Workforce Development Group; Toronto Workforce Innovation Group; Workforce Planning Board of York Region and West Gwillimbury

Employment Ontario.

Das, B.L. 1998. *An Introduction to the WTO Agreements*. Penang: Third World Network.

De Wel, Bert, Judith Kirton-Darling, Alain Mestre, Abbe Panneels, Philip Pearson and Sebastien Storme. 2011. *Collective Bargaining and the Green Economy: A European Trade Union Perspective*. Brussels: ITUC-GURN Workshop. <ituc-csi.org/IMG/pdf/Collective_bargaining_and_the_green_economy.pdf>.

Decaillon, Joel, and A. Panneels. 2010. *Employment and Climate Policies in Europe, Climate Change, Impacts on Employment and the Labour Market — Responses to the Challenges*. Brussels: ITUC-GURN Workshop.

Demerse, Clare. 2011. *Reducing Pollution, Creating Jobs: The Employment Effects of Climate Change and Environmental Policies*. Drayton Valley, Alberta: Pembina Institute.

___. 2010. "Leaked Government Document Says Canada Should End Fossil Fuel Subsidies." Pembina Institute Climate Change Blog, May 26. <climate.pembina.org/blog/92>.

Department of Geography and Environmental Studies. n.d. *Environments: A Journal of Interdisciplinary Studies*. Waterloo, Ontario: Wilfrid Laurier University. <environmentsjournal.ca/index.php/ejis/index>.

DesJarlais, Claude, and Anne Blondlot (eds.). 2010. *Savoir s'adapter aux changements climatiques*. Montreal: Ouranos. <ouranos.ca/fr/pdf/53_sscc_21_06_lr.pdf>.

DesJarlais, Claude, Alain Bourque, Réal Décoste, Claude Demers, Pierre Deschamps and Khanh-Hung Lam (eds). 2004. *Adapting to Climate Change*. Montreal: Ouranos. <ouranos.ca/en/pdf/ouranos_sadapterauxcc_en.pdf>.

Deutsche Bank Research. 2008. *Climate Change and Tourism: Where Will the Journey Lead?* Frankfurt, Germany: Deutsche Bank Research.

Direct Marketing Association U.K. 2009. *Green Matters Special Issue: PAS 2020*. New York: Direct Marketing Association.

Doern, Bruce G., and Monica Gattinger. 2003. *Power Switch: Energy Regulatory Governance in the Twenty-First Century*. Toronto: University of Toronto Press.

Dubois, G., and J. Ceron. 2006. "Tourism and Climate Change: Proposals for a Research Agenda." *Journal of Sustainable Tourism* 14, 4.

Dupressoir, Sophie, Ana Belèn-Sanchez, Patrick Nussbaumer and Jorge Riechmann. 2007a. *Climate Change and Employment. Impact on Employment of Climate Change and CO₂ Emission Reduction Measures in the E.U.-25 to 2030: Synthesis*. Brussels: European Trade Union Congress; Syndex; ISTAS; Social Development Agency; Wuppertal Institute.

___. 2007b. *Climate Change and Employment: Impact on Employment in the European Union-25 of Climate Change and CO₂ Emission Reduction Measures by 2030*. Brussels: European Trade Union Congress; Syndex; ISTAS; Social Development Agency; Wuppertal Institute.

Dziczek, Kristin, Sean McAlinden, Bernard Swiecki and Yen Chen. 2008. *Beyond the Big Leave: The Future of U.S. Automotive Human Resources*. Ann Arbor, MI: Center for Automotive Research. <cargroup.org/?module=Publications&event=View&pubID=80>.

ECO Canada. 2012. *Trends in the Green Economy*. Calgary: ECO Canada.

___. 2010. *Defining the Green Economy: Labour Market Research Study*. Calgary: ECO Canada.

___. 2007. *Profile of Canadian Environmental Employment 2007*. Calgary: ECO Canada.

The Economist. 2009. "The Grass Is Always Greener: Saving the Planet and Creating Jobs May Be Incompatible." April 2. <economist.com/node/13404568>.

Electricity Sector Council. 2008. *Building Bright Futures: Powering Up the Future. 2008*

Labour Market Information Study Full Report. Ottawa: Electricity Sector Council.

___. 2007a. *Human Resource and Skill Needs Facing the Ontario Electricity Sector*: Appendix F of the report of the agency review panel on Phase II of its review of Ontario's provincially owned electricity agencies. Toronto: Ontario Ministry of Energy.

___. 2007b. *Labour Market Demand and Transitions in the Electricity Industry: Final Report*. Ottawa: Canadian Electricity Association.

Engel, Ditha, and Daniel Kammen. 2009. *Green Jobs and the Clean Energy Economy*. Copenhagen: Climate Council's Thought Leadership Series. <climatechange. ca.gov/eaac/documents/member_materials/Engel_and_Kammen_Green_Jobs_ and_the_Clean_Energy_Economy.pdf>.

Environment Canada. 2009. *Sulphur in Liquid Fuels 2007*. Ottawa: Environment Canada. <ec.gc.ca/Publications/default.asp?lang=En&xml=87ED17E7-714E-4A04-A596-77CA82D690B6>.

___. 2008. *Canada's Greenhouse Gas Emissions: Understanding the Trends, 1990–2006*. Ottawa: Environment Canada. <ec.gc.ca/Publications/default. asp?lang=En&xml=75805F15-908C-4FB1-A285-6D437FF04C93>.

EPA (United States Environmental Protection Agency). 2009. *Potential for Reducing Greenhouse Gas Emissions in the Construction Sector*. Washington, DC: EPA. <nepis.epa. gov/Adobe/PDF/P10043HN.PDF>.

___. 1999. *Tier 2 Sulfur Regulatory Impact Analysis: Executive Summary*. Washington, DC: EPA. <epa.gov/tier2/frm/ria/exec-sum.pdf>.

European Commission. 2008. "Climate Change and International Security: A Paper from the High Representative and the European Commission to the European Council (S113/08)." March 14. <consilium.europa.eu/uedocs/cms_data/docs/ pressdata/en/reports/99387.pdf>.

European Industrial Relations Observatory. 2009. "Germany." <eurofound.europa. eu/eiro/2009/country/germany.htm>.

Evans, Bryan, and John Shields. 2011. "From Pragmatism to Neoliberalism: Ontario's Hesitant Farewell to Dr. Keynes." In Patrice Dutil (ed.), *The Guardian: Perspectives on the Ministry of Finance of Ontario*. Toronto: University of Toronto Press.

EWEA (European Wind Energy Association). 2009. *Wind at Work: Wind Energy and Job Creation in the EU*. Brussels: EWEA. <ewea.org/fileadmin/ewea_documents/docu-ments/publications/Wind_at_work_FINAL.pdf>.

Fankhauser, S., F. Sehlleier and Nicholas Stern. 2008. "Climate Change, Innovation and Jobs." *Climate Policy* 8.

FCM (Federation of Canadian Municipalities). 2003. *Municipal Building Retrofits: The Business Case*. Ottawa: FCM. <gmf.fcm.ca/files/Capacity_Building_-_MBRG/ MBRG_thebusiness_case_En.pdf>.

FedEx Corporation. 2008. "Global Citizenship Report." Memphis, Tenn.: FedEx. <citizenshipblog.fedex.designcdt.com/sites/default/files/fedex_citizenship_2008. pdf>.

Forest Products Association of Canada. 2011. "Key Economic Facts — Canada's Forest Products Industry 2010." <fpac.ca/index.php/en/>.

___. 2009. *Sustainability Report 2009*. Ottawa: Forest Products Association of Canada. <fpac.ca/index.php/en/publications>.

Frechtling, D., and E. Horvath. 1999. "Estimating the Multiplier Effects of Tourism Expenditures on a Local Economy through a Regional Input-Output Model." *Journal of Travel Research* 37, 4.

Fu, G.Z., A. Chanand and D.E. Minns. 2003. "Life Cycle Assessment of Bio-ethanol Derived From Cellulose." *International Journal of Life Cycle Assessment* 8, 3.

GAO (United States Government Accountability Office). 2008. *U.S. Postal Service: Mail-related Recycling Initiatives and Possible Opportunities for Improvement.* (Report #GAO-08-599). Washington, DC: U.S. GAO.

Gardner Pinfold Consulting Economists Limited. 2009. *Economic Impact of Offshore Oil and Gas Development in Nova Scotia, 2002–2006.* Halifax: Nova Scotia Department of Finance.

Gardner, T. 2010. "U.S. Proposes Grading Cars on Emissions, Efficiency." Reuters, August 30.

Geraeds, Gert-Jan. 2009. "Tackling Climate Change on Three Fronts: Politics, Public Opinion, and Science." *Researchtrends* October. <massey.ac.nz/~ychisti/RT2009.pdf>.

GHK Consulting Inc. 2009. *Thematic Expert Work on Green Jobs for DG, EMPL/D1, Commissioned by the European Employment Observatory.* London, U.K.: GHK. <eu-employment-observatory.net/resources/reports/GreenJobs-MEDHURST.pdf>.

Giddens, Anthony. 2011. *The Politics of Climate Change.* 2nd edition. Cambridge: Polity Press.

___. 1994. *Beyond Left and Right: The Future of Radical Politics.* Stanford: Stanford University Press.

Gill, Stephen. 1995. "Globalisation, Market Civilisation and Disciplinary Neoliberalism." *Millennium* 5, 24 (Winter).

Global Climate Network. 2010. *Low-Carbon Jobs in an Interconnected World.* Discussion Paper 3. London, U.K.: Global Climate Network.

Global Insight. 2008. *U.S. Metro Economies: Current and Potential Green Jobs in the U.S. Economy. A Report prepared for the United States Conference of Mayors Climate Protection Center.* Lexington, MA: Global Insight. <usmayors.org/climateprotection/documents/Green%20Jobs%20FINAL.pdf>.

GLOBE Foundation of Canada. 2010. *British Columbia's Green Economy: Building A Strong Low-Carbon Future.* Vancouver: GLOBE Foundation.

Goodall, Amanda H. 2008. "Why Have the Leading Journals in Management (and other Social Sciences) Failed to Respond to Climate Change?" *Journal of Management Inquiry* 17, 4.

Gossling, Stefan. 2011. *Carbon Management in Tourism: Mitigating the Impacts on Climate Change.* Abingdon, England: Routledge.

Gossling, Stefan, and C.M. Hall. 2006. *Tourism and Global Environmental Change: Ecological, Social, Economic and Political Interrelationships.* Abingdon, England: Routledge.

Gower, S.T. 2006. *Following the Paper Trail: The Impact of Magazine and Dimensional Lumber Production on Greenhouse Gas Emissions, a Case Study.* Washington, DC: H. John Heinz III Center for Science, Economics and the Environment.

Gregory, D., E. Hildebrandt, K. LeBlansch and B. Lorentzen. 1999. "Industrial Relations and the Protection of the Environment: Research Findings from a New Policy Field." *European Journal of Industrial Relations* 5, 2.

___. 1996. "Industrial Relations and the Environment — Some Theses." *European Review of Labour and Research* 2, 3.

Grinspun, Ricardo, and Robert Kreklewich. 1994. "Consolidating Neoliberal Reforms: 'Free Trade' as a Conditioning Framework." *Studies in Political Economy* 43.

Gunton, T. 2003. "Megaprojects and Regional Development: Pathologies in Project

Planning." *Regional Studies* 37, 5.

HAC (Hotel Association of Canada). 2009. "HAC Joins the Partnership for Global Sustainable Tourism Criteria." Media release, April 2. <hotelassociation.ca/reports/news%20releases/HAC%20Green%20Key%20GSTC%20Release.pdf>.

Hak, Gordon. 2007. *Capital and Labour in the British Columbia Forest Industry: 1934–1974.* Vancouver and Toronto: UBC Press.

Hall, C.M., and J.E.S. Higham. 2005. *Tourism, Recreation, and Climate Change.* Clevedon. Buffalo: Channel View Publications.

Hamilton, J.M., D.J. Maddison and R.S. Tol. 2005. "Effects of Climate Change on International Tourism." *Climate Research* 29, 3.

Harris/Decima and Canada Post. 2008. *The New Environmentalism: Survey Sponsored by Canada Post.* <canadapost.ca/cpo/mr/assets/pdf/business/newenvironmentalismpaper_en.pdf>.

Hayter, Roger. 2000. *Flexible Crossroads: The Restructuring of British Columbia's Forest Economy.* Vancouver: UBC Press.

Heintz, J., H. Garrett-Peltier and B. Zipperer. 2011. *New Jobs, Cleaner Air: Employment Effects Under Planned Changes to the EPA's Air Pollution Rules.* Amherst, MA: CERES; University of Massachusetts Political Economy Research Institute.

Held, David, Angus Hervey and Marika Theros (eds.). 2011. *The Governance of Climate Change: Science, Economics, Politics and Ethics.* Cambridge: Polity Press.

Henschel, Chris, and Tim Gray. 2007. "Forest Carbon Sequestration and Avoided Emissions." Background paper for the Canadian Boreal Initiative/Ivey Foundation Forests and Climate Change Forum, Kananaskis, Alberta, October. Toronto: Ivey Foundation. <forestsandclimate.org/background.pdf>.

Herman, Lawrence. 2011. "Green Energy Act — Japan's Challenge in the WTO." *Cassels Brock Newsletter*, June 13. <casselsbrock.com/CBNewsletter/Green_Energy_Act__Japan_s_Challenge_in_the_WTO>.

Heynen, Nik, James McCarthy, Scott Prudham and Paul Robins. 2007. *Neoliberal Environments: False Promises and Unnatural Consequences.* New York: Routledge.

Holmen Enterprises Inc. 2006. *Recommended National Education Benchmark for New Home Builders and Renovators and Assessment of Provincial Courses against the Recommended Benchmark.* Ottawa: Canadian Home Builders' Association. <chbabc.org/uploads/files/Recommended%20National%20Education%20Benchmark%20for%20New%20Home%20Buil.1.pdf>.

Holmes, John. 2004. "The Auto Pact from 1965 to the Canada — United States Free Trade Agreement (CUSFTA)." In M. Irish (ed.), *The Auto Pact: Investment, Labour and the WTO.* The Hague: Kluwer Law International.

Hooper, Richard, Dame Deirdre Hutton and Ian R. Smith. 2008. *The Challenges and Opportunities Facing the U.K. Postal Service: Independent Review of the U.K. Postal Services Sector.* <berr.gov.uk/files/file46075.pdf>.

Howlett, Karen, and Steve Ladurantaye. 2011. "How McGuinty's Green-Energy Policy Cost Him a Majority in Ontario." *Globe and Mail*, October 8. <theglobeandmail.com/news/politics/ontario-election/how-mcguintys-green-energy-policy-cost-him-a-majority-in-ontario/article2195401>.

Howlett, Michael. 2001. *Canadian Forest Policy: Adapting to Change.* Toronto: University of Toronto Press.

Humphreys, E.R., T.A. Black, K. Morgenstern and T. Cai. 2006. "Carbon Dioxide Fluxes in Coastal Douglas-Fir Stands at Different Stages of Development After

Clearcut Harvesting." *Agricultural and Forest Meteorology* 140.

Hutton, W. 2012. "A Catastrophe in Global Warming Falls off the Agenda." *The Guardian*, June 24. <guardian.co.uk/commentisfree/2012/jun/24/will-hutton-climate-change-action>.

ILO (International Labour Organization). 2011. *Towards a Greener Economy: The Social Dimensions*. Geneva, Switzerland: ILO. <ilo.org/wcmsp5/groups/public/---dgreports/---dcomm/---publ/documents/publication/wcms_168163.pdf>.

Industry Canada. 2010. *Canadian Wind Energy Sector Profile 2010*. Ottawa: Industry Canada, in partnership with KPMG and the Canadian Wind Energy Association. <ic.gc.ca/eic/site/wei-iee.nsf/vwapj/profile_2010_profil_2010_eng.pdf/$file/profile_2010_profil_2010_eng.pdf >.

___. n.d.a. "Canadian Industry Statistics: Definition Construction (NAICS 23)." <ic.gc.ca/cis-sic/cis-sic.nsf/IDE/cis-sic23defe.html>.

___. n.d.b. <ic.gc.ca/eic/site/mse-epe.nsf/eng/home>.

Intergovernmental Panel on Climate Change. 2007a. *Climate Change 2007: Impacts, Adaptation and Vulnerability. Contribution of Working Group II to the Fourth Assessment Report of the Intergovernmental Panel on Climate Change*. M.L. Parry et al. (eds.). Cambridge, U.K.: Cambridge University Press <ipcc.ch/publications_and_data/publications_ipcc_fourth_assessment_report_wg2_report_impacts_adaptation_and_vulnerability.htm>.

___. 2007b. "Summary for Policymakers." In M.L. Parry et al. (eds.), *Climate Change 2007: Impacts, Adaptation and Vulnerability. Contribution of Working Group II to the Fourth Assessment Report of the Intergovernmental Panel on Climate Change*. Cambridge, U.K.: Cambridge University Press.

___. 2001. *Climate Change 2001: Synthesis Report*. A contribution of working groups I, II and III to the Third Assessment Report of the Intergovernmental Panel on Climate Change. R.T. Watson and the Core Writing Team (eds.). Cambridge and New York: Cambridge University Press and <grida.no/publications/other/ipcc_tar/>.

International Brotherhood of Electrical Workers. n.d. "Working Green." <ibew.org/WorkingGreen/index.htm>.

Jackson, Tim. 2009. *Prosperity without Growth: Economics for a Finite Planet*. London: Earthscan.

Jacobs, Michael. 2001. "The Environment, Modernity and the Third Way." In Anthony Giddens (ed.), *The Global Third Way Debate*. Cambridge: Polity Press.

Jordan, Bill. 2010. *Why the Third Way Failed: Economics, Morality and the Origins of the "Big Society."* Bristol: Polity Press.

Jotzo, F. 2012. "Australia's Carbon Price." *Nature Climate Change* 2.

Kammen, Daniel, K. Kapadia and M. Fripp. 2006 [2004]. *Putting Renewables to Work: How Many Jobs Can the Clean Energy Industry Generate?* Berkeley: University of California, Berkeley.

Kleiner, Morris M. 2006. *Licensing Occupations: Ensuring Quality or Restricting Competition?* Kalamazoo, MI: W.E. Upjohn Institute for Employment Research.

Konkin, Doug, and Kathy Hopkins. 2009. "Learning to Deal with Climate Change and Catastrophic Forest Disturbances." *Unasylva* 231/232. <fao.org/docrep/011/i0670e/i0670e04.htm>.

Kruse, Claudia. 2004. *IIGC Briefing Note: Climate Change and the Construction Sector*. London: ISIS Asset Management PLC.

Kumar, Pradeep, and John Holmes. 1998. "The Impact of NAFTA on the Auto Industry in Canada." In S. Weintraub and C. Sands (eds.), *The North American Auto Industry Under NAFTA.* Washington, DC: CSIS Press.

Laing, M. 2006. "Government Procurement at GATT/WTO." *Asian Journal of WTO and International Health Law and Policy* 1, 2.

Lang, Isa. 2008. "Wrestling with an Elephant: A Selected Bibliography and Resource Guide on Global Climate Change." *Law Library Journal* 100, 4.

Lee, J.G., and K. Xu. 2005. "Design for the Environment. Life Cycle Assessment and Sustainable Packaging Issues." *International Journal of Environmental Technology & Management* 5, 1.

Lehr, Ulrike, et al. 2008. "Renewable Energy and Employment in Germany." *Energy Policy* 36, 1.

Leiper, N. 1999. "A Conceptual Analysis of Tourism-Supported Employment Which Reduces the Incidence of Exaggerated, Misleading Statistics About Jobs." *Tourism Management* 20, 5.

Lemmen, D.S., F.J. Warren, J. Lacroix and E. Bush (eds.). 2008. *From Impacts to Adaptation: Canada in a Changing Climate 2007.* Ottawa: Government of Canada. <nrcan.gc.ca/earth-sciences/climate-change/community-adaptation/assessments/132>.

Lipsig-Mummé, Carla. 2012. "Greening Work in Three Dimensions." Foundation lecture, Institute on Workforce Futures, Macquarie University, Sydney, Australia.

____. 2011. "Work in a Warming World: A Green Turn for the Canadian Economy." Plenary speaker, Knowledge Talks: Senior Seminar Series, Human Resources and Skills Development Canada, June 9.

____. 2008a. "Adapting Employment to Fit a Warming World." Toronto Star, February 1.

____. 2008b. "But What About the Jobs? Negotiating Climate Change in a Warming World." *Australian Options* 54 (Spring).

Lipsig-Mummé, Carla, and John Mummé. 2009. "Inquiry into the Effects of Climate Change on Training and Employment Needs." Invited submission to the Australian Senate Committee on Employment, Education and Industrial Relations. Canberra, Australia.

Lorenz, Andrea. 2007. "Competency Pays! The Petroleum Competency Program Provides a Win-Win-Win Situation For Employees, Service Companies, and Producers." *Onstream* (Spring).

Lorinc, John. 2011. "Ontario's Search for a Solar System." *Globe and Mail Report on Business Magazine,* February 24. <theglobeandmail.com/report-on-business/rob-magazine/ontarios-search-for-a-solar-system/article1919546>.

Lynch, Amanda. 2008. "Climate Change: Mapping the Context." Submission to the *Garnaut Review.* Victoria, Australia: Monash University.

M.K. Jaccard and Associates. 2008. *Preliminary Report: Exploration of a Policy Package to Reduce Canadian Greenhouse Gas Emissions 25% below 1990 levels by 2020.* Vancouver: MK Jaccard and Associates.

MacDermott, C. 2013. "Ontario's Environment and the Wynne of Change. *Sierra Club Prairie,* January 29. <prairie.sierraclub.ca/en/node/5767>

Macdonald, Douglas. 2011. "Harper Energy and Climate Change Policy: Failing to Address the Key Challenges." In Christopher Stoney and G. Bruce Doern (eds.), *How Ottawa Spends 2011–2012: Trimming Fat or Slicing Pork?* Montreal: McGill–Queen's University Press.

MacLean, H.L., and L.B. Lave. 1998. "A Life Cycle Model of an Automobile."

Environmental Science & Technology 32, 3.

Mangmeechai, A., and H.S. Matthews. 2007. *Life Cycle Analysis of Energy and Greenhouse Gas Emissions of Ground Shipping in the United States: U.S. Postal Service Case Study*. Paper presented at the InLCA/LCM Conference, October 2–4, Portland, OR.

Marchak, Patricia M. 1997. "A Changing Global Context for British Columbia's Forest Products Industry." In T. Barnes and R. Hayter (eds.), *Troubles in the Rainforest: British Columbia's Forest Economy in Transition*. Victoria: Western Geographical Press.

___. 1983. *Green Gold: The Forest Industry in British Columbia*. Vancouver: UBC Press.

Marshall, Dale. 2011a. "Populism Beats Good Policy: The Ontario Progressive Conservative Platform." Notes from the Panther Lounge Blog, May 30. Vancouver: David Suzuki Foundation. <davidsuzuki.org/blogs/panther-lounge/2011/05/populism-beats-good-policy-the-ontario-progressive-conservative-platform>.

___. 2011b. "The Ontario NDP Platform: Politics Trump Good Energy Policy … Again." Climate and Clean Energy Blog, July 12. Vancouver: David Suzuki Foundation. <davidsuzuki.org/blogs/climate-blog/2011/07/the-ontario-ndp-platform-politics-trump-good-energy-policyagain>.

___. 2011c. "Backgrounder: Ontario's Green Energy Act." Climate and Clean Energy Blog, August 23. Vancouver: David Suzuki Foundation. <davidsuzuki.org/blogs/climate-blog/2011/08/backgrounder-ontarios-green-energy-act>.

___. 2011d. "Ontario Liberal Platform Maintains Green Energy Focus." *Climate* and Clean Energy Blog, September 9. Vancouver: David Suzuki Foundation. <davidsuzuki.org/blogs/climate-blog/2011/09/ontario-liberal-election-platform-a-mixed-bag>.

___. 2002. *Making Kyoto Work: A Transition Strategy for Canadian Energy Workers*. Vancouver, BC: Canadian Centre for Policy Alternatives.

Mattera, Philip. 2009. *High Road or Low Road? Job Quality in the New Green Economy*. Washington, DC: Good Jobs First. <goodjobsfirst.org/pdf/gjfgreenjobsrpt.pdf>.

Maxton, G.P., and J. Wormald. 2004. *Time for a Model Change: Re-engineering the Global Automotive Industry*. Cambridge: Cambridge University Press.

Mcavoy, Christine. 2011. "Suzuki Warns Tory Scheme to Cancel Green Energy Plans Is 'Absolute Insanity.'" *Toronto Star*, July 21. <thestar.com/news/canada/politics/article/1028008--suzuki-warns-tory-scheme-to-cancel-green-energy-plans-is-absolute-insanity>.

McBride, Stephen. 2010. Personal communication to Carla Lipsig-Mummé.

McColl, D. 2009. *Green Bitumen: The Role of Nuclear, Gasification and CCS in Alberta's Oil Sands: Summary Report*. Calgary, AB: Canadian Energy Research Institute.

McMonagle, R. 2005. *Job Creation Potential of Solar Energy in Canada*. Ottawa: Canadian Solar Industries Association.

McQuaig, Linda. 2012. "Stephen Harper Turns Environmentalists into Public Enemies." *Toronto Star*, June 4. <thestar.com/opinion/editorialopinion/article/1205794--stephen-harper-government-turns-environmentalists-into-public-enemies>.

Molot, Maureen A. 2008. "The Race to Develop Fuel Cells: Possible Lessons of the Canadian Experience for Developing Countries." In L. Mytelka and G. Boyle (eds.), *Making Choices about Hydrogen: Transport Issues for Developing Countries*. Tokyo: United Nations University Press.

Molot, Maureen A., and L. Mytelka. 2007. "Do Clusters Matter in a Globalized Industry? Hydrogen Fuel Cell Clusters and the Auto Industry in Canada." Paper presented at the International Studies Association Conference, Chicago.

Monbiot, George. 2006. *Heat: How to Stop the Planet from Burning*. Toronto: Doubleday.

Montreal Gazette. 2012. "Editorial: Environmental Cuts Raise Troubling Questions." May 28. <montrealgazette.com/technology/Environmental+cuts+raise+troubling+questions/6691262/story.html>.

National Academy of Sciences. 2002. *Effectiveness and Impact of Corporate Average Fuel Economy (CAFE) Standards*. Washington, DC: National Academy Press. <nap.edu/catalog.php?record_id=10172>.

National Energy Board. 2009. *2009 Reference Case Scenario: Canadian Energy Demand and Supply to 2020*. Calgary: National Energy Board.

Natural Resources Canada. 2010. *Biomass, Bioenergy and Bioproducts*. Ottawa: Natural Resources Canada. <cfs.nrcan.gc.ca/pages/65>.

___. 2007. *The State of Canada's Forests Annual Report 2007*. Ottawa: Canadian Forest Service. <publications.gc.ca/collections/collection_2007/nrcan-rncan/Fo1-6-2007E.pdf>.

___. 2006. *Canada's Energy Outlook: The Reference Case 2006*. Ottawa: Natural Resources Canada.

___. n.d.a. "National Forest Carbon Accounting, Monitoring and Reporting System." <carbon.cfs.nrcan.gc.ca/FAQ_e.html#5b>.

___. n.d.b. "Forest Inventory" <cfs.nrcan.gc.ca/pages/97>.

___. n.d.c. "Overview of Canada's Energy Policy." <nrcan.gc.ca/energy/policy/1352>.

New York Times. 2012. "Global Warming and Climate Change." June 27. <topics.nytimes.com/top/news/science/topics/globalwarming/index.html>.

Newcomb, B. 2004. *Economic Impacts of Offshore Oil & Gas Development on Nova Scotia 2001–2003: A Progress Report*. Halifax: Nova Scotia Department of Energy.

Norges Bank Investment Management. 2011. *Government Pension Fund Global Annual Report, 2011*. <nbim.no/en/press-and-publications/Reports/810/1062/>.

Nowicka, P. 2007. *The No-Nonsense Guide to Tourism*. Toronto: Between the Lines/New Internationalist Publications.

NRTEE (National Round Table on the Environment and the Economy). 2012. *Reality Check: The State of Climate Progress in Canada*. Ottawa: NRTEE.<nrtee-trnee.ca/wp-content/uploads/2012/06/reality-check-report-eng.pdf>.

NTTC (National Travel and Tourism Coalition). 2010. *Looking to 2020: The Future of Travel and Tourism in Canada Whitepaper*. Ottawa: NTTC. <tiac.travel/_Library/documents/NTTC_Whitepaper_Final.pdf>.

O'Brien, Karen. 2010. "Responding to the Global Environmental Change: Social Sciences of the World Unite!" *UNESCO World Social Science Report 2010*. Paris: UNESCO and the International Social Science Council.

OECD (Organisation for Economic Co-operation and Development). 2012a. *Environmental Performance Review: Germany 2012 Highlights*. Paris: OECD. <oecd.org/environment/environmentalcountryreviews/oecdenvironmentalperformancereviewsgermany2012.htm>.

___. 2012b. *OECD Environmental Outlook to 2050: The Consequences of Inaction*. Paris: OECD. <oecd.org/environment/environmentalindicatorsmodellingandoutlooks/oecdenvironmentaloutlookto2050theconsequencesofinaction.htm>.

___. 2010. *OECD Economic Surveys: Canada, 2010*. Paris: OECD. <oecd.org/eco/economicsurveyofcanada2010.htm>.

____. 2008. *Eco-Innovation Policies in Canada*. Paris: OECD Environment Directorate <oecd. org/dataoecd/27/14/42876916.pdf>.

Office of the United States Trade Representative. 2011. "China Ends Wind Power Equipment Subsidies Challenged by the United States in WTO Dispute." Media release, June. <ustr.gov/about-us/press-office/press-releases/2011/june/china-ends-wind-power-equipment-subsidies-challenged>.

Oxfam International. 2009. *Suffering the Science: Climate Change, People and Poverty*. Briefing Paper 130. London: Oxfam International.

Parfitt, Ben. 2010a. "'Living Assets' Are Key in the Fight against Climate Change." Vancouver: Canadian Centre for Policy Alternatives. <policyalternatives.ca/publications/commentary/living-assets-are-key-fight-against-climate-change>.

____. 2010b. *Managing B.C.'s Forests for a Cooler Planet: Carbon Storage, Sustainable Jobs and Conservation*. Vancouver: Canadian Centre for Policy Alternatives. <policyalternatives.ca/sites/default/files/uploads/publications/reports/docs/ccpa_bc_managingforests.pdf>.

Partington, P.J., and Matthew Bramley. 2010. *Canada's Main Sources of GHG Emissions*. Drayton Valley, AB: Pembina Institute. <climate.pembina.org/pub/1966>.

Patay, Migali, and Oliver Sartor. 2012. *Australia's Clean Energy Future Package: How Does it Compare with the EU's Approach?* Paris: CDC Climat Research Group. Climate Brief #15, May. <cdcclimat.com/IMG//pdf/12-05_climate_brief_15_-_ets_australia.pdf>.

Patenaude, Genevieve. 2011. "Climate Change Diffusion: While the World Tips, Business Schools Lag." *Global Environmental Change* 21.

Pearce, Alicia, and Frank Stilwell. 2008. "Green Collar Jobs: Employment Impacts of Climate Change." *Journal of Australian Political Economy* 62.

Penney, Jennifer, Ireen Wieditz, Brent Gilmour, Jeff Evenson and Karen Lior. 2007. *Skills for Energy Efficient Construction: A Report on Trades Training for Energy Efficient Buildings in the Greater Toronto Area*. Toronto: Clean Air Partnership, Canadian Urban Institute, Toronto Training Board. <cleanairpartnership.org/pdf/skills_05_2007.pdf>.

Perez-Garcia, Jorge, Linda A. Joyce, David McGuire and Xiangming Xiao. 2002. "Impacts of Climate Change on the Global Forest Sector." *Climatic Change* 54.

Pew Center on Global Climate Change. 2009. *Green Jobs*. Arlington, VA: Pew Center.

PHRCC (Petroleum Human Resources Council of Canada). 2010. *Petroleum Labour Market Information Supply/Demand Analysis 2009–2020*. Ottawa: PHRCC.

Plume, Andrew. 2009. "Where Government, Industry and Academia Meet." *Researchtrends* October. <massey.ac.nz/~ychisti/RT2009.pdf >.

Pollin, Robert, and Heidi Garrett-Peltier. 2009. *Building the Green Economy: Employment Effects of Green Energy Investments for Ontario*. Toronto: Green Energy Act Alliance, Blue Green Canada, World Wildlife Federation. <assets.wwf.ca/downloads/building_the_green_economy.pdf>.

Pollin, Robert, Heidi Garrett-Peltier, James Heintz and Helen Scharber. 2008. *Green Recovery: A Program to Create Good Jobs and Start Building a Low-Carbon Economy*. Amherst, MA: University of Massachusetts, Political Economy Research Institute; Washington DC: Center for American Progress. <peri.umass.edu/fileadmin/pdf/other_publication_types/peri_report.pdf>.

Preston, Alison. 2009. "Labour Markets and Wages in 2008." *Industrial Relations Journal* 51, 3.

Prism Economics and Analysis. 2007a. *A Labour Market Investigation of the HVACR Sector.* Ottawa: Construction Sector Council. <csc-ca.org/en/products/labour-market-investigation-hvacr-sector>.

____. 2007b. *Environmental Scan of the Ontario Concrete Forming Industry, Commissioned by the Ontario Cast in Place Concrete Development Council.* Toronto: Prism Economics.

____. 2005. *Training Trust Funds: A Review of Their History, Legal Foundations, and Implications for Trade Union Training Strategy.* Ottawa: Canadian Labour Congress. <ogrady.on.ca/Downloads/Papers/Training%20Trust%20Funds.pdf>.

____. 1997. *A National Inventory of Training Resources for Carpenters.* Commissioned by the National Industrial Adjustment Committee of the Carpentry Craft. Toronto: Prism Economics.

Province of British Columbia. 2010. *Clean Energy Act, 2010,* Statutes of British Columbia, Chapter 22. <bclaws.ca/EPLibraries/bclaws_new/document/ID/freeside/00_10022_01>.

Province of Ontario. 2012. "McGuinty Government Earns Top Marks for Clean Air, Water and Energy Actions." Media release, June 8. <ontario.ca/ene/en/2012/06/ontario-named-canadas-greenest-province.html>.

____. 2011. "Green Energy Act Creates 20,000 jobs." Media release, July 25. <news.ontario.ca/mei/en/2011/07/green-energy-act-creates-20000-jobs.html>.

____. 2009. *Green Energy Act, 2009,* Statutes of Ontario 2009, Chapter 12. <e-laws.gov.on.ca/html/statutes/english/elaws_statutes_09g12_e.htm>.

Quenqua, Douglas. 2007. "The Power of Perception." *DM News* December 17. <media.haymarketmedia.com/Documents/1/DM_PB_Survey_525.pdf>.

R.A. Malatest and Associates. 2010. *Analysis and Assessment of Labour Market Transition Programs for Laid-off Forest Products Workers.* Ottawa: Forest Products Sector Council.

Radwanski, Adam. 2011. "McGuinty's Treacherous Path: Where Party Line Meets Compromise." *Globe and Mail*, October 7. <theglobeandmail.com/news/politics/mcguintys-treacherous-path-where-party-line-meets-compromise/article556453/>.

Räthzel, Nora, and David Uzzell. 2013. *Trade Unions in the Green Economy: Working for the Environment.* London: Routledge.

Renner, Michael. 2008. *Green Jobs: Working for People and the Environment.* Washington, DC: Worldwatch Institute.

Richardson, Katherine, Sill Steffen, Hans Schellnhuber, Joseph Alcamo, Terry Barker, Daniel M. Kammen, Rik Leemans, Diana Liverman, Mohan Munasinghe, Balgro Osman-Elasha, Nicholas Stern and Ole Wæver. 2009. *Synthesis Report from Climate Change: Global Risks, Challenges and Decisions. Copenhagen, March 10–12, 2009.* Copenhagen: University of Copenhagen. <climatecongress.ku.dk/pdf/synthesisreport/>.

Riley, M., A. Ladkin and E. Szivas. 2002. *Tourism Employment: Analysis and Planning.* Clevendon, U.K.: Channel View Publications.

Ritson-Bennett, Sheila. 2011. "A (Trade) Climate for Renewable Energy? WTO Jurisprudence in Relation to Domestic Renewable Energy Measures." LL.M. diss., University of Edinburgh.

Robitaille, Lise, and Jose Etcheverry. 2005. "Training, Education, and Public Awareness: Key Components for Developing a Strong and Vibrant Canadian Solar Industry." Paper presented at the Solar Energy Society of Canada Conference, Burnaby, B.C. <sesci.ca/sites/default/files/pdfs/Sol_Spring06_paper.pdf>.

Rogers, Joel. 2007. *Seizing the Opportunity (For Climate, Jobs, and Equity) in Building Energy Efficiency.* Madison, WI: Center on Wisconsin Strategy.

Roland-Holst, D. 2008. *Energy Efficiency, Innovation, and Job Creation in California.* Berkeley: University of California at Berkeley. Center for Energy, Resources, and Economic Sustainability (CERES).

Roy, F., and C. Kimanyi. 2007. "Canada's Changing Auto Industry." *Canadian Economic Observer* (May). Ottawa: Statistics Canada.

Rushton, Sean. 2007. "The Economy and the Environment: Working Hand in Hand." *Research Perspectives online* (Spring). <research.uottawa.ca/perspectives/10202>.

Rutherford, Tod, and John Holmes. 2012. "(Small) Differences that (Still) Matter? Cross-Border Regions and Work Place Governance in the Southern Ontario and U.S. Great Lakes Automotive Industry." *Regional Studies.*

Sandborn, Calvin. 2012. "The Case for Strong Environmental Assessment." *Vancouver Sun*, June 4. <vancouversun.com/news/case+strong+environmental+assessment/6728921/story.html>.

Scott, Daniel. 2008. "Adaptation." In M. Simpson et al. (eds.), *Climate Change Adaptation and Mitigation in the Tourism Sector: Frameworks, Tools and Practices.* Paris: UNEP, University of Oxford, UNWTO, WMO.

Scott, Daniel, and S. Beckman. 2010. "Adapting to Climate Change and Climate Policy: Progress, Problems and Potentials." *Journal of Sustainable Tourism* 18, 3.

Scott, Daniel, J. Dawson and B. Jones. 2008. "Climate Change Vulnerability of the U.S. Northeast Winter Recreation — Tourism Sector." *Mitigation and Adaptation Strategies for Global Change* 13, 5–6.

Scott, Daniel, and B. Jones. 2007. "A Regional Comparison of the Implications of Climate Change for the Golf Industry in Canada." *Canadian Geographer* 51, 2.

Scott, Daniel, and Geoff McBoyle. 2007. "Climate Change Adaptation in the Ski Industry." *Mitigation and Adaptation Strategies to Global Change* 12, 8.

Scott, Daniel, Geoff McBoyle and M. Schwartzentruber. 2004. "Climate Change and the Distribution of Climatic Resources for Tourism in North America." *Climate Research* 27, 2.

Scott, Daniel, P. Peeters and Stefan Gossling. 2010. "Can Tourism Deliver Its 'Aspirational' Greenhouse Gas Emission Reduction Targets?" *Journal of Sustainable Tourism* 18, 3.

Scott, Daniel, et al. 2005. "Climate Change and Tourism and Recreation in North America." In Colin Michael Hall and James E.S. Higham (eds.), *Tourism, Recreation, and Climate Change.* Clevedon; Buffalo: Channel View Publications.

Sedjo, Roger, and David Bael. 2007. *The Impact of Globalization on the Forest Products Industry.* (WP-2007-36). Pittsburgh: Sloan Industry Studies Association. <isapapers.pitt.edu/151/>.

Sheill, L., and R. Somerville. 2012. *Bailouts and Subsidies: The Economics of Assisting the Automotive Sector in Canada.* (IRPP Study No. 28). Ottawa: Institute for Research on Public Policy.

Simpson, Michael C., Stefan Gossling, Daniel Scott, C.M. Hall and E. Gladin (eds.). 2008. *Climate Change Adaptation and Mitigation in the Tourism Sector: Frameworks, Tools and Practices.* Paris: UNEP, University of Oxford, UNWTO, WMO. <unep.fr/shared/publications/pdf/DTIx1047xPA-ClimateChange.pdf>.

SLS Consulting. 2008. *Informing the Dialogue: Facts about Mail and the Environment.* Washington, DC: SLS Consulting.

Smith, M., and J. Crotty. 2008. "Environmental Regulation and Innovation Driving Ecological Design in the U.K. Automotive Industry." *Business Strategy and the Environment* 17, 6.

Sosnow, Cliff. 2011. "Mesa Power Brings Claim under NAFTA over Ontario's Green Energy Program." *Blakes Bulletin: International Trade and Investment online*, July. <blakes.com/english/legal_updates/international_trade/jul_2011/Mesa.pdf>.

Spears, John. 2012. "Ontario Lags on Conservation, Says Environmental Commissioner." *Toronto Star*, June 5. <thestar.com/business/article/1205997--green-report-liberals-fail-to-keep-conservation-commitments-says-ontario-environmental-commissioner>.

SQW. 2008. *Today's Investment Tomorrow's Assets: Skills and Employment in the Wind, Wave and Tidal Sector*. London: British Wind Energy Association. <bwea.com/pdf/publications/BWEA%20Skills%20Report%20FINAL%2016oct.pdf >.

Stanford, Jim. 2010. "The Geography of Auto Globalization and the Politics of Auto Bailouts." *Cambridge Journal of Regions, Economy and Society* 3.

Statistics Canada. 2009a. *Canadian Tourism Satellite Account 2004*. (Catalogue #13-604-M - No. 063). Ottawa: Statistics Canada. <statcan.gc.ca/pub/13-604-m/13-604-m2009063-eng.pdf>.

___. 2009b. *Energy Statistics Handbook, 4th Quarter, 2009*. (Catalogue #57-601). Ottawa: Statistics Canada.

___. 2009c. *National Input-Output Tables 2006*. (Catalogue #15F0041XDB). Ottawa: Statistics Canada.

___. 2009d. "Table 3.50-1: Energy and Greenhouse Gas Intensity, by Industry, Canada — Primary Sector." *Human Activity and the Environment: Annual Statistics* <statcan.gc.ca/pub/16-201-x/2009000/t223-eng.htm>.

___. 2009e. *Electric Power Generation, Transmission and Distribution 2007*. (Catalogue # 57-202-X). Ottawa: Statistics Canada, Manufacturing and Energy Division.

___. 2008. *Human Resource Module of the Tourism Satellite Account, Update to 2006*. (Catalogue #13-604-M - No. 059). Ottawa: Statistics Canada. <statcan.gc.ca/pub/13-604-m/13-604-m2008059-eng.pdf>.

___. 2007. *Labour Force Survey: Total Employment in Canada by Age Group and Gender for NAICS 2211*. Ottawa: Statistics Canada.

___. n.d.a. "CANSIM Table 282-0012: Labour Force Survey Estimates (LFS), Employment by Class of Worker, North American Industry Classification System (NAICS) and Sex, Annual (Persons)." Ottawa: Statistics Canada.

___. n.d.b. "CANSIM Table 281-0024 Employment (SEPH), Unadjusted for Seasonal Variation, by Type of Employee for Selected Industries Classified Using the North American Industry Classification System (NAICS)." Ottawa: Statistics Canada.

Stern, Nicholas. 2007. *The Economics of Climate Change: The Stern Review*. Cambridge, U.K.: Cambridge University Press. <webarchive.nationalarchives.gov.uk/+/http://www.hm-treasury.gov.uk/stern_review_report.htm>.

Strategic Directions Inc. 2003. "Labour Market Assessment of the Oil and Gas Industry Supply and Service Sector in Newfoundland and Labrador." A report prepared for the Petroleum Industry Human Resources Committee (PIHRC) and Newfoundland Ocean Industries Association (NOIA). St. John's, Newfoundland: PIHRC and NOIA.

Sturgeon, T., J. van Briesebroeck and G. Gereffi. 2008. "The North American Automotive Production System: Canada's Role and Prospects." *International Journal of Technological Learning, Innovation and Development* 2.

Sustainable Prosperity. 2012. *The United Kingdom (U.K.) Climate Policy: Lessons for Canada.* Ottawa: University of Ottawa. <sustainableprosperity.ca/dl821&display>.

Sweeney, B. 2010. "Comparing Employment Relations in a Cross-Border Region: The Case of Cascadia's Forest Products Industry." PhD. diss., Queen's University, Kingston, Ontario.

Syndex. 2011. "Social Partnership Initiatives in Europe on Climate Change and Employment." Summary report for a conference in Brussels, March 1 and 2, 2011. <resourcecentre.etuc.org/linked_files/documents/IP1%20-%20Study%20-%20 Initiatives%20involving%20social%20partners%20in%20Europe%20on%20 climate%20change%20policies%20and%20employment.pdf>.

Syndex, S. Partner, WMP Consulting. 2009. *Climate Disturbances, the New Industrial Policies, and Ways Out of the Crisis.* Brussels: European Trade Union Confederation.

Talaga, Tanya. 2010. "Four More Ontario Coal-Fired Generating Units Shut Down." *Toronto Star*, October 1. <thestar.com/news/ontario/article/869588--four-more-ontario-coal-fired-generating-units-shut-down>.

Thomson, K. 2010. "Failure to Reduce Carbon Emissions Will Lead To Job Losses and Lower ... Living Standards." Speech to the House of Victorian Parliament, Australia, June 21.

Thornley, P., J. Rogers and Y. Huang. 2008. "Quantification of Employment from Biomass Power Plants." *Renewable Energy* 33, 8.

TIAC (Tourism Industry Association of Canada). 2009. *Tourism & Travel Trends 2008.* Ottawa: TIAC.

___. 2008a. *Green Your Business: Toolkit For Tourism Operators.* Ottawa: TIAC; Canadian Tourism Commission; Parks Canada.

___. 2008b. *The Report on Canada's Tourism Competitiveness: A Call for Action for the Canadian Tourism Industry.* Ottawa: TIAC.

Timilsina, G., et al. 2008. *The Canadian Nuclear Industry: Contributions to the Canadian Economy: Final Report.* Calgary, Alberta: Canadian Energy Research Institute.

Todgham-Cherniak, Cyndee. 2010. "The U.S. and E.U. Join Japan's WTO Complaint against Ontario's *Green Energy Act.*" Trade Lawyers Blog, October 1. <tradelaw-yersblog.com/blog/article/the-us-and-eu-join-japans-wto-complaint-against-ontarios-green-energy-act>.

Transport Canada. 2008. *Strategic Review of Canada Post Corporation: Report of the Advisory Panel to the Minister.* Ottawa: Transport Canada. <cpcstrategicreview-examenstrate-giquescp.gc.ca/finalreport/rpt-eng.pdf>.

Tuerck, David, Benjamin Powell and Paul Bachman. 2009. *"Green Collar" Job Creation: A Critical Analysis.* Boston: Beacon Hill Institute, Suffolk University. <beaconhill. org/BHIStudies/GreenJobs09/BHIGreen_Collar_Job_Critique090625.pdf>.

Tufts, Steven. 2010. "Schumpeterian Unionism and 'High-Road' Dreams in Toronto's Hospitality Sector." In A.C. Bergene, S.B. Endresen and H. Merete (eds.), *Missing Links in Labour Geographies.* Farnham, U.K.: Ashgate.

___. 2009. "Hospitality Unionism and Labour Market Adjustment: Toward Schumpeterian Unionism?" *Geoforum* 40, 6.

___. 2007. "Emerging Labour Strategies in Toronto's Hotel Sector: Toward a Spatial Circuit of Union Renewal." *Environment and Planning A* 39, 10.

___. 2003. "SARS & New Normals: Healthcare and Hospitality Workers Fight Back." *Our Times* 22, 4.

UNEP (United Nations Environment Programme). 2011. *Towards a Green Economy: Pathways to Sustainable Development and Poverty Eradication*. Nairobi, Kenya: UNEP. <un.org/esa/dsd/resources/res_pdfs/publications/sdt_cc/cc_global_green_new_deal.pdf>.

___. 2009a. *Global Green New Deal: A Policy Brief*. Nairobi, Kenya: UNEP. <unep.org/pdf/A_Global_Green_New_Deal_Policy_Brief.pdf>.

___. 2009b. "Green Policies and Jobs: a Double Dividend?" In *World of Work Report 2009: The Global Job Crisis and Beyond*. Geneva: International Labour Organization.

___. 2008. *Green Jobs: Towards Decent Work in A Sustainable, Low-Carbon World*. Nairobi: UNEP/ILO/IOE/ITUC. Washington, DC: Worldwatch Institute. <unep.org/labour_environment/PDFs/Greenjobs/UNEP-Green-Jobs-Report.pdf>.

___. 2007. *Labour and the Environment: A Natural Synergy*. Nairobi: UNEP. <unep.org/labour_environment/pdfs/unep-labour-env-synergy.pdf>.

___. 2006. *Buildings and Climate Change: Status, Challenges and Opportunities*. Paris: UNEP, SBCI.

___. n.d. Green Economy Initiative website. <unep.org/greeneconomy/>.

UNITE HERE Toronto Task Force on the Hotel Industry. 2006. *Industry at the Crossroads: A High Road Economic Vision for Toronto Hotels*. Toronto: UNITE HERE.

United States Bureau of Labor Statistics. 2010. *Measuring Green Jobs*. Washington, DC: U.S. Bureau of Labor Statistics. <bls.gov/green/>.

United States Congressional Budget Office. 2011. *Estimated Impact of the* American Recovery and Reinvestment Act *on Employment and Economic Output from January 2011 through March 2011*. Washington, DC: U.S. Congressional Budget Office.

United States Department of Commerce, Economics and Statistics Administration. 2010, *Measuring the Green Economy*. Washington, DC: U.S. Department of Commerce.

Universal Postal Union. 2010. *Greening the Post Press Kit*. <upu.int/en/activities/sustainable-development/environment/key-documents.html>.

___. 2006. "The UPU Publishes its Postal Statistics for 2006." *Post and Parcel*, December 10. <postandparcel.info/20020/companies/the-upu-publishes-its-world-postal-statistics-for-2006/>.

University of British Columbia (UBC) Sustainability Office and Academic Programs Working Group. 2009. *Sustainability Labour Market Trends: A Canadian and International Perspective*. Vancouver: UBC Press.

University of Pennsylvania Think Tanks and Civil Society Program. 2011. "2011 Global Go To Think Tanks Rankings Report." <gotothinktank.com>.

UNWTO (World Tourism Organization) and the United Nations Environment Programme (UNEP). 2008. *Climate Change and Tourism: Responding to Global Challenges*. Madrid: World Tourism Organization. <uneptie.org/shared/publications/pdf/WEBx0142xPA-ClimateChangeandTourismGlobalChallenges.pdf>.

USW (United Steelworkers). 2010. *Raw log Exports: Bad Economics, Bad for the Planet*. Vancouver: USW District 3.

Vancouver Sun. 2008. "Government Brings in Low-carbon Fuel Bill." April 2. <canada.com/vancouversun/news/business/story.html?id=23e7f256-4ebc-4468-974a-c4219d78b13b>.

Victor, P. 2008. *Managing without Growth — Slower by Design not Disaster*. Cheltenham: Edward Elgar.

Wall, Geoff. 2006. "The Tourism Industry and its Vulnerability and Adaptability to

Climate Change." *Acta Touristica* 18, 2.

Wall, Geoff, and C. Badke. 1994. "Tourism and Climate Change: An International Perspective." *Journal of Sustainable Tourism* 2, 4.

Wall, Geoff, R. Harrison, V. Kinnaird, and G. McBoyle. 1986. "The Implications of Climatic Change for Camping in Ontario." *Recreation Research Review* 13, 1.

Wall, Geoffrey, and Alistair Mathieson. 2006. *Tourism: Change, Impacts and Opportunities*. Toronto: Prentice Hall.

Watt, Douglas. 2005. *The Labour Market Information (LMI) Program: Acting on Human Resource Information to Build and Maintain Capacity in the Canadian Construction Sector*. Ottawa: Conference Board of Canada. <conferenceboard.ca/documents. aspx?DID=1435>.

Weiss, L. 2005. "Global Governance, National Strategies: How Industrialized States Make Room to Move under the WTO." *Review of International Political Economy* 12, 5.

Wells, Jill. 2003. "Social Aspects of Sustainable Construction: An ILO Perspective." *Industry & Environment* 26, 2. <uneptie.org/media/review/vol26no2-3/voL26_no2-3.htm>.

Western Economic Diversification Canada. 2008. "Renewal of Quesnel Historic Site to Bring Jobs and Training." Media release, May 22. <wd.gc.ca/eng/77_10410. asp>.

Whaples, Robert. 2009. "The Policy Views of American Economics Association Members: The Results of a New Survey." *Econ Journal Watch* 6, 3: 337–48. <econjwatch.org/articles/the-policy-views-of-american-economic-association-members-the-results-of-a-new-survey?ref=date-archive>.

White, Rodney. 2010. *Climate Change in Canada*. Don Mills, ON: Oxford University Press.

White, Sarah, and Jason Walsh. 2008. *Greener Pathways: Jobs and Workforce Development in the Clean Energy Economy*. Madison, WI: Center on Wisconsin Strategy; The Workforce Alliance; The Apollo Alliance.

Wilke, M. 2011. *Feed-in Tariffs for Renewable Energy and WTO Subsidy Rules: an Initial Legal Analysis*. (Issue Paper #4). Geneva: International Centre for Trade and Sustainable Development.

Williams, C. 2007. "Fueling the Economy." *Perspectives on Labour and Income* 8, 5. (Catalogue #75-001). Ottawa: Statistics Canada.

Williams, Patricia. 2008. "Survey Finds Licensing, Climate Change among Top Concerns of Worldwide Plumbing Industry." *Daily Commercial News*, October 6. <dailycommercialnews.com/article/id30811>.

Williamson, T.S., et al. 2009. *Climate Change and Canada's Forests: From Impacts to Adaptation*. Ottawa and Edmonton: Natural Resources Canada, Canadian Forestry Service Northern Forestry Centre and Sustainable Forest Management Network.

Wills, Rebecca, and James Wilsdon. 2003. "Technology, Risk and the Environment." In Anthony Giddens (ed.), *The Progressive Manifesto*. Cambridge: Polity Press.

Winfield, Mark. 2012. *Blue-Green Province: The Environment and the Political Economy of Ontario*. Vancouver: UBC Press.

___. 2011. "Ontario's Energy Election." *Toronto Star*, September 26. <thestar.com/opinion/editorialopinion/article/1060025--ontario-s-energy-election>.

Wood Manufacturing Council. 2005. *National Human Resource Sector Study for the Advanced Wood Products Manufacturing Sector*. Ottawa: Wood Manufacturing Council. <wmc-cfb.ca/reports>.

Woodbury, R., L. Bartram, R. Cole, R. Hyde and D. MacLeod. 2008. *Buildings and*

Climate Solutions. Victoria, BC: Pacific Institute for Climate Solutions, University of Victoria. <pics.uvic.ca/sites/default/files/uploads/publications/WP_Sustainable_Buildings_November2008.pdf>.

Workforce Information Council. 2009. "Measurement and Analysis of Employment in the Green Economy: Workforce Information Council Green Jobs Study Group Final Report." Washington, DC: United States Bureau of Labor Statistics.

Working for America Institute. 2003. *U.S. Hotels and Workers: Room for Improvement*. Washington, DC: Working for America Institute.

World Bank. 2012. *State and Trends of the Carbon Market 2012*. Washington DC: World Bank.

World Travel and Tourism Council. 2012. *Travel and Tourism Economic Impact: 2012, Canada*. London: WTTC. <wttc.org/site_media/uploads/downloads/canada2012.pdf>.

WRI (World Resources Institute). 2005. *Greenhouse Gas Emissions 2005*. Washington, DC: WRI.

WTO (World Trade Organization). 2010. *Dispute Settlement: Dispute DS412. Canada — Certain Measures Affecting the Renewable Energy Sector*. Filed by Japan. September. <wto.org/english/tratop_e/dispu_e/cases_e/ds412_e.htm>.

___. n.d.a. *U.S. Section 301 Trade Act (DS152)*. <wto.org/english/tratop_e/dispu_e/cases_e/1pagesum_e/ds152sum_e.pdf>.

___. n.d.b. *Agreement on Subsidies and Countervailing Measures ("SCM Agreement")*. <wto.org/english/tratop_e/scm_e/subs_e.htm>.

Yakabuski, Konrad. 2009. "Inside This Building Technology Exists That Could Transform the Forestry Sector." *Globe and Mail*, June 18.

Yates, Charlotte, and S. Vrankulji. 2006. *Labour as a Competitive Advantage in the Canadian Automotive Parts Industry: A Study of Canada and Four Local Labour Markets (Brantford, Stratford, Guelph, Windsor)*. Hamilton, Ontario: Labour Studies Program, McMaster University.

Yuen, Jenny. 2009. "Gore Green with Envy." *Toronto Sun*, November 25.

Zuboff, Shoshana. 1988. *In the Age of the Smart Machine*. New York: Basic Books.

ACKNOWLEDGEMENTS

Climate@Work has been a collaborative project. Thanks first to the Social Science and Humanities Research Council of Canada for financial and administrative support for Work in a Warming World, a Community–University Research Alliance project. Thanks as well to the Tri-Councils and David Moorman and Jacques Critchley for their creative generosity and financial support in the earliest days of the work.

Colleagues in Canada, the U.K. and Australia were generous with their ideas and their time: Charles Campbell, Linda Clarke, Bob Hatfield, Gerry Hunnius, Andrea Kosavic, Donald Lafleur, Amanda Lynch, John Mummé and Stepan Wood.

We've benefitted from fine research assistance by Conrad Page, Jessica Edge, Dave Huntington, Victor LaPierre, Carol Ma, Stephanie Tombari, Jen Vermilyea, Heather Whiteside, Justine Mannion, as well as administrative support from Annette Dubreuil and Sabreena Delhon.

Thanks finally to Ann Kim, Work in a Warming World's coordinator, who organizes us.

CONTRIBUTORS

Geoff Bickerton is the director of research for the Canadian Union of Postal Workers. He is active on the Steering Committee of Work in a Warming World (W3). For many years he was active in the disarmament movement, serving as secretary-treasurer of the Ottawa Disarmament Coalition for over a decade. He was active in the struggle against free trade and served as co-chair of the strategy committee of the Pro Canada movement and as a member of the executive of the Action Canada Network.

John Calvert is an associate professor in the Faculty of Health Science at Simon Fraser University. He is a member of the board of the Morgan Centre for Labour Studies at SFU, a research associate of the Canadian Centre for Policy Alternatives and a member of the board of the Wilderness Committee, BC's largest membership-based environmental NGO. Dr. Calvert has published four books, most recently *Liquid Gold: Energy Privatization in BC*. As a co-investigator of the SSHRC-funded W3 research team, he is examining how the construction industry and its workforce have been addressing climate change, in Canada and internationally.

Marjorie Griffin Cohen is a professor of political economy and gender, sexuality and women's studies at Simon Fraser University. Her research focuses on political economy and public policy. She has been on the boards of New Grade Energy (Sask), B.C. Hydro and B.C. Power Exchange.

Meg Gingrich studied in the Ecosystems, Governance and Globalization program at Stockholm University from 2007 to 2009, where she wrote her master's thesis on trade union action on climate change. She worked as a research assistant for the Work in a Warming World project, based out of York University and for the Service Employees International Union's research department. She works as a researcher at the United Steelworkers Canadian National Office in Toronto.

John Holmes is a professor of geography at Queen's University, where he served as head of the department from 1993 to 2004 and as president of the union representing academic staff at from 2005 to 2007. At Queen's, he is affiliated with the graduate program in industrial relations in the School of Policy Studies. He has held visiting appointments at the Universities of Sussex, Wales and Manchester. In 2007, he was the invited visiting professor in the Institute of Political Economy at Carleton University. His primary research focuses on the contemporary restructuring and reorganization of production and work in North America. Empirical research and writing has focused primarily on the automobile industry.

Austin Hracs is a development analyst at Millier Dickinson Blais Inc., in Toronto, Ontario. Austin worked at Queen's University as a research associate in the Department of Geography, where he obtained his MA, and as an analyst for the housing industry, where he examined regional economic and housing trends in Ontario and across the southern United States. In his current role, Austin contributes to economic strategies, municipal cultural plans and regional workforce strategies for communities across Canada. His work centres on developing tangible and realistic policies to better leverage community resources.

Carla Lipsig-Mummé is a professor of work and labour studies and director of the Work in a Warming World research program based at York University, Canada. Carla has been a union organizer, negotiator, researcher and labour educator in Canada, the U.S. and Australia. Founding director of the Centre for Research on Work and Society, she has also written widely on international labour, community unionism, homeworking, youth and labour, the work/climate relationship and labour and the state in Canada, Quebec, Australia and Russia. In 2009 she jointly authored a report for the Australian Senate Committee on Employment, Education and Industrial Relations' Inquiry into the Effects of Climate Change on Training and Employment Needs. *Climate@Work* is Carla's second book.

Stephen McBride is a professor of political science and Canada Research Chair in Public Policy and Globalization at McMaster University. He has published widely on issues of global and Canadian political economy and public policy. His most recent books are (with Heather Whiteside) *Private Affluence, Public Austerity: Economic Crisis and Democratic Malaise in Canada* and (co-edited with Gary Teeple) *Relations of Global Power: Neoliberal Order and Disorder*.

John O'Grady is a founding partner of Prism Economics and Analysis, an independent consulting firm that specializes in labour market analysis. His published work focuses on labour relations and labour market issues. He has undertaken commissioned research work for a range of organizations in the construction industry and in the public sector. He was previously a visiting senior researcher at the Economic Council of Canada, research director at the Ontario Federation of Labour and the representative in Asia of the Canadian Labour Congress and the International Confederation of Free Trade Unions. He served as chair of the Institute for Work and Health, president of the Toronto Business Development Centre and advisor to the Funding Review of the Ontario Workplace Safety and Insurance Board.

Elizabeth Perry is a professional librarian, researcher and editor. In a long career at the library of the Centre for Industrial Relations and Human Resources, University of Toronto, she provided research support to faculty, students and industrial relations practitioners across Canada. In 2000, she began writing for an international internet audience in a weekly column for the HR.com website.

Later, she initiated an electronic newsletter called the *Weekly Work Report* (now named *The Perry Work Report*) at the U of T and subsequently served as editor of the *Work and Climate Change Report*, produced by the Work in a Warming World research program at York University. Her current interest is in the climate change crisis, and her goal is to inform Canadians about alternative public policy options.

Sarah Ryan is a communications specialist with the Canadian Union of Postal Workers. She finished a year working with UNI Global Union's Post & Logistics sector. In 2011, she received an MA from Carleton University's Institute of Political Economy.

John Shields is a professor in the Department of Politics and Public Administration at Ryerson University, where he has taught for the last twenty-five years. He is a past research director of CERIS – The Ontario Metropolis Centre (a SSHRC Centre of Excellent on immigration and settlement) and holds the rank of CERIS Senior Scholar. For a term, he was managing editor of the *Journal of International Migration and Integration* published by Springer in the Netherlands. John has published five books and some ninety articles, chapters and research papers. The focus of his recent work has been on Canadian public policy, immigration and settlement studies, neoliberal restructuring and labour market change.

Steven Tufts is an associate professor in the Department of Geography at York University. His research interests are related to the geographies of work, workers and organized labour. His current projects involve the use of strategic research by labour unions and labour union renewal in Canada, the integration of immigrants in urban labour markets, labour market adjustment in the hospitality sector, the impact of climate change on workers and workplaces, and the intersection between labour and right-wing populism. He has contributed to a number of edited collections and published articles in journals such as *Geoforum*, *Antipode* and *Environment and Planning A*.